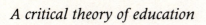

A critical theory of education

Advances in Contemporary Educational Thought Series
Jonas F. Soltis, Editor

The Cultural Dimensions of Educational Computing:
Understanding the Non-Neutrality of Technology
C. A. Bowers

Power and Criticism:
Poststructural Investigations in Education
Cleo H. Cherryholmes

The Civic Imperative:
Examining the Need for Civic Education
Richard Pratte

Responsive Teaching:
An Ecological Approach to Classroom Patterns
of Language, Culture, and Thought
C. A. Bowers
David J. Flinders

A Critical Theory of Education:
Habermas and Our Children's Future
R. E. Young

A critical theory of education

HABERMAS AND OUR CHILDREN'S FUTURE

ROBERT E. YOUNG
The University of Sydney

TEACHER'S COLLEGE, COLUMBIA UNIVERSITY
NEW YORK AND LONDON

First published in the United States of America in 1990 by
Teachers College Press,
1234 Amsterdam Avenue, New York, NY 10027.

Manufactured in Great Britain.

Library of Congress Cataloging in Publication Data

Young, R. E. (Robert E.), *1940–*
    A critical theory of education: Habermas and our children's
future / by R. E. Young.
      p.   cm.
    Includes bibliographical references.
    ISBN 0-8077-3018-1
    1. Habermas, Jürgen.   2. Education–Philosophy.   3. Critical
theory.   I. Title.
LB880.H2572Y68   1990
370'.1––dc20   89-39146
                                       CIP

1 2 3 4 5 93 92 91 90

CONTENTS

Foreword   vii

Preface   ix

1   The modern educational crisis   1
2   From interests to practice   26
3   Emancipation and education   45
4   Traditional schooling and responsible critique   68
5   Traditional teaching and learning   87
6   Critical teaching and learning   99
7   Contexts for research and action   126
8   The organisation of educational enlightenment   149
    Concluding remarks   167

Index   172

To Mary

FOREWORD

While still recent, the *rapprochement* between analytic and continental philosophy in philosophy in general and philosophy of education in particular is a recognised fact of contemporary scholarship. Not so many years ago, however, the work of R. S. Peters in the United Kingdom and Israel Scheffler in the United States represented the cresting wave of an analytic approach to philosophy of education in the English-speaking world. The only alternative to riding this new wave seemed to be risking drowning in an old-fashioned schools approach or slogging one's way through the linguistic seaweed of phenomenological and existential writings.

Interestingly, it was in Australia, not in England or America, that another philosophical alternative, the work of the neo-Marxists of the Frankfurt School of critical theory in Germany, attracted the attention of a significant number of English-speaking education scholars early on. R. E. Young's book from Australia reaps the benefit of this long-term, shared interest in the theory of critical theory as it is found in its major spokesman, Jürgen Habermas, and as it gets translated into ideas about the human enterprise of education. In this book, Young gives us the first full exposition of Habermas' major ideas in the context of educational thought.

This is a useful and impressive work. It brings heretofore untranslated German work in critical theory to English-speaking education scholars. It brings a thorough and thoughtful understanding of the work of Jürgen Habermas to bear on the development of a sophisticated educational theory and praxis. Young displays a sensitive understanding of the current state of educational philosophy and politics in Germany and America. By also treating schooling and scholarship in Australia, the United Kingdom, France and Sweden, Young bridges international boundaries and raises the discussion of the aims of education to a universal human level.

He uses Habermas' central ideas about the ideal speech situation and communicative action to argue against the views of Mill and Peters (not to mention Aristotle) that young children are not yet rational enough to engage in pedagogically sound rational dialogue. Young sees the purpose of a critical theory of education as the development of capacity for genuine autonomy through communications. He therefore takes a cautious developmental approach to the opening of young minds to ideological critique.

His references to John Dewey are not window-dressing. Dewey's ideas about progressive education were generated from the same belief in the ability of human beings to make a better world that Habermas (and his spokesman, R. E. Young in this book) uses to underwrite a theory of democratic society and a problem-solving form of education. Young also offers an examination of the idea of 'action research' from a Habermasian perspective, a practical consideration of the relation of teachers to administrators, and a normative and transformative view of educational research, all of which should be of interest to qualitative researchers.

This is a book that should be read by anyone who wants to understand Habermas and the basic philosophical ground work of what is happening today in educational thought under the general rubric of critical theory. It is a book which will advance the cause of international understanding and scholarship in educational theory.

Jonas Soltis, Editor
Advances in Contemporary Educational Thought Series

PREFACE

The purpose of this book is to outline a critical theory of education based on the social philosophy of the contemporary German theorist, Jürgen Habermas, and to show that this is a theory relevant to our times.

Habermas' views have often been misunderstood in the English-speaking world and a great deal of educational theory which they have inspired in Germany, like much of Habermas' own writing on education, remains untranslated. Habermas' work is often difficult for the reader not familiar with the continental tradition in philosophy.

Clearly, one of the tasks of this book will be to try to overcome these problems, and to present Habermas' ideas clearly, against their own background, and in a manner which allows their significance for our own tradition to be understood. A book which did this and which sketched the main implications of these ideas for contemporary educational problems would already be more than amply justified; if, in addition, it led us to feel that at least some of the ideas discussed had some practical potential, it would be doubly so.

Another of the book's tasks is to present, for the first time, a balanced and relatively complete sketch of what a Habermasian critical theory of education would look like. Too often, only parts of Habermas' work have been selected for inclusion in an educational theory while other parts, perhaps necessary to a proper balance, have been ignored. This is not to assert that we must adopt an uncritical attitude to Habermas' work, or to say that any educational theory must take all or nothing from it. We must leave such matters to time and the development of educational thought. But it *is* to maintain that we will not know what the potential of a theory of education such as Habermas', which places *educational processes* at the centre of possibilities for human progress, might be until we try to describe a theoretical programme which calls upon all of the theoretical resources it offers us. For this reason it would be beside the point to spend too much time on the work of non-Habermasian theorists, or on the task of delineating in just what ways such theorists might share common ground or differ from the Habermasian viewpoint. Otherwise valuable thinkers such as Apple, Popkewicz and Giroux are not discussed in this book.

Another limitation of the book is that it does not follow up in any great detail the many avenues for practical application it opens up; it is intended to do this in a later work. But I would want to assert that the kind of theory developed in this book is a theory with practical intent. Enough of the possibilities for concrete, situated practice are indicated to provide support for this claim. Here and there, too, reference is made to practical critical programmes actually in place and to empirical studies already carried out.

The book draws extensively on the German literature in critical theory of education, but it does so selectively, in the light of Habermas' later work. That literature is complex and extensive. As is the case in the English-language work, the term 'critical' is used by some to refer to anything vaguely Marx-influenced and by others to refer only to the 'Frankfurt School' and its successors, such as Habermas, Offe and Wellmer. It is always the narrower sense that is intended in the present work.

Since the German literature is almost completely untranslated I have had to provide my own translations. Let the reader be warned I am no Germanist. Where I have provided the translation this is indicated by an asterisk: e.g. (Gamm, 1978: 14*). Cited works and the full references for quoted works appear in chapter notes. There is no bibliography, but the name index indicates where an author's work has been cited in the notes and the full reference will generally be found at the earliest citation in the chapter notes.

I would like to thank many people, both in Germany and elsewhere, for their encouragement and help over the years in my study of German educational thought and in the writing of this book, especially Professor Habermas and his colleagues at Starnberg and Frankfurt. However, the responsibility for the arguments presented is mine.

CHAPTER 1

THE MODERN EDUCATIONAL CRISIS

We are all workmen: prentice, journeyman
or master, building you – you towering nave.
And sometimes there will come to us a grave
wayfarer, who like a radiance thrills
the souls of all your hundred artisans
as tremblingly he shows us a new skill. . . .

Then hammerstrokes sound, multitudinous
and through the mountain echoes blast on blast
Only at dusk we yield you up at last
and slow your sleeping contours dawn on us.

God, you are vast.

(Rainer Maria Rilke)[1]

As educators we can choose to participate in history, in the slow and uncertain reconstruction of God, or we can turn our backs on it. If we choose history we choose a task which is terrible, because it is virtually endless, and such a choice carries with it a risk that we, like Sisyphus, will devote our lives to climbing a little higher, to building the walls a little higher, only to have them fall, carrying us down with them. And if we choose this task, we will have little more in the way of architect's plans to work from than hunches, or momentary visions of the wholeness we seek to create and we will find that we can communicate even these few precious insights only in a stammer, since our voices are no longer in harmony and we possess, as Rilke puts it, 'only fragments of [God's] old name'.[2]

No one can be more aware of this risk, more surely antiutopian, even to the extent of being perceived as pessimists, than those who, like the early critical theorists, have built and have seen their work reduced to rubble. One could understand such people being overtaken by so pervasive a caution, that they became willing to live in mean huts constructed from the broken blocks and columns of a grander possibility. In a community of this kind we would not be suprised to learn that to build higher or more nobly than your forebears was a crime. Each generation would have the task of replacing the old, but never transcending it.

In the history of European thought, static and dynamic theodicies have long contended with each other. On the one hand, a world which was fallen, a 'vale of tears', an unchanging antechamber to Heaven or Hell, on the other, a realm of historical possibility, of the building of the Holy City here on earth. The Renaissance advent of a vigorous humanism gave new life to the dynamic alternative. Later, the European Englightenment ushered in a new, secular consciousness, but one which nevertheless inherited the old struggle for a sense of meaning and direction in human affairs. Hegel retained a secular version of the mystical theodicy of salvation history, to define the choice that presents itself to members of the human species. Beginning from the dynamic conception that whether we like it or not, we are authors of our own history,[3] the great questions, for Hegel, and later for Marx, were these: Can we also be the aware 'subjects' of our own history? Granted, we make our fate, can we control it? And if so, by what art or science?

Educators have always faced a double task. As succeeding generations of children enter their classrooms, the huts must be rebuilt – the children must be prepared to take their place in the society that already exists. At the same time, it has usually been recognised that the society which exists is only an imperfect representation of what it could be. At times, and for some educators, the imperfections seem slight and the basic institutions seem sound. They do not seek to discover the latent plan in the fragments of column, frieze or lintel that lie around them. At other times, and for other educators, the task seems greater, the labour more tremendous. Some of these would be willing to pile fragments upon one another heedless of the possibility of their all coming tumbling down. And there are times, like the present, when educators are so deeply divided in their vision of the educator's task that it is appropriate to say that education is in crisis.

The word crisis is often used loosely.[4] There is said to be a crisis every time there is 'trouble, trouble right here in River City', as the itinerant music teacher in *The Music Man* puts it. But crisis is a term which is aptly applied to the condition of education today. Whether we take the original Greek meaning of the word – as a moral dispute that has developed to the stage where it demands decisive resolution – or the classical, medical meaning – of a stage in the evolution of a disease where the fate of the patient hangs in the balance – or the more contemporary notion of a state of conflict and disturbance of some part of our normal functioning that is decisive for its continuity or change – the term crisis is the only one that is apt.

While differences of opinion about education have always existed, these have only cyclically reached a degree of stridency that rises above the boredom level on the floor of parliament or congress. A great deal of the time, schools and universities have drifted in the political backwaters, suffering, perhaps, from malaise, but evoking no passion from any quarter of the political compass. Then, suddenly enough, they became objects of the most rigid attention, occupying the minds and studding the speeches of everyone from the most senior politicians to the editorial writer of the local newspaper. Such fluctuations can mask the fact that the present problems are expressions of the very same crisis that education faced in the 1960s – the educational crisis of modernity.[5]

Schools became caught up in a whirlwind in the 1960s, but the whirlwinds died away to a gentle breeze. Now in the 1980s the winds are again beginning to howl about the classroom windows. It may well be that this storm, like the storm of 1968, will pass, and that its sound and fury will have threatened more damage than it will actually cause. The walls of our school systems are stronger than would-be educational reformers of Left or Right might want to believe. It may also be the case that the choleric voices which proclaim the inadequacy of our education systems have no more to offer than River City's new music teacher, who could not play or read a note.

As in 1968, our schools and universities are experiencing a crisis, although today, the crisis is manifesting itself less in student street theatre than in the financial statements of institutions. But it is not simply the subjective experience of crisis that justifies the use of the word. Crisis is an appropriate term, because the present struggle, like that of the 1960s, is a struggle about the moral foundations of education, about its relation to the freedom of the individual and the purpose of the state. It is a struggle which demands, and is receiving at the hands of certain governments, determined, if illusory resolution.[6] It has provoked a situation, especially in universities, where many responsible commentators are beginning to fear for the life of these institutions. It is manifested in disturbances of normal functioning that are likely to be decisive for our educational futures and to some extent for the future of our respective nations.

THE CRISIS TENDENCIES OF CAPITALISM

Habermas' analysis of the crisis tendencies in advanced or late capitalism, *Legitimation Crisis* (*LC*), provides a remarkably prescient account of this pattern of crises.

Capitalism still suffers from recurring crises of economic accumulation. Although Marx may have been wrong in arguing that such tendencies were unavoidable, from time to time capitalist economies have been threatened by catastrophic falls in growth and profit. Habermas argues that under the conditions of extensive involvement of governments in the management of the economy and the mitigation of class conflict through the welfare state, economic crisis turns into a 'rationality crisis', as members of society look to governments and economic experts for explanations and solutions, only to recognise that both are relatively helpless. The legitimacy of government is threatened by this and so we see, today, as Habermas predicted before the end of the long economic boom had become clear (he was writing *LC* in 1971–2), a growth in the number of calls for governments to retreat from control over people's lives. The intrusion of governments, and their perceived failure to manage crime, poverty and the economy, leads to a crisis of motivation and meaning. Young people begin to ask whether or not it is meaningful to work hard at school when there may be no prospect of a job at the end of it. In turn jobs are reduced to incomes and the idea of 'vocation' disappears.

This cascade of crisis tendencies is cyclical, tied as it is to the economic cycle, but each turn of the wheel leaves a residue of cynicism and loss of meaning. In later work, Habermas distinguished more clearly between the motivational and legitimation crises produced cyclically, and a longer-term process of destruction of values by the intrusion of the political–economic system into the life–world. It is the everyday interactions with people who are really important to us which give meaning and provide motivation in life and it is from this level of life, the 'life–world', that the economic and political system has been borrowing significance for so long. The invasion or colonisation of this world, by political administration and by the forces of the system control such as money exchange and power, has gradually reduced the capacity of the life–world to give meaning to life. This robs educational and occupational interaction of some of the organising values like respect for elders, or norms of interpersonal conduct, such as honesty in speech, upon which they might draw. In times like the present, the longer-term process and the cyclical process come together, with the longer-term process generating the underlying problems of meaning and the cyclical one generating the immediate atmosphere of crisis and more deeply influencing the particular political form the crisis takes on.[7]

The solution of the immediate economic or political problems, which may occur rather automatically with the next turn of the economic cycle or with shifts in political control, is not at the same time a solution of the underlying problem. This deeper problem is a general problem of modernity and it will not be easily resolved by traditional, cyclical solutions. They may make the problem worse. It was this longer-term process, in the absence of economic crisis, which manifested itself most directly in the crisis of the 1960s.

At that time, the crisis began in the 'free speech' movement at Berkeley as a confrontation between authoritarian forms of educational administration and a student consciousness liberated from a failing traditional value system. Its development in the United States and Australia, under the impact of the draft of 19- and 20-year-olds for the Vietnam War, was hastened. It began as a critique of specific cultural and administrative forms and developed broader themes, such as those associated with the Civil Rights Movement in the US. It was a crisis confined mainly to adolescents and young people, a stratum freed for the first time from the constraints of traditional morality, at a moment in their lives when they had little or no commitment to the existing structure of occupational and financial status, and under political circumstances which were perceived as illegitimate and, indeed, life-threatening. Only in its mature phase did this process connect broader political and economic conditions with the particular issues with which the crisis began. Today, under conditions which threaten the status of the older generation, many of whom are those same 1960s adolescents grown older, the crisis is perceived more broadly from the beginning as a crisis for all our institutions.[8]

THE EDUCATIONAL CRISIS OF MODERNITY

The political and cultural response to the 1960s manifestation of the crisis was many-sided, but may be summed up in terms of the expansion of the welfare state, the liberalisation of education, and the penetration of counter-cultural symbols into mass entertainment and consumerism. One of the effects of this domestication of revolt was to increase the eventual cultural vulnerability of advanced capitalist societies in the event of the inevitable, cyclical economic downturn.

The present manifestation of the modern educational crisis, coming after a period of accommodation, occurs under different economic and political conditions from those of the 1960s. The educational crisis of 20 years ago did not initially manifest itself in the political sphere, nor was it brought into being by the educational policies of government or because it was part of the agenda of a political movement. It began among students and a small minority of faculty and spread into wider fields of domestic and foreign policy. Only in its fully developed stage did it lap up against the shores of economics. The present manifestation has its origins in economic crisis and in the response to that crisis of an emerging political movement: neoconservatism. In this manifestation, the nature of the political and economic links of the educational crisis are explicit. It is publicly recognised, from the beginning, that our educational problems are only a part of a wider political–economic crisis complex.[9]

Shorn of its more aberrant outliers, the old working class movements' post-1960s solution to the cluster of economic and cultural problems of that time was to develop further the welfare state, to encourage cultural pluralism, and to attempt to overcome inequalities of life chances by social intervention such as affirmative action, school bussing and the like. In the United States context, such policies, although sometimes bipartisan, were associated more with the Democratic party, the so-called 'liberals', than with the Republicans. In the United Kingdom (and Australia), where a more direct link between a stronger labour movement and a political party developed, labour parties were associated with this sort of policy, more clearly than conservative parties, despite, again, a degree of bipartisanship during the 1960s and early 1970s.

In education, these policies found very limited and imperfect expression in a range of specific innovations and in the consolidation of the general comprehensive form of the secondary school. The curriculum was broadened by the introduction of a wider range of either non-academic or non-traditional subjects particularly at senior high-school level. Financial support for the higher education of economically disadvantaged groups (and, specifically in the US, 'minorities') was greatly extended, and in the US quotas and affirmative action programmes actually brought some change in the level of access to higher education of disadvantaged groups.

Generally speaking, though, by 1978 much of the change in levels of access to senior high school and tertiary education had already occurred. The policies of welfare state expansion, in education, as elsewhere, had only marginal effects on the problems they were designed to solve. Problems of motivation and legitimacy remained. Absolute poverty was alleviated, but relative poverty remained; in the UK and Australia little further progress in equalising educational opportunity occurred after the early 1970s; in the US progress of this kind may well have peaked a little later. When it came to administrative and pedagogical reform schools proved more intransigent than anticipated.[10]

The modern comprehensive school is a very imperfect realisation of the educational goals of the 1960s, but even so, it is this type of school and the practices associated with it that are currently under attack. To understand the nature of the neoconservative challenge it is necessary to recognise that it is being mounted in the context of a general social critique centred on problems of labour and economic nationalism, in a particular foreign policy climate. Ironically, the sophistication of this critique owes a great deal to the systematisation of social and political analysis by post-1960s progressives, responding to the perceived inadequacy, and self-indulgence, of 1968.

What is at stake is the set of answers we give to the Hegelian questions. Whether we can make our history or whether such a belief has already led in the last few decades to a situation in which we must unmake a great deal of it. Whether we can control our fate to such a degree as to dare to begin reconstructing God or whether our control is so limited that we must proceed with the utmost caution. And finally, whether we possess in reason and art a fallible but useful means for this task, or whether, reason being limited to the domain of necessity and art to idiosyncracy, our means fall so far short of our aim as to force us to abandon it.

MODERNITY AND ITS DISCONTENTS

One of the characteristics of current discussion is the re-emergence of eighteenth- and nineteenth-century themes – a going back to and a going over the fundamental assumptions of the democratic state, of the idea of the liberty of the individual, of the role of mass schooling in the education of an enlightened citizenry and the like. The very roots of modernity, from Mill and the French *philosophes* to the fathers of modern democratic constitutionalism, are being inspected anew.

The fading optimism of the sixties image of humanity is brought face to face with the anthropological pessimism of conservatism. The rational hubris of the Enlightenment's 'social physics' has dissolved into post-modern irrationalism and attempts manipulatively to reassert traditional values. As Habermas points out, the democratic utopias peopled by rational educated citizens, which were the dream of the Enlightenment, have everywhere been overtaken by a pervasive sense of limitation:

> The future is occupied with the merely negative; on the threshold to the 21st Century we find the terrifying panorama of a world-wide threat to the interests of life in general: the spiral of the arms race, uncontrolled proliferation of automatic weapons, structural impoverishment of developing countries, unemployment and growing social imbalance in developed countries, problems of overburdening the environment, and the nearly catastrophic operations of high technology are the catch words that penetrate by way of the mass media into public consciousness. (Habermas, 'The new obscurity . . .' 1986: 2)

The reasons for the exhaustion of the utopian energy of the Enlightenment, Habermas argues, are to be found in the contradictory by-products of its very success. The development of medicine, technology, industry, communications media and information processing have led to the emergence of institutional complexes; these in turn both require and constitute new managerial systems which penetrate more widely into more and more aspects of daily life, destroying the primal communal and institutional sources of motivation and, hence, hope.

Many commentators, especially among French post-modernists such as Foucault, believe that this exhaustion is the product of more than a merely passing pessimism.[11] But Habermas argues that it is the result of the exhaustion of a particular utopian ideal, a one-sided and incomplete form of vision shared by both the New Right and the Old Left – a form of colour-blindness in which the analyst sees only the world of work and material productivity, and understands social process solely in terms of the movement of the 'media' of money and power – that is, in economic and political terms. Both the New Right and the Old Left fail to realise that the developmental impulses in modern society, which are now showing signs of exhaustion, are not the only developmental possibilities inherent in modernity. Indeed, it can be argued that we have possessed the material means to solve most of our material problems since at least 1950. The unbalanced development of our material possibilities has everywhere run up against its own limitations.

The central focus of the first great utopian impulse of the Enlightenment was the problem of labour. This classical problem of modernity was addressed by Marx, Weber and others in terms of the social organisation of labour. The utopian ideals of the European democratic labour movements centred around the vision of a society of free and equal labour. In the West, this vision worked itself out in the reform of capitalist society, through the movements of political labour and the development of the welfare state, including the provision of public education and the accompanying transition from birth to achievement criteria in determining status and life chances. Habermas argues that this vision has now become obscured because the limits of the emancipatory possibilities of the welfare state, as well as those of the labour movement, have been reached or even, in retrograde ways, exceeded. The partial association of educational success and occupational advancement which occurred is now diminishing. The response of some sections of the New Right to problems consequently arising has been to try to reverse the developmental process and recapture or freeze the developmental process in some prior stage – to reinvent, say, the 1950s. Other sections wish to push forward to a technocratic libertarian state.

The response of the Old Left is to try to deny that the utopian possibilities of the socialisation of labour, under the present conditions of limited cultural development, have been exhausted. A typical response of this group is one which coincides with a part of the New Right's educational agenda. It involves a further attempt to replace autonomous standards internal to education with a government-decided set of economic and technological priorities. The essentially consensual life–world of the school is to be increasingly penetrated by contractual and legal oversight and made an administratively account-able and measurable part of the production system.

The goal of neutralising class conflict has been achieved by the welfare state largely through the political labour movement, through redistri-bution of wealth and government support for non-market sectors of the economy such as education and training, through legislation governing aspects of occupational health and safety, and through collective bargaining and/or arbitration. These policies gain their legitimation from representative electoral processes and from the relative degree of success of the state in regulating class conflict and ensuring the general conditions for the accumulation of capital in the face of recurring downturns in the business cycle. The growth of the economy is, in turn, a precondition of the redistributive policies of the welfare state which serve to support the public institutions relied on by the workers and disadvantaged sections of society. The accumulative process is also a precondition of the government's financial capacity to buy off influential, often affluent, but potentially disruptive, pressure groups.

However, the limitations of the state in both the political sphere of regulating class conflict and the economic sphere have become increasingly obvious. The state has been unable to protect its own economy against international economic influences and the policies of multinational capitalism. Internally, it has been unable to satisfy either its clients – or the capitalists whose co-operation has been necessary for the welfare-state compromise to work.

> In a situation in which an insufficient willingness to invest, economic stagnation, rising unemployment, and a crisis in the public budget can be suggestively connected in the perception of the public with the costs of the welfare state, we can see clearly the structural limitations within which the social welfare state compromise has to be worked out and maintained. (Habermas, 'The new obscurity . . .' 1986: 7)

The state lacks the power to contest the basic mode of functioning of the economic system. As business leaders are so ready to point out, the state is dependent on capitalist sentiment. It cannot guarantee work. The number of supporters of the welfare state, among liberals and even labour voters, begins to diminish:

> The upwardly mobile voter groups, who have directly reaped the greatest benefits of the formation of the social welfare state, are capable in times of crisis of developing a mentality concerned with protecting their standard of living. They may also join together with the old middle class, and in general with those classes oriented toward productivity, into a defensive block against underprivileged or excluded groups. (Habermas, 'The new obscurity . . .' 1986: 8)

As this occurs, the state further tightens the net of legal and administrative controls and interventions into the lives of its clients. The development of more pervasive computerised surveillance and dossiers on citizens is an example of this. But even its more benevolent actions are self-contradictory. In providing income support in the form of pensions and grants, it replaces family relationships with bureaucratic ones – this reduces the dignity of recipients. A similar process is developing with regard to the 'pedagogical privacy' of the classroom and the collegial individualism of the relatively anarchical arena of higher education. The product of this process of intervention is the generation of new forms of problem and the destruction of traditional and interpersonally constructed sources of socially valuable norms:

> In short, inherent in the project of the social state is a contradiction between goal and method. Its goal is the establishment of forms of life which are structured according to egalitarian standards and which at the same time open up arenas for individual self-fulfillment and spontaneity. (Habermas, 'The new obscurity . . .' 1986: 9)

THE NEW RIGHT AND THE OLD LEFT

Habermas identifies two groupings on the basis of their response to this problem. The 'legitimists', who seek to preserve the welfare state and to find ways of pushing forward its reformist programme centred as it is on the freeing of labour from dependency, and the neoconservatives, who want to wind down the welfare state. Politically, these tendencies may be connected respectively to the left of the Democratic party in the United States, to elements in the Left and centre Left of the labour parties, of Britain and of Australia, and to the Republican Party in the US and to the various conservative parties in Britain and Australia.

The neoconservatives, the New Right, espouse a freeing of 'economic energies' (e.g. the ill-fated supply-side economics) which will result, they believe, in new growth. But, as Habermas points out, in the United States (and in Britain and Australia), this has resulted in redistribution of income to the rich and growth of the dependent and economically marginal underclass. This is accompanied by a shift away from the parliamentary process, in principle answerable to the public, towards a series of private negotiations, and an increasing marginalisation of the state, as one partner in these deals among others (corporatism), or as a neutral referee or stake-holder, as it was considered to be in, say, the *laissez-faire* period of British nineteenth-century politics.

The educational policy associated with this is part of a general cultural policy. It has two thrusts. First, intellectuals are discredited as a non-productive class, or at least, the non-technical, 'political' intellectuals who concern themselves with questions of the kind discussed in this book. The constant denigration of sociologists (except in America, where sociologists have led the intellectual Right) by those, often economic journalists, who are spokesmen [sic] for the New Right is an example of this. In the area of curriculum it is reflected in a push for more technically-oriented and supposedly economically relevant learning, for a depoliticisation of the humanities and social curriculum, and for the restoration of traditional values. The economic and technical part of this agenda is shared by the Old Left.

However, the neoconservative attack on the intellectuals is simply scapegoating:

> Neoconservativism shifts onto cultural modernism the uncomfortable burdens of a more or less successful capitalist modernisation of the economy and society. . . . The neoconservative does not uncover the economic and social causes for the altered attitudes towards work, consumption, achievement and leisure. Consequently, he attributes all of the following – hedonism, the lack of social identification, the lack of obedience, narcissism, the withdrawal from status and achievement competition – to the domain of 'culture'. . . . These discontents have not been called into life by modernist intellectuals. they are rooted in deepseated reactions against the process of societal modernisation. Under the pressures of the dynamics of economic growth and the organisational accomplishments of the state, this social modernisation penetrates deeper and deeper into previous forms of human existence. (Habermas, 'The new obscurity . . .' 1982: 7)

Second, there is a push for a revival of approved folk culture. Both the populism of nation, family, and conventional morality on the one hand, and the rejection of social science, values exploration, personal development and political subject matter in the curriculum on the other, reflect this trend. Here we may interpret this as an attempt to reinstate private value systems as an autonomous source of the morality which is seen to be threatened by the extension of the welfare state. When the family is again supported by the laws, when the tax system and everything else, deregulated, the social workers sacked, and the government regulations removed from factory, farm and home, the gap will be filled by a revived folk-culture.

It is difficult to see this attempt to reassert traditional values as a move to the promotion of maturity. Perhaps only those who, like many New Right intellectuals, have once rebelled against tradition and have now returned to it in their maturity, recognising its value for the first time, could really believe that it is anything other than a recipe for immaturity when imposed on people in their formative years.

It could, perhaps, more cogently be argued that the particular kind of intellectuals who are being rejected are precisely those who are speaking on behalf of the suppressed side of the potentialities of modernity – the possibilities inherent in a post-conventional morality and a mature social and political discourse within the realm of a genuine process of public formation of will and conscience. However, the neoconservative programme may well succeed, despite its economic marginalisation of a significant proportion of citizens, because it does clearly recognise the fear of freedom increasingly felt by many under the impact of the extension of the state into daily life and the destruction of the traditional moral basis of marriage, the family, parenthood and social life which this entails. Indeed, those who make up New Right have been characterised as liberals who, in the circumstances of the 1980s, have become frightened of their own liberalism.

The Old Left fails to recognise the existence of this fear of freedom, this felt need to go back to folk-certainties, rather than forward, though *anomie*, to a mature post-conventional state of moral thought. But it also fails to recognise a growing fear *for* freedom, which its increasingly statist solutions to social problems engender in a third group which Habermas identifies – the critics of growth. The critics of growth generally take a different view from both neoconservatives and the Old Left. They are critics of economic growth but proponents of personal and communal growth. They reject further economic growth as a major goal in advanced societies, because they argue that our lives have already become too thoroughly dominated by commodities – to the extent that many of our personal relationships have become commodified. They seek to regain, at a new level, the balance of material and personal wellbeing which may have obtained in an earlier, smaller-scale, village society. In this purpose they are also anti-statist, but not in the same way as the neoconservatives. They seek to oppose the bureaucraticisation of life but not only state bureaucratisation. They seek the reconstitution of private, economic community, too; 'they demand that the inner dynamics of sub-systems steered by power and money should be broken, or at least, restrained through forms of reorganisation that are closer to their base and are self-administered' (Habermas, 'The new obscurity . . .' 1986: 13).

One of the themes common to many members of this third category is that of social and personal development. The development generally envisaged is not simply linear growth but a transformation of perspective – a conversion. Habermas seeks to resolve the problems of one-sided modernisation by means of an evolution to a qualitatively new level of development involving new levels of problem-solving [learning]. This theme is sometimes expressed by critics of growth in terms of the dawn of a new age or the emergence of a new 'paradigm'. The centre of the struggle between the three tendencies is cultural and educational. The New Right seeks to solve the problems of the present crisis of capital accumulation by re-creating a vigorous, entrepreneurial capitalism fuelled by a renewal of 'the Protestant ethic' in the working population. They attack the 'new class' of sociologists, social workers, feminists and intellectuals: 'The new class and its hostile culture must be tamed or forced out of all sensitive areas' (P. Steinfels, *The Neo-Conservatives*, 1979: 55 quoted in Habermas 1983: 77). The Old Left seeks to continue the programme of redistribution and socialisation of the economy. Parts of the Old Left look explicitly to countries like Sweden where the process of socialisation of labour and the bureaucratisation of social life is most fully advanced while still retaining a democratic electoral structure. In the present economic circumstances, they, too, seek to solve the problem of capital accumulation by a revalorisation of capital through planning and social contracts aimed at increased productivity as well as the direct containment or lowering of real labour costs. The renewal of the productive power and the international competitiveness of the old capitalist economies of Europe and the English-speaking world is a bipartisan goal. However, the cultural goals of the Old Left in general are concerned primarily with issues of equity, but they have extended their concern to social and racial as well as social-class equity. For reasons of political inclusiveness, this group nominally supports some of the causes of the critics of growth, but its attention is centred on the state and the political economy of labour rather than on the person or the community. In contrast, the New Right seeks to emphasise competitive vigour and to celebrate the culture of the entrepreneur. The critics of growth are, as yet, institutionally fragmented. Some have sought to find a political vehicle in labour parties which, seeking to maintain as broad a base as they can, have supported them. Other have sought to influence events through centrist parties, such as those found in Britain and Australia, or through even more narrowly based parties, such as the Greens. Generally speaking, this group has a project which seeks to direct attention to non-growth areas of life – the environment, peace, personal development, community development, the folk arts, etc. This cultural programme tends to assume and rely on a reasonable degree of equity and welfare state support for disadvantaged groups but its developmental thrust is directed elsewhere.

Perhaps the example of the Feminist Movement is the most interesting here. Of the two ruling political tendencies the Old Left is the most hospitable to feminism, but its hospitality is not without strings. The price of an alliance between feminism and the Old Left is the acceptance of an analysis of the situation of women essentially in political–economic terms – in terms of class and class conflict. But feminism, as a movement, has demonstrated its capacity to make progress through the exercise of means outside the established structures of administrative authority and economic power, suggesting the possibility that any acceptance of an analysis limited to media of power and money might effectively domesticate the Women's Movement.[12]

HEGEL, MARX AND THE FRANKFURT SCHOOL

Clearly, neoconservatism is informed by a degree of pessimism about human nature, and by an individualistic, and relatively narrow understanding of our capacity to solve problems by a reason which goes beyond the absolute givenness of traditional values or expansion of technology. This pessimism concerning the scope of our capacity for rational problem-solving is so pervasive in the English-speaking world that it has become the unacknowledged background for much of the debate. In our characteristic fear of Utopian Grand Theory we have turned our backs on the very kind and level of reasoning with which our forefathers constructed the democratic institutions we presently enjoy. Only the largely relativist and irrationalist tendencies of some of the critics of growth move outside this charmed circle of 'positive reason'. However, critical thought offers an alternative perspective on the crisis, based not on irrationalism but on a return to that broader conception of reason which characterised much of the thought of the founders of the modern democratic state.

The centre of growth of critical thought is the recognition, central to Hegel's thought, and given concrete form by Marx, that 'through the multiple effort to preserve their life by the labour of their own hands, men make themselves the authors of their own historical development, without however recognising themselves as the subjects of that development' (*T & P*: 218). The historical development that humankind achieves is a development that encompasses the self-formation of a plastic humanity, rather than adaptation to the limits of a fixed, or essential nature inclined possibly to evil. It also encompasses the making of knowledge and the achievement of new levels of knowing. And it indicates the recognition that there is a continuing tension between the fact of historical self-formation and the actual level of awareness of this.

Hegel postulates a universal tendency for the creations of our own authorship to become autonomous objects – to become objectified – and to face us blandly, as if we had not created them, and worse, to turn on us and cause us to suffer. In a review of Tom Wolfe's *Bonfire of the Vanities*, which is about New York, Anatole Broyard wrote:

> In 1970 in *The Uses of Disorder*, Richard Sennett argued that it was part of a big city's function to confuse, interrupt and frustrate us, because this forces us to improvise. Such improvisation led us to high culture. . . . In Wolfe's view, the . . . disorder uses us. The disorder is no longer convertible.[13]

In New York, disorder has become autonomous. A creation of human provenance, it has now lost even its capacity to provoke creative responses. New York's loss of meaning represents the omega point towards which our society at large is rushing with ever greater speed.

It is this tendency to perpetual imprisonment in the present historical level of our own self-formation, and the fact that we are sentenced to stay in this prison as a result of our uncritical acceptance of given levels of development as indicative of 'our nature', 'our society', 'our culture', that is the first, perennial feature of the human historical process. The second is the motivation – born in suffering and our response to it – to transcend the distortions and inadequacies of our present level of self-formation. Neoconservatism's recognition of this perennial reality is distorted. The social conservatives' notion of transcending suffering by a linear development of our economic and technological powers within an essentially fixed framework of social institutions is a limited one. Similarly, the notion of transcending suffering by the further development of rational–legal organisation – by more bureaucracy – characteristic of the Old Left, is also limited. Neither approach can cope with the autonomous meaninglessness that has swallowed New York. The idea of linear progress and development can only take any epoch a certain way before the demand for a transcending level of awareness of the existing historical mode of self-formation becomes overwhelming. As Habermas argues,[14] the essential and recurring contradiction of our humanity consists in our being a causally-determined natural species, yet morally free – free, even, to participate in causing our future selves. Our past pattern has been marked by a tendency to allow this contradiction to reach crisis before we take the necessity for its transcendence seriously. It is our constant attempts to free ourselves from the limiting conditions of each epoch of our own self-formation that is the motive force of our history as humanity (rather than our simple chronology as a species which undergoes changes). As Marx saw, the truth of the insights which are the fruit of this awareness, this meta-vision of our possibilities, is demonstrated only in the historical practice of living it. The vision of the Enlightenment may have taken a one-sided form, but it was a progressive vision. Those who lived under that vision created a great deal of 'progress'. In a time of exhaustion of that vision we are either seeking to give it new life, but essentially in its old one-sided form, or to transcend it.

Even his enemies tend to accept that Marx was one of the most powerful critics of the political and economic forms taken on by the new societies of the Enlightenment. He saw quite clearly that the political liberation of the mass of the people, through the popular franchise which accompanied the economic ascendency of the bourgeoisie, was only half liberation. As long as this mass remained economically dependent, the development of its human possibilities remained chained to the six-day, eighty-hour week and the starvation wages of the mid-nineteenth century. His analysis of capitalist economies pointed to the perpetuation of this dependency as long as capitalism prevailed. Eventually there would be an inevitable rupture between the class of economic dependants and the class of owners of the capital means of production. This would occur because the class of owners of capital would always remain small and the dependent class would always remain large. The dependent class would also remain grossly exploited because the laws of capitalism would force owners to keep wages as low as possible. Sooner or later the vast majority would act in their own interests. The history of revolutionary activity, especially in the nineteenth century (e.g. 1848), despite disappointments, led to the belief that such action might well come sooner than later.

The working class, the proletariat, was the class which, due to the structure of capitalism, was bearer of historical destiny – it would take the next step. The next step, however, would also be the last, because for the first time in history, the interests of the class which took control of society would be (virtually) universal. It would mean a society governed in the interests of all, in which, for the first time, the structure of labour and the political structure would be governed by a coincidence of universal interests.[15]

The events in the decades after Marx's death in 1883 did not bear out the expectations which his work aroused in his followers. From the perspective of Germany in the 1920s and 1930s, faced with the betrayal of the democratic promise of the Russian Revolution by Lenin, and later Stalin, the revolutionary failure of the German working class in 1918–19, and that same working class's later welcoming of Hitler, a small group of Marxist-influenced intellectuals at the Institute for Social Research in Frankfurt (the Frankfurt School) recognised the need for a thoroughgoing revision of Marxism.[16]

This group of thinkers, among them Fromm, Marcuse, Adorno and Horkheimer, were guided in their revision by two central insights. First, that the tendency of Marx at times to see his work as objective and scientific, in the manner of the scientific community of his time, and the maturation of this tendency at the hands of some of his followers, particularly in the Soviet Union, into a rigid and dogmatic science of dialectical materialism, was responsible for a great many of the shortcomings of Marxist theory, explaining, in particular, its tendency to postulate 'iron laws' of capitalist development and its failure to adapt them under the pressure of historical events. Second, that Marx's contradictory view of consciousness discouraged the development of an understanding of the consciousness of the proletariat and led to a practical failure of revolutionary parties to influence this consciousness, or to create an effective critique of the mass-produced consumer culture which actually came into being.

The central criticism that members of the Frankfurt School, and in particular Adorno and Horkheimer[17], levelled against Marxism was that it had become infected with the very same epistemological views that had infected capitalism itself – the one-sided subjective development of reason: the limitation of reason to its instrumental, positive role. They sought to reinstate a broader conception of reason, which has been present in European thought since at least the time of Aristotle. In this view, reason could be instrumental and positive, but it could also be political and ethical. Like Kant and Hegel, they wanted to retain the notion of a universal reason committed to ethics. This was essential to any possibility of rational social progress. Unlike Kant, they sought to rescue political–ethical reason by unifying it with instrumental reason rather than radically separating it. They felt that such a separation was the first step towards making ethical reason vulnerable to the later movement of instrumental reason which seeks to eject political–ethical thought from the palace of reason altogether. They thereby wished to keep open the idea of a critical meta-awareness, which addressed itself to a continual confrontation of the existing state of affairs with its own contradictions, of the seemingly 'natural' crystallisations of social institutions with the possibilities that had been excluded by this historically temporary condition. They wished to keep open the possibility of going beyond the fragile 'half-democracy' in which human progress had become bogged down.

A by-product of this critique of instrumental reason was a recognition, held in common by some strands of thought in the sociology of knowledge, that suppressed political and ethical considerations inevitably found their way by subterranean routes into the 'findings' of positive reason. Following Lukacs, when reason was held to be the product of individual minds without at the same time a recognition that these minds were the minds of historical, socially-formed beings, it was labelled 'subjective'.[18] Objective reason was the term used to describe the actual movements of thought in their social as well as individual reality. From the standpoint of Habermas' later discussion of Hegel, it is possible to see this concept of 'objective reason' as useful but fictive:

> the philosophy of history creates the fiction of historical subjects as the possible subject of history, as though objective tendencies of development [e.g. of reason], which actually are equivocal, were comprehended with will and consciousness by those who act politically and were decided by them for their own benefit. From the lofty observation post of this fiction the situation is revealed in its ambivalences which are susceptible to practical intervention, so that an enlightened mankind can elevate itself then to become what up to that point it was only fictitiously. (*T & P*: 252)

Positive reason is content with the assumptions and limits characteristic of its own epoch – it is subjective. It concentrates on developing the implications of these in the fullest possible degree. Only when the limits and contradictions of these assumptions are no longer avoidable will the need to invoke a more critical understanding of reason become clear. When critical reason becomes active, the self-understanding of thinkers becomes changed reflexively, by an awareness of the epoch-specific character of their limitations. In this state, thought approaches objective reason. But the epoch-specific limitations of reason are not simply the limits of existing scientific concepts or theories. They also include limitations engendered by the social and moral circumstances, by the interplay between instrumental and political–ethical considerations, by the historical, cultural and social imbeddedness of thinkers.

Under such circumstances, the Frankfurt thinkers believed that the appropriate method of critique was immanent critique, which proceeds through forcing existing views to their systematic conclusions, bringing them face to face with their incompleteness and contradictions, and, ultimately, with the social conditions of their existence.[19] After their long stay in exile in America, where they fled after leaving Germany in 1933, Adorno and Horkheimer recognised more clearly, that the problems of capitalism could no longer be seen in terms of the material deprivation of the working class which Marx had observed 60 years earlier. They turned to Marx's earlier analysis of alienation, defining the problems of capitalist society as problems which flowed from the dynamics of capitalism as a system characterised by cultural and technological conditions resulting from the one-sided development of reason: a productive, hedonistic, consumer society characterised by moral and personal childishness – a rich kid who never grew up.

While societies like the United States might be seen as democratic, they were democratic in only limited ways. The mass franchise was a manipulated franchise, a product of the mass management of public opinion. The reigning personality type, which schools helped to shape, was one which felt at home in relationships of either domination or subordination, rather than mature autonomy and equality. The dominant mode of interaction in such societies was manipulation and the dominant character type was manipulative – literally, proceeding as if people were things to be controlled by 'pressing the right buttons'.[20]

Adorno and Horkheimer described the consumer capitalism they found in the United States in terms of the one-sided development of the possibilities inherent in the American Revolution. They attempted to trace the connection between 'economic life, individual psychic development and cultural change'. Positive reason was unable to do this, since it had abandoned the possibility of ethical reason and, because of the legacy of Marxist-Leninist thought, had grown suspicious of all attempts to understand society as a whole. Instead, it limited itself to reflecting the society as it was. As Habermas later pointed out:

> The hitherto undisputed attempts of the great theories to reflect on the complex of life as a whole is henceforth itself discredited as dogma . . . the spontaneity of hope, the act of taking a position, the experience of relevance or indifference, and above all the response to suffering and oppression, the desire for adult autonomy, the will to emancipation, and the happiness of discovering one's identity – all these are dismissed for all time from the obligating interest of reason. (*T & P*: 262–3)

The earlier internal critique of capitalism, which could have carried it towards more progressive possibilities had stalled in the welfare state compromise. It had moved forward initially under the pressure of working-class political movements informed by holistic thinking, but these movements had lost their vision in the manipulated culture of private consumerism, to which even education is beginning to succumb. One of the main sources of critical reason which could have prevented this – the intellectuals – had also been culturally neutralised by the impact of a triumphant positivism. The key to unlock the door to progress lay in the keeping of reason. The critique of positive reason was the key to critique in general.

By a set of interlocking self-limitations, positive reason supported the social status quo and promoted the treatment of human beings as things. By its doctrine of evidence it limited evidence to sensory experience. Expressed in the social sciences as behaviourism,[21] and extended to the contradictory notion of 'verbal behaviour', this led to a science of public opinion that accepted the givens of the historical moment in lieu of any vision of the potentialities. Despite the fact that we know from our own experience how fickle public opinion is, the public opinion survey, capturing the present opinions of samples of the population, became the dominant mode of sociological research, aimed at testing theories of society whose validity was nevertheless not believed by their creators to be limited to the present moment.

The positivist vision of evidence is like the vision of the typical photojournalist. Recently, *Life Magazine*, in 'The year in pictures' reviewed the events of 1987. It published a picture of Colonel North, standing at attention in full-dress uniform, viewed from a camera angle slightly below the waist, looming heroically against a marble background and flanked by the US flag. But the environmental, social and economic news of 1987 seldom got a picture. Indeed, the stock-market crash was illustrated by graphs. In photojournalism, only individuals make history, not social, economic or political processes or systems. The camera deals only with appearances and even, then, as the picture of Colonel North shows, it does not deal with them in a value-free way.

In its early stages positivism was characterised by a belief in the value freedom of its activities. Under criticism because of the obvious falsehood of this view, the defence was to distinguish between the scientific contexts of 'discovery' and 'verification'.[22] The former, in which hypotheses were created, was a value-influenced and human process, but the latter, in which strenuous attempts were made to falsify them, was one in which the hypotheses would be refined and values removed. This defence may have failed in fact, because it did not show how the human social process of testing hypotheses could be any more secure against values than the process of discovery, but it succeeded subjectively because it provided a continuing basis for the separation of science from 'politics', which was necessary if the resolute refusal of positive science to deal rationally with values was to be maintained. This refusal took the form of an ethical 'decisionism'.[23] Scientists could only make a personal decision about values, such as their decision to pursue the truth through science, or the decision made by the developer of the atomic bomb, Oppenheimer, to try to prevent his work being misused by politicians. This decision might be informed by reason but was seen as essentially non-rational in its basis. Science, per se, could deal with values only as the psychological states of individuals induced in them by learning experiences or perhaps in some cases genetically programmed. As such, the realm of ethics and political commitment was seen as accessible *to science* only as a realm available for empirical generalisation, law-like explanation, and manipulation. In this way, whatever the impact of personal statements by scientists to the contrary, positive science lent itself to the further development of an alienated culture of manipulation. In the science of education, this led to a view of pedagogy as manipulation, while curriculum was divided into value-free subjects and value-based subjects where values were located decisionistically. The older view of pedagogy as a moral/ethical and practical art was abandoned.

The appropriation of the findings of such a science by the advertising industry, by those who manage political campaigns and by an increasingly research-guided entertainment industry, was the bridge whereby this dwarfed vision of ethical and political reason entered the popular culture, providing social support for manipulative personal relations, thus completing the circle of limitation which has robbed advanced capitalism of its progressive possibilities. Under the prevailing conditions of reason, no amount of technological or economic increase or expansion and refinement of the bureaucratic organs of the state, can provide progress. Those of the Old Left who seek to breathe new life into the social–democratic settlement, including as it does the meritocratic role of schooling, which characterised the welfare state structures of the New Deal (in America) or the post-World War II

Welfare State of Britain and Australia, have failed to realise that the methodology they seek to use is responsible for the problems they want to solve. The New Right have also failed to realise the nature of the problem. They seek to wind down the existing extent of rational manipulation by the state, including the attempts by the state to manipulate equality of opportunity, but wish to give added impetus to the technological and cultural processes which have, in fact, been part of the cause of our present problems. However, the attempt, on the part of some sections of the New Right, to reinstate traditional, non-manipulative values in interpersonal relations indicates that they may see a little further than the Old Left, despite the fact that they are mistaken when they attribute the breakdown of old values to the activity of 'subversive' intellectuals, rather than to the forces at work which drive capitalism towards a more diversified and ever hungry consumerism. Unfortunately, it seems unlikely that it will prove possible to reinstate the old values. The social relationships of the village society which supported and validated them have gone. Without these, the old values can never be perceived with anything other than a nostalgic sense of artificiality. The only way forward is through the present state of societal *anomie* to a new, post-conventional maturity and a democratic reconstitution of popular culture as a culture of critical reconstruction.

THE LIMITATIONS OF CRITIQUE

The most potent accusation made against critical theory is the charge that it is biased towards the merely negative. It is potent because it can be made by a critic who otherwise accepts the argument of critical theory. While Adorno and Horkheimer may be able to help us diagnose the systematic interlocking of social, cultural and epistemological factors which have produced the present crisis, the poetic completeness of their vision prevents us from seeing any opportunity for effective action. However, as Henry Giroux points out, the conflict and contradiction in various cultural spheres is as much a source of opportunity for transcendence as the general or overall form of such spheres may be a cause for critique.[24] From their standpoint as Germans, and as not wholly integrated visitors on the American scene, Adorno and others may have underestimated the potential of the American working class to bring about change, due to a natural enough tendency to overstress the homogeneity of American life and to a focus on its ills. In addition, as Habermas has argued, their self-limitation to immanent critique led to a methodological stress on the merely negative, to the identification of gaps, contradictions and incompleteness.[25] To get any sustained view of transcending possibilities, and thus to have a more positive vision, it was necessary to develop some normative vision, some potential for a transcending method.

The problem of finding some surer guide to transcending our existing state of development than is provided by the identification of contradictions is the key problem for any critique. All possibility of progress seems to involve some method which, however fallibly, fitfully and reversibly, allows us to go beyond the merely negative, but, and this is the rub, such methods, all too often have become the vehicle of inquisition, pogrom or crusade. Throughout history we have attempted to find some absolute standpoint, an Archimedean point outside the relative world of history, to provide a sure and certain method. The meaning of the Enlightenment is to be found just as much in the abandonment of the previous certainties of religion (in its absolute, timeless forms), as in the new faith in the goddess of reason that it ushered in. Now we are witness to the dethronement of reason. Adorno was able to live with a negative method. Horkheimer borrowing a mystical optimism from Benjamin, thought that the shadowy lineaments of the new could emerge from the relentless critique of the old. Habermas, not satisfied with this, sought to develop a vision of method unstained by the possibility of fanaticism or one-sided appropriation. He found this method in the neo-Kantianism of Karl-Otto Apel's account of transcendental aspects of human speech. Despite criticisms which have forced a weakening of originally stronger claims, Habermas has clung to the insight that it is in the facts of human speech that the possibility of freedom and respect for each human being's potential contribution to the experience of the species rests.

He has connected his view of the potentialities of speech with the possibility of evolutionary progress through communicative action. At the heart of this vision lies a communicative understanding of reason and a view of the crisis of modernity as a crisis of learning which need not, but might, be resolved by a shift to a higher level of learning:

> The educational history (*Bildungsgeschichte*) of humanity develops in the same way as that of society – as Hegel grasped in *The Phenomenology of Spirit*. The education of individuals takes place, at a given developmental state of civilisation, in the manner of a reproduction of a model of experience that is constitutive of it. (Habermas, 'Pädagogische "Optimismus"...' 1961: 256*)

Despite individual regressions and the failure of some sectors of public life to have yet reached genuinely democratic levels of will-formation, the developmental problem which faces modern society and education is that of institutionalising – Talcott Parson's code for making a permanent and entrenched part of normal life – rational problem-solving procedures in more and more spheres of life.

We are at the threshold of a learning level characterised by the personal maturity of the decentred ego and by open, reflexive communication which fosters democratic participation and responsibility for all. We fall short of this because of the one-sided development of our rational capacity for understanding. Fragments of a more mature learning level are all around us. Much of the thinking has already been done, but the task of actually realising or institutionalising greater maturity remains. The present situation in the democracies is one characterised by attacks on some of the structures which have already partially institutionalised greater social and personal maturity.

In such terms, the present crisis may properly be called a crisis of educational rationality. The modern educational crisis is a product of the one-sided development of our capacity for rational management of human affairs and rational problem solving. The institution of mass schooling can be either a source of the problem or a possible vehicle for the changes in learning level we require.[26] Traditionally, education has had a commitment to reason, to rational problem solving. It has had this commitment precisely to the degree that it has had a commitment to knowledge and truth.

The present crisis is manifesting itself as a general social crisis in economic, political and motivational dimensions. It is accompanied by a sense of loss of meaning. Both the New Right and the Old Left have turned to cultural and educational management and manipulation in an attempt to extend further the steering power of the system, to replace lost motivation and meaning by a managed traditionalism in the case of the New Right and by a strategy of attempting to increase corporate commitment in the case of the Old Left. The crisis is thus an educational crisis, because powerful groups seek to employ educational means to bring about what they would see as a satisfactory resolution to current problems. But it is also an educational problem in a more direct way, as teachers have known for some time. The school system is in the front line of loss of motivation and meaning. For schooling to continue to be educational it must solve the modern educational problem. It needed neither the Old Left nor the New Right to tell teachers there is an educational crisis in schools.[27]

If critical theory is headed in roughly the right direction, the problem can only be solved by a shift to a new learning level. Schools, as always, are under a double obligation, are burdened by a double task. To resolve their own problems they must transcend their present incomplete and one-sided level of development, and they must also do this if they are to make a contribution to the solution of the problems of the society in which they are found. Conversely, their capacity to do this is limited by the immaturity of the society with which they are intermeshed and the corresponding limitations of the individuals which it has produced.

Clearly, any progress which might be made will be slow, and incremental. But it would be valuable to be reasonably sure of the blueprint which is to be followed; to have a glimpse, as Rilke would say, of God's 'sleeping contours'. The critical theorist of education is a grave wayfarer who offers, tremblingly, a vision and a new skill for this vast task.

NOTES

1. R. M. Rilke, *Poems from the Book of Hours*, trans. Babette Deutsch, New York: New Directions Press, 1941: 29. Reprinted by permission of New Directions Press.
2. *Ibid.*
3. J. Habermas, *Theory and Practice (T & P)*, London: Heinemann Educational Books, 1974. (Original German versions of the articles concerned appeared in 1968–71.) The argument of this chapter is based largely on *T & P*: 214–16, with some added ideas from later work, such as Habermas' 'Neoconservative culture criticism in the United States and West Germany', *Telos*, **56** (Summer), 1983: 75–89 and 'The new obscurity: the crisis of the welfare state and the exhaustion of utopian energies', *Philosophy and Social Criticism*, **11** (2), 1986: 1–18.
4. See Habermas' discussion of the term 'crisis', *T & P*: 215–16. For a recent Marxist analysis see R. Sharp, *Capitalist Crisis and Schooling*, Melbourne: Macmillan, 1986. See also H. Weiler's analysis in 'Education, public confidence and the legitimacy of the modern state: do we have a crisis?', *Phi Delta Kappan*, September 1982: 9–14.
5. This is also D. Misgeld's view in 'Emancipation, enlightenment and liberation: an approach toward foundational enquiry into education', *Interchange*, **6** (3), 1975: 23–37.
6. For instance, the recent educational legislation in Great Britain and Australia setting up new national educational planning and advisory bodies, weighted towards industry and economic priorities.
7. J. Habermas, *Legitimation Crisis (LC)*, London: Heinemann Educational Books, 1976 (original German version 1973). Some of Habermas' later ideas on life-world colonisation only subliminally present in *LC* have been added here.
8. There is an extensive literature on the educational crisis of the 1960s, but Habermas' own work on this is interesting. J. Habermas, L. Von Friedeburg, C. Oehler and F. Weltz, *Student und Politik*, Berlin: Luchterhand, 1961, and 'Student protest in the Federal Republic of Germany', *Towards a Rational Society (TRS)*, London: Heinemann Educational Books, 1971, 13–30. See also H. Weiler, *op. cit.* and 'Legalisation, expertise, and participation: strategies of compensatory legitimation in education policy', *Comparative Education Review*, **27** (2), 1983: 259–77, but I would argue that the New Right has given up this strategy for that described by C. Offe (see Chapter 3).
9. See for instance the following Australian New Right publications (readers familiar with New Right educational writers in Britain and the US can make their own comparisons): R. Baker, 'Why the cultural debate matters', *IPA Review*, Winter 1986: 26–7. T. Duncan, 'Conflicting visions of Australia', *IPA Review*, Winter 1986: 20–5. D. Kemp, 'Education and values', *IPA Review*, Winter 1986: 52–5. S. Moore and L. Kramer, 'Betraying the young: Literature programmes in schools', *IPA Review*, Autumn 1986: 23–6. G. Partington, 'The peace educators', *Quadrant*, January–February 1986: 58–66.
10. This analysis is based in part on H. Weiler, 1982, 1983. See notes 4 and 8 above.
11. Such as that associated with the post-modernist movement, e.g. M. Foucault, 'Das Verschwinden des universellen Intellektuellen', *Frankfurter Rundschau*, **27** (6), 1981:

3–17. See also J. Habermas, *The Philosophical Discourse of Modernity (PDM)*, Oxford: Polity Press, 1987 (original German version 1985) which contains extensive discussions of post-modernism, and R. Bernstein (ed.) *Habermas and Modernity*, Oxford: Polity Press, 1985, which contains papers by Giddens, Rorty and others on Habermas' view of modernity.

The following section is based largely on my article 'The New Right and the Old Left: a plague on both their houses', *Discourse: The Australian Journal of Educational Studies*, **7** (1), 1987: 24–36.

12. See J. Habermas 'New social movements', *Telos* (Fall 1981): 33–7 and *op. cit.*, 1986.

13. This review appeared in the New York Times in late January, 1988.

14. *T & P*: 246.

15. This piece of vulgar Marxism must be excused. It has been included for the purposes of exposition.

16. For a history of the Frankfurt School see M. Jay, *The Dialectical Imagination*, Boston: Little, Brown, 1973.

17. The following section is based on T. Adorno and M. Horkheimer, *Dialectic of Enlightenment*, New York: Herder and Herder, 1972, on T. Adorno's *Negative Dialectics*, New York: Seabury Press, 1973, and on the treatment of the Frankfurt School in D. Held, *Introduction to Critical Theory: Horkheimer to Habermas*, London: Hutchison, 1980. See also M. Jay, *Adorno*, London: Fontana, 1984.

18. The locus classicus is G. Lukacs, *History and Class Consciousness*, London: Merlin Press, 1971. See also mention in *T & P*: 157 and a discussion by David Ingram in *Habermas and the Dialectic of Reason*, London: Yale University Press, 1987: Chapter 5.

19. For an accessible discussion of Horkheimer's idea of immanent critique see D. Held, *op. cit*: 183–7, and for a discussion of Adorno, Horkheimer and Habermas on the issue of immanent critique see R. Roderick, *Habermas and the Foundations of Critical Theory*, London: Macmillan, 1986.

20. On the social psychology of Adorno see T. Adorno, E. Frenkel-Brunswick, D. Levinson and R. Sanford, *The Authoritarian Personality*, New York: Harper Bros, 1950.

21. See J. Habermas, *Zur Logik der Sozialwissensschaften (ZLS)*, Beiheft [Monograph] 5, Philosophische Rundschau, **14**, 1966–7, J. Palermo, 'Pedagogy as a critical hermeneutic', *Cultural Hermeneutics*, **3**, 1975: 137–46.

22. For a discussion of the role of this distinction see A. Kaplan, *The Conduct of Inquiry*, San Francisco: Chandler, 1964: 13–18.

23. Habermas discusses this in *T & P*: 276–9 and more extensively in Chapters 4–6 of *Knowledge and Human Interests (K & HI)*, London: Heinemann Educational Books, 1972 (original German version 1968) as well as in *TRS*. Much of the argument in *ZLS* is also relevant.

24. H. Giroux, *Critical Theory and Educational Practice*, Geelong: Deakin University, 1983.

25. J. Habermas, 'Ideologies and society in the post-war world', an interview with G. Freudenthal, Jerusalem, 16 December 1977, in P. Dews (ed.) *Habermas: Autonomy and Solidarity: Interviews*, London: Verso, 1986, 49.

26. *T & P*: 31–2: 'The structure of the general system of education (*Bildungssystem*) might possibly be more important for the organisation of enlightenment than the ineffectual training of cadres or the building of impotent parties.'

27. See H. Weiler, *op. cit.*, also S. Shapiro, 'Crisis of legitimation: schools, society and declining faith in education', *Interchange*, **15** (4), 1984: 26–39, 'Habermas, O'Connor and Wolfe, and the crisis of the welfare capitalist state: conservative politics and the roots of educational policy in the 1980's', *Educational Theory*, **33** (3 & 4), 1983: 135–47. D. Dawkins, *Economics, Politics and Education*, Geelong: Deakin University, 1986.

Also cited in Chapter 1: J. Habermas, 'Pädagogische "Optimismus" vor Gericht einer pessimistischen Anthropologie', *Neue Sammlung*, **1**, 1961: 251–78.

CHAPTER 2

FROM INTERESTS TO PRACTICE

The soul of man must quicken to creation
Out of the formless stone, when the artist unites himself with stone,
Spring always new forms of life . . . .

Out of the sea of sound the life of music,
Out of the slimy mud of words, out of the sleet and hail of verbal
    imprecisions,
Approximate thoughts and feelings, words that have taken the place of
    thoughts and feelings,
There spring the perfect order of speech, and the beauty of incantation.

(T. S. Eliot)[1]

In a seldom quoted commencement address to the New School of Social Research, New York, in 1980, Habermas paid tribute to the influence of Hanna Arendt on his thinking. In her major work, *The Human Condition*, Arendt explored the nature of praxis as distinct from poiesis. Poiesis is making, it involves technique and craftmanship, whereas praxis is acting or doing, and it includes political–ethical actions based on prudent practical judgements. Habermas points out that she wished, by revisiting this Aristotelean distinction, to resist the 'specific modern temptation of reducing the political practice of citizens to just another kind of instrumental action or strategic interaction' – that is, action oriented to finding the most efficient means to a predetermined goal. Arendt develops an understanding of practice which 'articulates the historical experiences and the normative perspectives of what we call today participatory democracy'.[2]

This understanding is based on her analysis of what it means to be human. For Arendt, the human condition is one of plurality, symbolic relationships and renewal through the birth of new generations. To live in a society we must solve the problem of plurality – we must connect the perspectives of social participants who inevitably view the world from different standpoints. It is through the construction of an intersubjective ground that we overcome the problems of plurality – without abolishing the reality of individual perspectives. To do this we must recognise that the web of significant relationships which give our lives meaning (son, mother, husband, lover, citizen, patriot) are essentially symbolic relationships sustained through physical media, rather than physical relationships, as such. We recognise that we construct these relationships as symbolic participants, with our own equal subjectivity, our own capacities to say 'yes' or 'no'. The very basis of this capacity to speak and listen is an assumption of symbolic reciprocity, of equal subjectivity, which keeps alive, no matter what the circumstances, the radical possibility of equality between human beings. We are not content with others' silences, we always seek their genuine agreement. We need to feel that they accept, and accept us. Finally, the truth of new individuals constantly reminds us of the possibility of new symbolic forms, of new and unanticipated ways of life. Recognition of this, in turn, means our human condition is marked by the development of protective institutions to control and manage this innovatory potential, lest it make the existing intersubjectivity vulnerable. Schools, of course, are among the organisations we have constructed, at least partly for this purpose of control. Again, to appropriate the Hegelian logic, we are potentially a self-forming species, if only we could recognise and vitalise our capacity to be aware of our authorship of history. The chief obstacle to this awareness is our tendency to objectify our own creations, and to regard them as natural and unchangeable aspects of the human condition. But history tells us that not only do 'things' change, we change too. Our self-knowledge, our learning capacity, our level of social discourse and reflection change. To this point in history, such changes have occurred in periods of turmoil resulting from the sudden releasing of tensions and the overcoming of contradictions which were a long time in the making. A more controlled and constructive process of change may be possible. To achieve a greater degree of control of the historical process we must learn to understand the nature of the contradictions we face at any given time, and we must institutionalise the process of reflection upon these, rather than institutionalising protections against change which, like poorly built dams, eventually burst, creating greater suffering. In science, in parliamentary processes, and in certain other spheres of life we have already created fragmentary discourses which have progressive potential. However, the objectifications of our age are not usually recognised as such without a process of critical reflection. Rather they form part of the taken-for-granted realm of background–knowledge – 'what everyone knows'. The process of critique can only pass beyond present relationships and present situations if we are able to get behind this 'taken for grantedness' and show that sections of the 'natural' world are not inevitable, and are, indeed, responsible for some of our problems. 'Out of the formless stone' of our symbolic creations we must cause to appear 'new forms of life'. For instance, it might be that out of the 'natural' femininity and masculinity of our definitions of woman-hood and manhood – a 'real' man, a 'lovely' woman – we must cause to appear a new form of life where feminine and masculine elements can be acknowledged in every person. It might also be that out of the definition of the generalised authority situation of the family, in terms of a ship's crew with the husband as the captain, we must cause to appear a new form of co-operative family life.

We can co-ordinate our actions, our creative action no less than everyday action,

> only on the condition that [we] reach a common definition of the situation with which [we] have to cope. [We] offer different interpre-tations and try to come to an agreement. In these interpretative achievements each actor draws from a common stock of knowledge which is provided by a cultural tradition shared with others. It is this background–knowledge which represents the context of the life–world, and in which any communicative action is imbedded . . . to those who act in concert the life–world is present as a background in the mode of implicit self-evidence. This certainty is in striking contrast to that of any piece of knowledge which is explicitly expressed in an utterance. Any such expression can be rejected . . . background assumptions and practices which are always taken for granted do not have this basic property of knowledge. (Habermas, 'On the German–Jewish heritage', 1980: 129)

Background–knowledge cannot normally be questioned, it can only break down. If we are to become aware of our imprisonment in existing states of affairs we must make at least some of this background–knowledge explicit and so subject to the possibility of critique. Usually we are forced to this only when we are under the pressure of a problem situation in which background–knowledge breaks down. Such situations are a fertile place for critique to start.[3]

This taken-for-granted knowledge and practice is often ideological. In one of the many senses of that much abused word, ideology refers to knowledge and practices which serve the interests of some groups or sections of society but not the interests of all. Ideology gets its power from the fact that this one-sided interest is disguised as either being actually in the interests of all or outside the realm of human control altogether – as a fact of nature. In this way, for instance, we could assert that all persons are born unequal, with unequal looks, intelligence or genetic potential. That being so, it is but a short step to explaining social inequality as a natural reflection of this fact of nature. However, the most powerful form which ideology can take is to be taken-for-granted – to be not only natural but unquestioned, even, unarticulated.

The social sciences, in attempting to establish just what are the facts of nature about human beings and what are changeable sets of historically created practices, have only one method available. They must borrow from philosophy the method, provided by Kant and employed by Hegel, of rationally reconstructing the pre-theoretic know-how of acting subjects – of asking, as does a grammarian in studying language, what rules and assumptions would people have to possess to be acting the way they do?

But Alfred Schutz, the founder of modern sociological phenomenology, was wrong in believing that access to this life-world could be had by reflection alone.[4] As ethnomethodology shows, it is only when that world becomes problematic, when its background–knowledge breaks down, that it is possible to observe conduct on the part of individuals which permits access to a reconstruction of that world.

In the early days, ethnomethodologists carried out research by 'making trouble' in everyday situations and sitting back to observe the 'fun'.[5] Leaving the ethics of such experimentation aside, these experiments involved using undergraduates to act in ways different from their usual forms of conduct and the observation of the consequent interactions. For example, undergraduates might be asked to act 'politely but distantly' at the family dinner table. This could result in all sorts of family feuds and crises as other members tried to interpret this conduct but it might reveal a great deal about the methodological character of the way other family members made sense of the student's conduct, and about the background assumptions upon which relationships in the family rested.

But, today, under the impact of the expansion of the money economy and the bureaucracy, more and more of the life–world and the spheres of interaction which proceed most fully under a debt to shared beliefs and norms, are coming under threat. There is no need to conduct ethically dubious social–psychological experiments to observe conduct which permits reconstruction of the life–world. It is possible to study the life–world in the evanescent light of its own destruction – as the breakdown of meanings gives rise to individual attempts to cope and an inchoate mass of social movements such as the peace movement, the environmental movement, religious fundamentalism, and feminism.

However, if such a study is not to be simply a lament for things passing, it must adopt a standpoint, some normative or meta-normative position upon which a defence of the life–world could be based. According to Habermas, such an Archimedean point is available in Arendt's analysis of Kant's conception of *Urteilskraft*, practical judgement. Kant argued that it is only through an 'enlargement of mind', a universalisation of perspective, that such a standpoint can be attained. It is achieved by comparing our judgement with the possible rather than the actual judgements of others, and putting ourselves in the place of any other man. . . . Critical thinking makes others present and thus moves potentially in a space which is public, open to all sides. (Habermas, quoting Arendt in *The Life of the Mind*, p. 257)

It is only in the creation of a public realm of discourse, open to all, in which citizens come together to pursue their common rather than private interests, getting to grips with the issues created by the destruction of meaning, that the reconstructed life–world can be studied and critically evaluated in a way which frees citizens from its reifying power.[6] As we will see in a moment, Habermas believes that this kind of open discourse is inherent in the nature of speech itself.

For Habermas, the post-Enlightenment creation of a concrete realm of public discourse, actually approximating to this ideal, was one of the most progressive and hopeful developments of our age. Conversely, the more recent failure of the twentieth-century attempt to extend this public domain from the bourgeoisie to the masses, or even to maintain it as an open domain for the middle classes, is a cause for alarm and regret. The conversion of the greater part of the public media into the privately-owned political tools of a few media moguls, so tellingly exposed in Orson Welles' movie *Citizen Kane*, and the symbolic take-over of so many issues and problem areas by coteries of experts and corresponding bureaucratic departments of state, has undercut the power of the public domain to provide a legitimate input to public policy.[7] Even the idea of public discussion and debate is no longer honoured except in the most perfunctory way, as governments cynically release 'green papers' or discussion documents and move towards legislation without allowing either time or facilities for any possible public consensus to emerge.[8]

Like the Frankfurt theorists before him, Habermas identifies the extension of instrumental forms of reason as one of the key ideological supports of the expansion of the interests of power and wealth. In *Towards a Rational Society* (*TRS*) he described the way in which the limited idea of bodies of knowledge built up through the employment of criteria of control over the physical environment had been extended to represent all possible knowledge in the doctrine of positivism. Such an approach, lacking as it does either an explicit internal dimension of reflection – within the scientific community itself – or an openness to the external, public sphere of reflection, because of its closedness to non-experts, has concealed the inner connection between rationality and meaning. It has produced a rationality which is meaningless and even meaning-destroying.

In a much later work, Habermas develops more formal philosophical arguments concerning the connection between meaning and truth, showing the necessary link between truth and the form of life of inquirers.[9] This is discussed further in Chapter 6. It is an example of the way in which Habermas has kept the same themes very much at the centre of his thought, while attempting to refine and restate them in response to criticism and his perception of the need to give greater precision to ideas which often began as broad, programmatic intuitions.

KNOWLEDGE AND HUMAN INTERESTS

To understand Habermas' present position and much of the response to his work by educationists, it is useful to discuss the development of his thought historically. So far in this chapter, we have been examining formative influences and pre-1980 ideas, in the light, admittedly, of a frame of relevance derived from access to later work on the modern condition. Now I want to begin a more or less sketchy summary of his thinking, from the lecture he gave on his inauguration as Professor of Philosophy at the Goethe University, Frankfurt, in 1965,[10] to the present day. In that lecture, he argued that the study of the nature and basis of human knowledge can only be pursued as a social investigation. Epistemology (the theory of knowledge) can only be pursued as social theory. On this basis he attacked positivism in its various forms (in *Zur Logik der Sozialwissenschaften*) including the critical rationalism of Popper, which itself had attacked other forms of positivism and come some way towards the position Habermas was seeking to develop. Unlike the mainstream positivists, Popper accepted that the scientific process was a critical one, involving an active process of examining the relation between our ideas and 'reality' – a postulated, independent world – and he recognised that our observation of that world takes place against a specific 'horizon of expectations' generated by theory and the critical debate about theory at any given time.[11]

Popper believed that theory comes up against 'reality' through tests which are conducted within the scientific community according to its developed conventions of method. While this process is fallible, because no absolute method is available, its mistakes are correctable through further critique and testing. The body of hypotheses that pass such tests form a 'third world' of knowledge, which has its own objective existence, independently of individual scientists. The driving force for this community and this process was a value decision by scientists to opt for a critical and rational search for knowledge. However, for Popper, the community of scientists itself lay outside the realm of science proper. The study of the social processes of the scientific community and the societies to which it belonged was the domain of a quite separate study in the sociology of knowledge. Epistemology could not be pursued as social theory. Study of the social realm merely allowed contingent explanation of particular contemporary directions of research, or the invention and attempt to test for certain hypotheses rather than others. It did not affect our overall understanding of the logic of scientific discovery.

Habermas argued that Popper had covered only half of the distance that it was necessary to cover in his move away from the mainstream position to some more satisfactory view of human scientific knowledge.[12] He failed to recognise and accept the full implications of his view that facts are objectifications constituted in a community against the horizon of expectations generated in critical discussion. The line Popper drew between the philosophy of science and the sociology of knowledge was a patently artificial one. McCarthy, translator and creative critic of Habermas, puts Habermas' critique of Popper in a nutshell:

> If Popper consistently pursued his insights that scientific discourse includes the critical discussion of alternative techniques of inquiry, competing theories, various definitions of basic predicates, in short, of different frames of reference and their elements; that 'it is only in the course of critical discussion that observation is called in as a witness'; and that even this witness depends on standards and rules then he could not limit rationality to trial and error in the sense of confrontation with the facts. If science is to serve as a paradigm of rationality, then all of the forms of argumentation involved in this process of critical discussion are rational. But the rational motivation of the acceptance of standards and rules, the criticism or support of attitudes and outlooks, cannot proceed by way of deduction and falsification. This is merely one element in a more comprehensive rationality. (McCarthy, 1978: 49)[13]

Habermas attempted to describe this 'more comprehensive rationality' in his most famous book, *Knowledge and Human Interests* (*K & HI*). In that book he argued that knowledge was created in communities of inquiry, guided by sets of rules or conventions for warranting propositions and theories. These sets of conventions were expressive of three deep-seated anthropological interests of the human species, in control, in understanding and in freedom from dogma.

The first two interests were characterised by a tendency to accept the given forms of the human world. They did not go beyond objectification to a transcending awareness of its human provenance, and thus its changeability.

> Positivism so lastingly repressed older philosophical traditions . . . that, given the self-abolition of the critique of knowledge by Hegel and Marx, the illusion of objectivism can no longer be dispelled by a return to Kant but only immanently – by forcing methodology to carry out a process of self-reflection in terms of its own problems. (*K & HI* : 69)

This objectification was, to a degree, less problematic, humanly speaking, in the physical than the social studies. In the latter, the tendency to accept descriptions of things as they are is more clearly a failure to explore things as they might otherwise be.

The empirical–analytical sciences, which proceed under a methodology based on predictive control, lead to a form of action based on prediction and manipulation.[14] A theory, consisting of a general rule, law or generalisation, together with a set of variable and fixed conditions under which it applies, allows the identification of some variable conditions which it is in the power of the person applying the knowledge to change (e.g. pull a lever with muscle power to unlatch the trapdoor of the gallows and allow the law of gravity to 'act' on the body of the condemned person until Newton's equal and opposite reaction occurs at the end of the rope). This form of action is called technical action. When it is extended to the human world it involves the creation of a technology based on laws of behaviour and conditions which can be changed. However benevolent the interest of the person pulling the levers, the mode of action is still the manipulation of changeable or variable conditions. The extension of this mode of action, to the status of a paradigm for all effective action-in-the-world, is called 'technicism'.

The second set of sciences, the hermeneutic (or interpretive) sciences which proceed under a methodology based on the development of understanding of texts and cultures (rather like the procedures linguists use to learn a new language), have a different relation to practice. Whereas technical action can only be manipulative, in the strict physical sense, hermeneutically-based action, which involves sending and receiving messages, may be manipulative in a metaphorical sense. One can pursue strategic goals of pursuading, warning, frightening, deceiving, etc., through sending and receiving messages. But one can, of course, pursue the goal of understanding and being understood. When one applies hermeneutic knowledge, the result is not a determinate, physically caused result, but a state of understanding of a message or a text. This understanding is not determinate, nor is it necessarily physically caused, although physical media and brain processes are obviously involved. In any case, the process itself and the development of hermeneutic knowledge is able to be carried out without reference to brain states. Perhaps the paradigm case of this kind of methodology is that of mathematics or logic itself.

Neither interest is sufficient to penetrate the screen of objectification. The first method, as discussed above, does not penetrate behind the given horizon of expectations of the contemporary scientific community; the second does not penetrate behind the façade of the existing culture or system of meaning as a product of communal or social objectification. Only the third method directly addresses the question of transcending the existent. The third method employs a critical methodology which, while it has a number of possible modes or stages, is ultimately secured in the structure of the community of criticism rather than in any methodological procedures directly applied to the object of critique itself, although it is assumed that the critical community applies whatever other methods are the state of the art.[15] The modes or stages of critical method employed by members of the Frankfurt School, and to an extent by Marx, involved the formation of various kinds of critical theorems, through the critique of political economy in Marx's case, and a wider range of types of cultural ideology critique on the part of Adorno and Horkheimer. Habermas, in his own critique of historical materialism reconstructs Marx's theory to produce a new kind of critical theorem. In *Knowledge and Human Interests*, the method of this reformulation is critical reflection – the systematic exploration by the knowing and acting subject of his or her formation as a person and/or of the social history within which that formation has taken place.

This process of reflection involves the development of a theory about self and society, about ideology and its formation (ideology critique). Habermas' critical theorem included the critique of instrumental reason, the analysis of the possibilities inherent in the ideal of a public domain and rational democratic citizenship and the critical contrasting of this with the actual state of affairs in public communication, and a reconstruction of Marx's argument about systematic distortions of interest due to the capitalist mode of production. Habermas argues that Marx's analysis placed too much emphasis on labour and work and not enough on communication and culture.[16] He reiterated a number of criticisms of Marx's political economics:[17]

1. The development of the state as an agent of the general management of capital rather than a mere superstructure has changed the dynamics of capitalism,
2. The rise in general affluence has reduced the significance of the purely economic component of class conflict,
3. The dissolution of the 'historical role' of the working class due to the more complex structure of (material) interests involved in the distortions of late capitalism has deprived critical theory of a clear audience, and
4. The historical facts of the Russian Revolution and the history of world communism have discredited dogmatic and antidemocratic versions of Marxism.

For Habermas, '. . . the four historical facts indicated above form an impenetrable barrier to any theoretical acceptance of Marxism . . .' (*T & P*: 198).

The problem with Marx's analysis lay in the materialist misconceptions to which his work was prone. Habermas' argument is a complex one, and by no means easy to summarise. The main thrust of his revision of Marx in *Knowledge and Human Interests* is to identify within it a form of instrumental reason based on Marx assuming

> empirically mediated rules of synthesis that are objectified as productive forces and historically transform the subjects' relation to their natural environment. What is Kantian about Marx's conception of knowledge is the invariant relation of the species to its natural environment, which is established by the behavioural system of action. . . . The conditions of instrumental action arose contingently in the natural evolution of the human species. At the same time, however, with transcendental necessity, they bind our knowledge of nature to the interest of possible technical control over natural processes. (*K & HI*: 35)

Marx's analysis rests on the conjunction of developments in both the forces of production (of which technological change is the epitome) and the relations of production (the social institutional framework of production). But the latter is not fully integrated into Marx's frame of reference. He does not develop his analysis of the way we make our history in terms of communication and culture as well as work. The full extent of the autonomy and reality of cultural processes is not recognised. It was this instrumentalism which prevented historical developments in Marxian analysis of the kind required to cope with the actual course of events.

For Habermas, an adequate understanding of our society and the state of our knowledge can be provided only by critical reason. Knowledge formulated under the guiding interests of instrumental reason cannot provide rational guidance in ethical–political matters. It cannot even provide an adequate understanding of its own production in the critical communication of a scientific community. Hermeneutic knowledge, of cultures, of systems of meaningful action and norms, and of texts, can overcome some of the limitations of instrumental reason.[18] It can provide rational understanding of systems of meaning. It can locate the meaning of relationships and deeds in a culture and a way of life, thus restoring an ethical dimension to our actions. It can also assist us to understand the social life and culture of the human enterprise called science, even if the participants in that process misunderstand themselves in terms of instrumental reason, or push other forms of understanding below the horizon of the taken-for-granted. What these forms of reason cannot do is provide a form of knowledge which permits us to proceed reasonably in developing and changing our culture, including the culture of science (attitudes, priorities). Like instrumental reason, which even in its Popperian form, pushes moral matters into a realm of irrational 'decisions', hermeneutic reason makes critique of culture a matter either of boldly accepting the priority of one culture over another, or of simply deciding, again without rational basis, to change something within a culture.

Habermas argues that we can do better than that. That it is possible to say something reasonable, if not absolute, about matters of practical importance (here 'practical' means ethical–political). He takes from Fichte the idea that the notion of reason contains within itself the notion of the autonomy of the reasoner – his or her freedom to use his or her reasoning mind without the results of reasoning being caused by forces external to the reasoning process. He joins this to the Hegelian notion, already discussed, of historical subjects becoming aware of their historical self-creation through reflection.[19] It is this capacity for critical reflection, which by its nature expresses an interest in autonomy, which is the basis of critical reason and the capacity of providing a unified understanding of knowledge which incorporates the insights of both instrumental and hermeneutic reason, but transcends them both.

The turning point of Habermas' debate with the hermeneuticist, Gadamer,[20] was the issue of decisionism and the possibility of a critical method which could actually overcome decisionism and realise the promise of transcending particular cultural frameworks.

Habermas looked to psychoanalysis for a model of critical method (but not for a model for a critical theorem).[21] In the therapist–patient relationship, he saw methodological procedures and safeguards which allowed the analyst to produce a critical theorem about the patient's problems which was not simply an ad hoc theory, imposed on the patient in the same way that a conquering nation may impose its culture on a conquered one. The safeguards consisted in the fact that analysis was voluntary and could be broken off at any time, that the correctness of the psychoanalytical theorem was determined by its free acceptance by the patient, (and by its healing power), and that society at large, and the professional peers of the analyst, enforced professional standards which also protected the patient's autonomy. The critical social theorist, he argued, was in much the same position as a psychoanalyst.

CRITICISM AND RESPONSE

Responses to the critiques of a capitalism guided by instrumental reason, of positivism and Marxism, and particularly the argument in *Knowledge and Human Interests* about the nature of human knowledge, were many-sided. Kellner and Roderick among others have shown how shallow was much of the criticism of his work in the English-speaking world.[22] Surprisingly, perhaps, similar problems of misapprehension arose in Germany, at least, in the field of educational thought.[23] It is unproductive to spend a greal deal of time demonstrating that any particular attempt to criticise or appropriate Habermas' work is based on fundamental misunderstandings of what he was attempting to say. Where I believe this to be the case the works concerned will simply be mentioned in end-of-chapter notes. Of course, it is a matter of judgement as to which misunderstandings are a result of Habermas' own lack of clarity or theoretical incoherence, and which fall quite outside any and every defeasible interpretation of it.

Roderick provides one of the best summaries of the critical reception of Habermas' work at the point where he had published *Knowledge and Human Interests*.[24] He identifies three major criticisms: first, Habermas seems to confuse two distinct kinds of reflection which are carried out in different ways. The first kind involves reflection on and reconstruction of the general or universal features of human nature and the possibility of knowledge. This is transcendental critique, even if the more absolute sense of transcendental is abandoned in favour of a more modest [?] attempt to speak of species universals. The second kind of reflection 'refers to the Marxian idea of a critique of ideology which involves reflection capable of freeing the subject from hidden constraints' (Roderick, 1986: 63). In Habermas' case these constraints were not to be found in the structure of the organisation of labour, to the extent they were for Marx, but in the structures of meaningful social action and speech. These are clearly two different kinds of enterprise requiring different kinds of argument and evidence.

It is problematic to try simply to link reflection to political action as Habermas seemed to want to do in *Knowledge and Human Interests*. While the second form of reflection is quite close to action, since it can directly free at least those who carry it out from the influence of ideology on their own actions, the first form of reflection is somewhat more distant. The truth about our transcendental capacities does not necessarily connect with action, even in the restricted sense just mentioned.

The second major criticism concerns the adequacy of the argument Habermas mounts for the transcendental basis of reflection – for the possibility of reflection which transcends cultural or sectional bias. Roderick summarises this criticism: it rests on the conflation of the two forms of reflection. The transcendental argument is a philosophical one which draws on the traditions of German idealism (particularly Kant), but Marx developed his critique of ideology through an explicit rejection of that philosophy and its method. Habermas' reinstatement of philosophy leads to an internal contradiction between the *raison d'être* of philosophy – the creation a theory free from history and culture (transcendental) – and the postulate of the historical formation of human consciousness (and of the partially ideological character of this):

> On the one hand, Habermas shares with Marx and the Frankfurt school the thesis of the social and historical contextuality of modes of thought. On the other hand, he rejects both the 'orthodox' Marxist claim to justify

critique with scientific standards and Adorno's claim that critique requires no systematic justification. To what critical standards can he then appeal? (Roderick, 1986: 65)

To put it another way, either nature is a constructed objectivity, as Husserl would have it, or it is the natural ground of our subjectivity. We are faced with what might be called the bootstrap dilemma. If our view of nature, including human nature, is constricted by the contextualised subjectivity of historical subjects, we would appear to contradict ourselves when we theorise our human nature as the ground of our historical subjectivity. How can we postulate transcendental conditions – conditions of our human nature – if that nature is subjectively constituted?

This dilemma appears to lie at the heart of the very idea of a critical theory. How can we transcend ourselves?

Horkheimer's original formulation of critical theory distinguished between an approach that grants priority to nature, as a whole within which history is to be included (traditional theory): and an approach that grants priority to the human historical world, as a whole within which interpretations of nature appear as human constructions (critical theory). (Roderick, 1986: 66–7)

The third major criticism concerns the adequacy or otherwise of Habermas' model for a transcending method – psychoanalysis. Psychoanalysis has itself come under fire because it sometimes fails to safeguard the autonomy of patients. Indeed, the model seems to assume an economically and politically independent middle-class analysand, who is psychologically able to reject the analysis. However, most social situations more closely resemble that which is found when psychoanalysis and other forms of psychiatry are practised in closed institutions. There the patients are not necessarily free to break off the analysis or reject the diagnosis/analysis that may have something to do, legally speaking, with their being there in the first place. In addition, when this dimension of power is added, we may take leave to doubt whether members of elite groups in society (the ruling class) are capable of responding to 'analysis'.

In later work, Habermas responded to these criticisms.[25] He distinguished between transcendental reflection, which is not united directly to praxis, and critical reflection, which can be more closely related. Critical theory, as such, is a study of transcendental or universal human competences. Such theory must produce *reconstructions* which examine both our powers and competences and, in a manner reminiscent of Piaget, our capacity for development – our developmental competence, if you like.

The Kantian idea of universal a priori contents of consciousness is reformulated here as empirically testable human universals, similar to Chomsky's attempt to understand universal features of language competence, but going beyond Chomsky's somewhat passive notion of competence to bridge the gap between knowledge and action. The Hegelian idea of a dialectic of the species' historical progress is reformulated in terms of the theory of moral development, modelled on Kohlberg. Instead of resting content with Kohlberg's account of moral development, which examines only the capacity to make moral judgements, Habermas goes beyond judgement to systems of action. In a similar way, his reconstruction of language goes beyond the capacity to produce or recognise grammatically correct utterances to a notion of *communicative* competence – the capacity to use such utterances competently in real-life situations. The rational reconstruction of speech asserts that such competence rests on a set of background assumptions of communication involving cognitive, moral and personal dimensions. These involve validity judgements about the truth, appropriateness and authenticity of utterances and speakers, which play an analogous role in the theory of knowledge to Kant's universals. The reconstruction of moral development reconstructs the Hegelian content in Habermas' earlier theory.

The second criticism was met by de-absolutising the discussion. Instead of speaking the language of subjective and objective reason, Habermas developed a less Hegelian account of the course and possible future course of social evolution. In this account, human consciousness is a part of nature, but a part which can exist at a number of evolutionary levels. We have now reached the level at which this fact of development may be effectively analysed. The subjectivity of our enclosure in history is a subjectivity characteristic of a particular developmental level – or learning level – and the social institutions characteristic of that level. The human historical world is at a given level and the interpretation of nature occurs at that level, but the level of development at present reached by the species-which-reflects-on-itself is itself a natural phenomenon. In short, the fact that we are a species in nature which progressively knows more and more about nature and itself and develops its methodology of knowing (its learning level) is just that – a fact – difficult though it may be to understand what this means. Essentially, critical theory is an attempt to cope with a further fact – we can know ourselves as precisely this kind of species – a learning species – and can understand our own method of learning.

In commenting on changes in the relation between theory and practice, since the classical period, Habermas expresses this view:

> theory, directed towards praxis and at the same time dependent on it, no longer embraces the natural, authentic or essential actions and institutions of a human race constant in its essential nature; instead, theory now

deals with the objective, overall complex of development of a human species which produces itself, which is yet only destined to attain its essence: humanity. What has remained is theory's claim of providing orientation in right action, but the realisation of the good, happy and rational life has been stretched out along a vertical axis of world-history; praxis has been extended to cover stages of emancipation. (*T & P*: 253)

Finally, Habermas' ideas on critical method went through a process of development culminating in an account of scientific argumentation and communicative action which reasserted the critical possibilities inherent in human communication itself, rather than in any more limited methodological tradition, such as psychoanalysis.

THE ORGANISATION OF ENLIGHTENMENT

The addressee, the audience, for Marx's critique was the proletariat. The critique was for them – i.e. for their interests, their situation. They could be expected to be motivated to act. Who is the addressee of Habermas' critique?[26] To put this question another way, Marx thought that the proletariat, once they understood his analysis of their situation, would act to change the social system (capitalism) which brought it about. What action does Habermas expect? In 1971 Habermas tackled this question in *Theory and Practice*.

The addressee of Habermas' theory is clearly universal, the oppressor *and* the oppressed. But the expectation that it is oppressed groups who will display the most immediate interest in enlightenment remains. In more recent work, Habermas appears to identify members of new social movements, such as feminism and environmentalism as potentially fruitful addressees of critical theory, but his analysis by no means suggests the working class is not still an important addressee, or indeed, that elements of the elite cannot also be involved in enlightenment. (However, critical reconstructions of the transcendental kind were only later distinguished from critical theorems of the ideology critique kind.) The formulation of critical theorems must be followed by the organisation of processes in which the theorems are applied and tested by reflection carried on within groups to which the processes of enlightenment have been directed and finally, these groups must select strategies and tactics and engage in political action and struggle. The conditions under which each stage of the process can occur are different.

A theory [critical theorem] can only be formulated under the precondition that those engaged in scientific work have the freedom to conduct theoretical discourse; processes of enlightenment (if they are to avoid exploitation and deception) can only be organised under the precondition that those who carry out the active work of enlightenment commit themselves wholly to the proper precautions and assure scope for communications on the model of therapeutic 'discourses'; finally, a political struggle can only be legitimately conducted under the precondition that all decisions of consequence will depend on the practical discourse of the participants . . . an organisation which tries to master all three of these tasks according to the same principle will not be able to fulfil any of them correctly. (*T & P*: 33–4)

In other words, there is no determinate relationship between theory and practice – no buttons which can be pressed to bring about enlightenment or changed social practices. First, some men and women must develop a critique, by reconstructing an understanding of the contradictions of the existing state of affairs (immanent critique) and by envisaging possibilities unrealised in it by drawing on counterfactual ideals of democratic participation inherent in human speech and language; then they must engage in communicating these insights, in such a way as those to whom they communicate can test the authenticity of the critical vision against their own experiences, in a situation free of coercion, for which, at least in the early development of Habermas' thought, the model still was the psychoanalytic dialogue; finally, the people concerned must organise themselves, as a party for change, to conduct further processes of enlightenment in the public domain, in so far as it is free, and to take political (but ethical and usually democratic) action to bring about changes which, at a tactical minimum, go as far as fostering the further organisation of enlightenment and the further opening up of the public domain, or perhaps even bring about changes in practice which alleviate the coercion and exploitation associated with the institutionalisation of the material interests of some rather than all. (In later work the distinction between kinds of reflection adds to this picture the work of reconstruction, by critical philosophy, of the normative basis of critique.)

EDUCATION AND ENLIGHTENMENT

From the beginnings of the period when the ideas of the Enlightenment began to find their way into the revolutionary (organisational) processes which gave us modern democratic states such as the USA and France, the importance of public education, or rather the education of a public as a basic means for the organisation of enlightenment was recognised.[27] In France, particularly, where the conception of human rights may not have been so fully part of the 'common sense' of the people as in the American colonies, it was felt that it was a philosopher's duty to promote common acceptance of the Rights of Man:

for only when reason 'hits the mark everywhere does it hit it properly, for only then will it form that power of public opinion, to which one can perhaps ascribe most of those changes which are truly advantageous for the peoples'. (Habermas quotes the Abbé Sieyes, *T & P*: 88)

But democracy can only move beyond its present half-developed state if the level of institutionally permitted learning in society is allowed to be raised, technical questions distinguished from ethical–political ones and discursive rather than instructional or indoctrinatory learning processes allowed to take place.[28]

> Non-reflexive learning takes place in action contexts in which implicitly raised theoretical (technical) and practical [ethical–political] validity claims are naively taken for granted and accepted or rejected without discursive consideration. Reflexive learning takes place through discourses in which we thematise practical validity claims that have become problematic or have been rendered problematic. (*LC*: 15)

While systems of public education, such as school systems, or systems of higher education, are not the only organisational medium in which such learning could be realised, they are, as indicated in an earlier quote from Habermas, a potential means.

They are a potential means of the organisation of enlightenment for several reasons. First, educational thought is still deeply influenced by classical and liberal traditions of the formation and development of the whole person, as expressed, for instance, in the German concept of *Bildung* (as enunciated by Kant).[29] These traditions enshrined notions of autonomy and of the responsibility of individuals for 'taking their rights' – at least, morally and intellectually – rather than receiving them. In the European educational tradition, which has to some extent been inherited by the English-speaking former colonies, the idea of each new generation transcending the old has also been present. Since Dilthey at least, it has been a recurring theme of the modern period. Here we have a universal addressee for a theory of social evolution or transcendence. Second, mass education systems are perhaps the only organised means, apart from the 'culture industry' and its mass media, on a sufficient scale to reach potential addressees of critique. Third, both educational academics and teachers possess a degree of institutionalised insulation from social norms and sanctions governing expression of opinion in other contexts of life.[30] Indeed, the school classroom has always been recognised as a territory where, to a degree, the exigencies of daily life are suspended – that, at least, is what is implicit in the epithet 'ivory tower' – and this insulation applies to students, too. Finally, I would argue that the schools keep alive an intuitive idea of critique, of the possibility of transcendence, which shows through in many unselfconscious 'child-centred' educational experiments. Schools have always been a site of a hope which sees beyond existing states of affairs. Teachers have always found in the freshness and openness of children a possibility of going beyond the present flawed, weary and soiled state of the world. It is the hope of critical theorists of education that educational institutions, and particularly schools, can play an important role in realising the 'perfect order of speech'.

NOTES

1. T. S. Eliot, *Collected Poems 1909–1962*, London: Faber & Faber, 1975: 183, quoted by permission of Faber & Faber.
2. J. Habermas, 'On the German–Jewish heritage', *Telos*, **44** (Summer 1980): 127–31. But on Habermas' reading of Arendt see M. Canovan, 'A case of distorted communication: a note on Habermas and Arendt', *Political Theory*, **11** (1), 1983: 105–16. The argument of this section of Chapter 2 is based on the *Telos* article on Arendt, but in a manner which connects it with the arguments in *T & P*, some of which were originally produced in the 1960s, later argument from *The Theory of Communicative Action (TCA)*, Vol. 1, London: Heinemann Educational Books, 1984 (original German version 1981) and Vol. 2, Oxford: Polity Press, 1987 (original German version 1982) and more recent discussions of modernity. I have also been assisted by K. Schaller's argument that critical theory of education can only by rescued by a phenomenological turn: 'Kritische Erziehungswissenschaft am Ausgang ihrer Epoche?', *Bildung and Erziehung*, **38** (3), 1985: 357–78.
3. The idea that areas of the life–world must first be experienced as problematic before being reconstructed is taken from P. Friere, *Pedagogy of the Oppressed*, Harmondsworth: Penguin, 1972, and J. Mezirow, 'A critical theory of adult learning and education', *Adult Education*, **32** (1), 1981: 3–24, but unlike Mezirow, who recommends 'making trouble', I have taken the view that such problematisation already exists in abundance and that it is ethically dubious deliberately to create it, at least, in the schooling of children, particularly since we have no absolute criteria for problematising whole forms of life: *TCA*: 73; *T & P*: 257.
4. See H. Garfinkel, *Studies in Ethnomethodology*, Englewood Cliffs NJ: Prentice-Hall, 1967, and Habermas' discussion of ethnomethodology in *TCA*: 115–33.
5. *Ibid.*
6. *T & P*: 28: 'The self-reflection of the lone subject therefore requires a quite paradoxical achievement: one part of the self must be split off from the other part.'
7. See Adorno's critique of the 'culture industry' in 'Cultural criticism and society,' 258–76 in P. Connerton (ed.) *Critical Sociology*, Harmondsworth: Penguin, 1976, and S. Aronowitz, 'Mass culture and the eclipse of reason: the implications for pedagogy', *College English*, **38** (8), 1977: 768–74.
8. The British White Paper on Higher Education was released at the beginning of the 1987 university vacation, allowing a very restricted time limit for the response. Six months later the same strategy was followed with a green paper in Australia. The document was so similar that it was widely joked it should be graded as a 'fail', because of plagiarism.
9. E.g. *TCA*.
10. The inaugural lecture was published as an appendix to *K & HI*.
11. See K. Popper, *The Logic of Scientific Discovery*, London: Hutchison, 1959, for the views which were relevant at the time of the *Positivismustreit*.
12. See Habermas' remarks in P. Dews (ed.) *Habermas: Autonomy and Solidarity*, London: Verso, 1986, 50.
13. T. McCarthy, *The Critical Theory of Jürgen Habermas*, London: Hutchison, 1978.
14. For the clearest discussion of the logic of theory/practice relationships see B. Fay, *The Theory of Social and Political Organisation*, London: Allen and Unwin, 1975.

15. There have been a lot of misunderstandings of Habermas on this point. He has never assumed that it is possible to engage in argumentation without giving reasons, or that reasons do not need to be 'grounded' in logical relation to other theory or 'founded' in accounts of experience. Nevertheless, his focus has been on the relation of such grounded and founded discussion to the methodological norms and horizons of expectation of the community of enquiry itself (to use Popper's terms).

    See also G. Skirbeck, 'Pragmatism in Apel and Habermas' in G. Floistad (ed.) *Contemporary Philosophy: A New Survey*, Vol. 4, The Hague: Nijhof, 1983, and M. Hesse's discussion 'Science and objectivity' in J. Thompson and D. Held, *Habermas: Critical Debates*, London: Macmillan, 1982. Since his switch to a communicative paradigm, most of the work written in English (including that by Hesse) relating Habermas' views to the philosophy of science has become redundant. The authors of that body of work must now take issue with Habermas' critique of epistemology and philosophy of 'consciousness'.

16. *K & HI*: Chapter 2; *T & P*: Chapters 6 and 7; *Communication and the Evolution of Society (C & ES)*, London: Heinemann Educational Books, 1979 (original German version 1976).

17. *T & P*: 195–8.

18. *K & HI*: Chapters 7 and 8.

19. *K & HI*: Chapter 9 and p. 315: 'the unity of knowledge and interest proves itself in a dialectic that takes the historical traces of suppressed dialogue and reconstructs what has been suppressed.'

20. As discussed in *ZLS* and *TCA*: 132–42. See also D. Misgeld, 'Habermas' retreat from Hermeneutics . . .', *Canadian Journal of Political and Social Theory*, **5** (1/2), 1981: 8–44.

21. *K & HI*: Chapters 10–12.

22. D. Kellner and R. Roderick, 'Recent literature in critical theory', *Philosophy and Social Criticism*, **23**, 1981: 141–70.

23. For discussion of some of these misunderstandings see particularly D. Held, *Introduction to Critical Theory: Horkheimer to Habermas*, London: Hutchinson, 1980, Part III.

24. R. Roderick, *Habermas and the Foundations of Critical Theory*, London: Macmillan, 1986, especially 62–9. But see also critics such as G. Kortian, *Metacritique: The Philosophical Argument of Jürgen Habermas*, Cambridge: Cambridge University Press, 1980. M. Theunissen, *Gesellschaft und Geschichte: Zur Kritik der kritischen Theorie*, Berlin, 1969, D. Held, *op cit.*.

25. Again, Roderick's summary is readable, *op. cit.* 69–73. See also Habermas' introduction to *T & P* and 'Reply to my critics' (*RTC*) in J. Thompson and D. Held (eds) *Habermas: Critical Debates*, London: Macmillan, 1982.

26. For a related discussion see U. Bracher, *Kritische Sozialforschung und ihr Adressat*, Frankfurt: Campus, 1978.

27. In 'Introduction: some difficulties in the attempt to link theory and practice', in *T & P*: 1–40.

28. *LC*: 14–16.

29. See Habermas' discussion in 'Pädagogische "Optimismus" vor Gericht einer pessimistischen Anthropologie: Schelsky's Bedenken zur Schulreform', *Neue Sammlung*, **1**, 1961: 252–78.

30. In German this is called *Schönraum* which involves *Karenz*, or restraint, on the part of teachers. See J. Habermas, 'Pädagogische "Optimismus". . .': 266–73. M. Brumlik also calls for this restraint in 'Verstehen oder kolonisieren – Uberlegung zu einem aktuellen Thema,' S. Müller and H. U. Otto (eds) *Verstehen oder Kolonisieren?*, Bonn: Deutschen Gesellschaft für Erziehungswissenschaft, 1985, 31–62.

CHAPTER 3

EMANCIPATION AND EDUCATION

Have ye courage, O my Brethren . . . *Not* the courage before witnesses, but anchorite and eagle courage, which not even a God any longer beholdeth? . . . He hath courage who knoweth fear but *vanquisheth* it; who seeketh the abyss, but with *pride*. He who seeks the abyss but with eagle eyes – he who with eagle talons *graspeth* the abyss: he hath courage.

(F. Nietzsche)[1]

Habermas is only the most recent in a long line of thinkers who recognised the critical potential of education. The presence in the classical tradition of a critical strand has already been noted. If educational theorists did not actually 'grasp the abyss', they sometimes looked at it with the eye of an eagle. Kant spoke of the courage to free oneself from one's self-imposed lack of freedom.[2] Schleiermacher developed Kant's ideas further, arguing that students should become responsible not only for actively educating themselves but also for improving the social group to which they belonged.[3] But the critical strand in the classical tradition was only one strand. It was woven together with strands of nationalism and dogmatism. In any case, the education of which the classical tradition spoke was not necessarily the education of the common people. It was only in connection with the development of the idea of democracy that the critical strand in educational thought, present since at least Plato's time, and given new life by Comenius' desire to 'amend human affairs' after the suffering and darkness of the Thirty Years War, became an unavoidable and central theme of educational thought.

The classical tradition, as the remark of Kant's alluded to above shows, also recognised the element of emotion and will – of courage to educate, above all, courage to educate oneself. The central metaphor of the Enlightenment is that of light breaking into the darkness – the light of reason breaking into the darkness of ignorance and blind tradition. As

Dieter Misgeld points out, this breaking in of light was not simply a passive, emotionally neutral process.[4] It was a matter of will. Ignorance and blind tradition were not abstract things. They were embodied in organised hierarchies of regal and ecclesiastical power. Those who would be enlightened had to have the courage to fight for the light. As Kant argued, the failure of emancipation was 'due, not to a lack of intelligence, but to lack of courage and determination to use one's intelligence without the help of a teacher. *Sapere audere*! Dare to use your own intelligence!' (Misgeld's translation, 1975, ff4: 36).

It is clear that the radical potential of the middle-class struggle against the *ancien régime* for freedom of thought and expression could not easily be confined to the property-owning classes. In America, particularly, but also in France, the capacity for enlightenment was generalised to the populace at large, in the development of the idea of popular democracy. However, populist elements in the new political thinking were matched by elements of nationalism and elitism. The role of education in the new states was ambiguous from the first.

As Dewey argued, the theoretical connection between democracy and mass education is well-known. But he also argued that the usual reason given for this is not the most adequate one:

> The superficial explanation is that a government resting upon popular suffrage cannot be successful unless those who elect and obey their governors are educated. Since a democratic society repudiates the principle of external authority, it must find a substitute in voluntary disposition and interest; these can be created only by education. But there is a deeper explanation. A democracy is more than a form of government; it is primarily a mode of associated living, of conjoint communicated experience.[5]

In contrast to Dewey's emphasis on a common way of life, the eighteenth-century ideal, associated with the name of Rousseau, tended to overemphasise the individual pursuit of happiness. Theoretically, of course, an emphasis on individual happiness was not supposed to be incompatible with a harmonious and progressive society. Genuine self-affirmation was possible only through the affirmation of others. Social harmony would be produced by nature, once social and institutional constraints on the individual were reduced. But the harmony referred to was not grounded in the functioning of existing social institutions; it was a utopian hope of universal harmony brought about by an eventual sharing of truth. The trick was to allow children enough freedom for this natural tendency to take its course. However, as Dewey points out, Rousseau's ideal required too great an act of faith:

> Merely to leave everything to nature was, after all, but to negate the very idea of education. . . . Not only was some method required but also some

positive organ, some administrative agency for carrying out the process of instruction . . . the movement for the democratic idea inevitably became a movement for publicly conducted schools. (Dewey, *Democracy and Education*: 93)

The result, perhaps unintended, was the identification of education with the purposes of the national state rather than the freeing of the powers of the individual:

Since the maintenance of a particular national sovereignty required subordination of individuals to the superior interests of the state both in military defense and in struggles for international supremacy in commerce, social efficiency was understood to imply a like subordination. The educational process was taken to be one of the disciplinary training rather than of personal development. (Dewey, *Democracy and Education*: 94)

Educational thinkers struggled to reconcile the two tendencies. Hegel attempted to reconcile them by arguing that the fulfilment of the individual lay in subordination to the state.[6] The chief function of the state was, in turn, the educational purpose of developing individuals, although, in practice, this simply justified a rather narrow, nationalistic curriculum. Later, too, the broader humanism of a Von Humboldt was transformed in practice to a mere embellishment on themes of national pride and social necessity.[7] For Dewey, the conflict between nationalism and elitism, on the one hand, and open social communication, on the other was the fundamental problem of organised education.[8]

The question that was central to Dewey's attempt to understand education in 1915 is just as relevant today, as the forces of nationalism, particularly economic nationalism, are again in the ascendant: 'Is it possible for an educational system to be conducted by a national state and yet the full social ends of the educational process not be restricted, constrained and corrupted?' He continues:

Internally, the question has to face the tendencies, due to present economic conditions, which split society into classes some of which are made merely tools for the higher culture of others. Externally, the question is concerned with the reconciliation of national loyalty, of patriotism, with superior devotion to the things which unite men in common ends, irrespective of national political boundaries. (Dewey, *Democracy and Education*: 97–8)

The modern educational crisis is a crisis of precisely the kind which Dewey was discussing. Two tendencies are at war with each other. An education which stresses the emancipation of the individual and through the universalisation of that emancipation, the development of autonomy-promoting social institutions, nationally and internationally, and an education which seeks to meet the more urgent economic and political needs of the nation in its contemporary situation. But, as Dewey points out, the specific form these tendencies take on can only be identified when we 'define the kind of society we have in mind' (Dewey, *Democracy and Education*: 97). The situation in late capitalist societies today is not that which Dewey faced. Processes of technological and structural change in the economy and of the decline of the deposit of traditional values upon which modern societies have drawn for so long have brought about a situation in which education is far more central to the fate of these societies than ever before. This is revealed by an examination of the motivational crisis of adolescence and problems of 'ungovernability' in late capitalism, to which we will now turn.

THE MOTIVATIONAL CRISIS OF ADOLESCENCE

In *Legitimation Crisis* Habermas examines the form the 'identity crisis' of adolescents takes on under the conditions of late capitalism.[9] He identifies two features of the system of attitudes and values which formerly underpinned the normal or conventional resolution of this crisis. In that resolution, young people adopted othodox patterns of adult motivation.

The first feature of the system of attitudes is a tradition of civil privatism, the second one of familial–vocational privatism. These traditions have been undermined by the loss of the traditional meanings upon which they were predicated. The result is that fewer young people are making either a relatively conflict-free or even satisfactory transition to adult life. One of the effects of this has already been mentioned – the crisis of motivation in schools.

Civil privatism is defined by an interest in the performance of the steering and maintenance apparatuses of the system (i.e. Dewey's national state) without a corresponding participation in the public support and creation of such apparatuses. It may be seen in calls for 'law and order' unaccompanied by any participation in either political processes affecting legislation or local action initiatives such as 'neighbourhood watch' programmes. Familial–vocational privatism is characterised by developed interests in consumption and leisure and a status orientation towards career opportunities.

Civil privatism is a necessary condition for the maintenance of the present level of limited democracy in capitalist societies because genuine participation in politics by all would be extremely problematic for ruling elites. Societies such as those of which we speak rely on a deal of apathy and on a residue of traditional values of subservience. In addition, new notions of complexity and expertise help to shield elite decision-making from demands for popular participation.

Familial–vocational   privatism   is   characterised   by   possessive individualism and a consumption-oriented materialism. The form taken by this kind of privatism varies systematically with social class. The middle-class ethos is status- and achievement-oriented while the working-class ethos is characterised by a degree of fatalism about status mobility chances. These differences are related to systematic differences in child-rearing patterns which lead to different motivational structures. As ideal types, in the middle-class we find 'the repressive authority of conscience and achievement orientations' and in the working class 'external superego structures and conventional work morality' (*LC*: 77).

But the reproduction of these attitudes was dependent on residues of tradition rather than on any specific institutional structures in capitalist society itself. The individualistic, consumer-oriented search for status does not, of itself, offer support in life's transcendental moments, or provide meaning for the pieties of group and political life. Only the continuation of traditional sources of meaning could do that. But it is precisely these sources of meaning which have lost their traditional institutional base, as the family, the church and the neighbourhood have lost their influence or significance. The rise of science as an alternative source of meaning, the professionalisation of helping relationships formerly the province of kin, the expansion of commodity forms into wider and wider areas of human interaction, the administrative regulation of marital and parental relationships and the commercialisation of culture have all been destructive of such meanings, breaking them up into fragments which can no longer function as parts of a systematic world-view for individuals.

Most recently, the values underlying privatistic attitudes have also begun to suffer more direct erosion. The ideology of achievement through education can only persuade if there is equal educational opportunity, or the appearance of it, particularly at the post-school level. It can only persuade if standards of evaluation do not discriminate against particular groups, such as ethnic minorities, if the labour market develops in line with the educational output and if the labour process itself is able to be related to educational qualifications.

This further loss of meaning is reflected at the level of the personality system of many young people, who have to come face to face with the contemporary situation equipped only with a pale remnant of once vigorous cultural resources. The possibility of a satisfactory transition to adulthood is diminishing. We are faced with a youth crisis. Unfortunately, the policies that governments are pursuing in attempts to resolve more general political and economic problems are likely to increase rather than reduce the pressure on young people.

UNGOVERNABILITY AND THEORIES OF CRISIS: CLAUS OFFE

Claus Offe provides a more recent account of the crisis situation in late capitalism than Habermas' 1975 discussion.[10] He argues that there is a degree of similarity between neoconservative theories of 'ungovernability' and the crisis theories of the 1968 leftist movement. The theories of the Old Left no longer seem viable. The self-assured belief in the imminent demise of capitalism through a crisis brought about by a sharpening of its internal contradictions seems today to have been unduly influenced by wishful thinking. Ironically, in the current economic crisis, the arguments of the Old Left have been revived by the New Right. They have been refined and adapted for conservative purposes. But in their resurrected form the source of crisis is seen as a result of 'the institutionalised arrangements of welfare state mass democracy' (Offe, 'Ungovernability . . .' 1985: 68).

In the neoconservative view, the state has failed. There is an overload of unrealistic public expectations. The very institutional structures which the Left sees as an ideological smokescreen for basic inequities, such as the provisions of the welfare state, are now rejected by the Right because the people they are intended to fool have begun to expect them actually to solve the problems of injustice. The dynamics of political pork-barrelling and campaign promises have awakened desires impossible to satisfy under capitalist conditions. The half-democracy we already have is also regarded as a part of the problem. It limits the ability of the state to solve its problems of control and direction. Only more obedience, commonness of purpose and less democracy can save advanced capitalist societies from being overtaken economically by the busy new economies of undemocratic, disciplined Asia. Indeed, the spectre of a shift in the geo-political centre of gravity to a point somewhere between China, Japan and India shrieks its way through neoconservative demonology.

Crisis symptoms arise because of the mismatch between the government's steering capacity and the sheer diversity and volume of claims made on it. Voters lose confidence in parties, and parties turn to methods for which they have no mandate. In principle it would seem that this loss of legitimacy and political commitment could be overcome either by a renewal of party loyalties and discipline, leading to greater social polarisation, or by a further breakdown in central parties and the development of single-issue political movements whose key aims do not involve the idea of winning a majority. Either 'solution' will make the problem worse.

The therapy offered by the neoconservatives is of two kinds. Either people must be induced to reduce their claims on government or they must be controlled through the strengthening of nationalism, competition and other forms of discipline. To achieve a reduction of claims there needs to be action in political power structures, market structures, socialisation processes and information provision. At the moment, the political structures are overburdened, so greater weight has to be placed on the other media of claims reduction. The first strategy aims to transfer claims on government to the market mechanism, the second to achieve cultural control of politically deviant groups, such as intellectuals of the Left, school teachers and curriculum makers, and the influential voices of the mass media.

A third strategy, which is complementary to the first two, attempts to apply new bureaucratic technologies directly to achieve greater steering power for the state – such technologies as cost–benefit analysis, closer fiscal management, and planning techniques. But the success of fine-tuning the bureaucracy is dependent on the mobilisation of consent. Without greater social integration the increase in the efficiency of steering mechanisms is not possible, so another aspect of the third strategy is the management of consent.

As Offe points out, there is a remarkable international convergence in these strategies. The Scandinavian social partnerships between labour unions and government, the 'social partnership' of Austria, and Germany's 'concerted action' are among the forms this process has taken. In Australia, too, the trade-union/government/business 'accord' is an example of a similar process. The British version of this, the 'social contract', which gives less weight to trade unions, nevertheless attempts to create a similar structure of consent management through a combination of direct appeal to voters and through national planning bodies such as the National Economic Development Council. More recently, the system of higher education has become the target of plans to increase the steering capacity of the state in the area of human resources production and at the same time to restrict the influence of 'subversive' intellectuals.

Offe suggests two basic questions need to be asked of these conservative policies and analyses: What causes capitalist societies to have control problems of this kind? And what justifies the expectation that the kind of strategies being implemented will work?

Several assumptions underlie the views of both the Right and the Left:

1. The relative affluence of such societies leads to demands for higher forms of fulfilment than the basic ones of food and shelter,
2. The expansion of technical rationality has destroyed traditional sources of normative control, and
3. The complexity of the system has finally outstripped the information management capacities of democratic forms of management.

But an examination of the proposed neoconservative remedies makes it clear just what set of demands is to be reduced – the demands of labour rather than capital. The contradiction between the interests of labour and capital cannot be wished away. It is still possible to analyse the process in terms of class conflict, at least in part. For the neoconservative analysis to work it would be necessary to show that class conflict is not a basic structural defect of capitalist societies or that the proposed remedies will abolish it.

Certainly, the idea that it is possible to restore traditional values in such a way as to allow the setting aside of class interests must founder on the rocks of the fact of entrenched cultural pluralism and the lack of credible institutional bases to give life to such values. Nor can the appropriation by the state of institutions, such as unions, in an attempt to manage this conflict prevent such institutions losing the allegiance of their members. As Offe argues:

> In the conservative world-view the crisis of governability is a disturbance in the face of which the false path of political modernisation must be abandoned and non-political principles of order, such as family, property, achievement and science, must again be given their due. (Offe, 'Ungovernability. . .' 1985: 81)

We can no longer afford egalitarianism, so the argument goes. The mass of the people are not all equally competent to govern and they must learn to stop asserting themselves, work harder, and be directed by the elite.

> The polemic against political modernisation, against equality, partici-pation and socialism, requires no consistent justification, no political programme, and no theory of a politically effected transition to other conditions. Its proponents are content to forge a negative political coalition of those who (actually or purportedly) are threatened by reform. (Offe, 'Ungovernability. . .' 1985: 81)

In the English-speaking world, the attempt to cope with educational demands has met with specifically educational versions of the strategies Offe identifies. The state has attempted to deal with rising educational expectations and the limited steering power it has over educational institutions and at the same time to use education as a means for dealing with rising expectations and limited steering power generally.

The part that educational policies play in this process clearly identifies the educational theory of neoconservatism as one of those theories of education which places the needs of the state first and the needs of individuals and their fullest development last. Neoconservative theory attempts to transfer the burden of educational expectations to the market (strategy 1), to achieve cultural control of subversive groups in education (strategy 2), to apply financial and economic planning techniques to education and to engineer or force the necessary consent to allow such planning to be effective (strategy 3). In addition, it attempts to use education as a means for general cultural control, through curriculum change and the shifting of output to technical and managerial studies. All of these strategies, incidentally, raise the level of tension for our youth.

In Australia, the management of higher education has come under the influence of a funding body made up essentially of representatives of the three major parties of the 'accord' – trades unions, business and government. No teacher, parent or social-service organisations are represented (strategy 3). The marketisation of education is pursued through the promotion of competition between government schools and between government and private school systems. In higher education this process can be accelerated by 'user pays' schemes and the privatisation of universities. In Australia and Britain private universities are emerging for the first time (strategy 1).

Control over 'subversive' groups has been attemptd in a number of ways: in the German state of Bavaria by direct banning from teaching posts in schools and universities of people who have been members of left-wing organisations (*Berufsverbot*), and by informal versions of the same process in some other states in Germany. Similar tendencies to McCarthyism are not unknown in the English-speaking world, but as yet they have given rise only to isolated occurrences. More subtly, perhaps, the tying of proportions of recurrent general and research funding to agreed course and research objectives (in Britain and Australia) provides a mechanism which is likely to have the effect of starving suspect disciplines like the social sciences and humanities (strategy 2). New budgetary procedures and planning processes, allied to biased criteria of assessment of performance, provide additional degrees of steerability. Similarly, seemingly neutral changes, such as the shift from funding student input to funding on the basis of graduate output, creates a pressure for changed educational practices likely to reduce student choice in the curriculum.

The debate about the role of the classics in American universities is not simply a debate about what constitutes a good general education. It is a debate about the restoration of traditional values. The output of neoconservative think-tanks and from writers such as Bloom is a clear sign that battle has been joined.[11] There will be an increasing attempt to stigmatise socialist and even liberal views and to legitimate the attempts of the state to reassert its control over and against democratic tendencies which limit it. In countries which feel economically threatened, the weapon of patriotism, coupled with anti-Asian racism, may be employed in this process. The fundamental contradiction of the neoconservative programme, which lies in its desire for both individual economic freedom and social and political discipline, will become more evident.

Offe rejects attempts to reinstate the theories of the Old Left. Theories which rely either on an ever increasing level of economic crisis or similar exponential growth of critical consciousness are unrealistic. There may be a better way of posing the problem:

> Social systems may be said to be ungovernable if the rules (norms) their members follow violate the underlying functional laws, or if they do not act in such a way that these laws can function at the same time. (Offe, 'Ungovernability . . .' 1985: 83)

That being so, there are two circumstances under which a crisis of ungovernability cannot arise. Either members of the system can develop an awareness and some degree of control of the conditions of system functioning or they can erect some kind of barrier to isolate system functions from culturally-guided action. The paradox of capitalism is that it tries to do both. First, the ownership and market system tries to provide a culturally and politically isolated functional mechanism. In turn, the normative and cultural sphere is relativised (and commodified) by the market. However, at the same time, the clockwork of the market must still be wound up and the clock set – the state must step in to control system functions. The parts of the mechanism of the clock are living labour power whose willingness to produce is variable – there is no such thing as a perfectly free or flexible market in labour. So the state seeks to organise labour, but the organisation of labour presses towards the opposite solution – one based on collective management and conscious control. The rhetoric of the free market must be accompanied by social and cultural repression of the market. But it is illusory to expect that a solution to this problem of basic policy contradiction can be found in 'trimming to size the rules and norms proper to action so that they might again harmonise with the functional imperatives and "objective laws" underlying the system' (Offe, 'Ungovernability . . .' 1985: 85). Neoconservatism and its remedies actually block access to the solution, which lies in subordinating system imperatives to democratically reached, and thus accepted, ethical–political rules: 'Advocating the adaptation of consciousness to any and all traditions and to claims of lowered expectations constitutes a pseudo-solution to the problem' (Offe, 'Ungovernability . . .' 1985: 86).

The resolution of the educational crisis is not to be found in the single-minded pursuit of planned linkages between educational institutions and the economy, particularly the export-oriented high-technology sector of the economy, through state control or market forces, nor does it lie in an all-out cultural campaign to sweep away subversives and reinstate the Protestant ethic. It lies in the further development of the organisation of enlightenment and the development of the personal maturity and social awareness of individuals and groups through an increase in the learning power of society.

Unlike either neoconservatism or some traditional forms of revolutionary Marxism, critical theory turns its face resolutely away from all forms of dogmatic authoritarianism, asserting the necessity of a transformation of conscious control over system imperatives through democratic communication processes. Its key concept, emancipation, encompasses more than the notion of either the economic control of the masses by an elite or the liberation of the masses by a vanguard.

LEFT AUTHORITARIANISM

Offe's critique applies equally to the Left. Various Left thinkers have put forward views about the functions of public education which seem to fit more comfortably with the statist solutions to the contemporary problem of modernity than with the alternative. For instance, Castles and Wüstenberg, in their widely read *The Education of the Future: An introduction to the theory and practice of socialist education*, define education as 'the planned and systematic shaping of consciousness' and add, 'socialists have always understood the importance of education as an instrument of social transformation' (S. Castles and W. Wüstenberg, 1979: 1).[12]

The first stage in this education would be installed in a state characterised by the 'dictatorship of the proletariat' (Castles and Wüstenberg, 1979: 5) in which the state would reshape the consciousness of the workers: 'the workers' horizon must not be', or must be, this or that – the state will decide the workers' thoughts. Such prescriptive language sits uncomfortably with talk elsewhere in their discussion of 'democracy'. The key, though, is the time dimension: 'Once polytechnic education has given everybody an understanding of the social aims and technological problems there can be no justification for excluding anybody from the organs of planning and decision-making' (Castles and Wüstenberg, 1979: 7). That 'once' is a very big word, it promises a process of entrenchment of dictatorship that may last a long time.

Like the Marxist analysis referred to above, other analyses which are based on a well-developed theoretical agenda leave the question of the control of education and its role in the transitional process towards a new society in the limbo of the implicit. Under conditions of capitalism they champion resistance to authority but little that is positive is said about the way schools would be managed in the transitional process. A detailed critical agenda, lacking safeguards against dogmatism, tends to be open to the accusation that the key issue for such an agenda is the use of schools and children as instruments in revolutionary praxis rather than a recognition of their role as subjects of communicative action. Unfortunately, critical theory of education has often lacked these safeguards, as a brief recapitulation of its development in Germany will show.

THE DEVELOPMENT OF A CRITICAL THEORY OF EDUCATION IN GERMANY

The development of critical theory of education has been complex. It is not possible fully to do justice to it here. In any case, the purpose of this book is not to provide a review of that literature or an historically situated analysis of its development, but to present a programmatic outline of a possible, and hopefully coherent, Habermasian critical theory of education. For this reason, the main purpose of the brief sketch of the German literature given below is to identify its central problems and the gaps in its development which any account making a claim to coherence must overcome.[13]

A number of writers in this tradition have made the point that Habermas' work does not provide all of the conceptual resources required for such a task. This is true, but I suspect that this point is sometimes inflated into a somewhat mystical defence of the 'uniqueness' of the secret sphere of the pedagogical relationship, the purpose of which seems to be to exempt it from critical scrutiny.[14] Nevertheless, the point remains: it is necessary to do a great deal of theoretical work to develop a critical theory of education from the Habermasian corpus, however promising that body of work with its emphasis on learning levels and historical processes of formation (*Bildung*) may be.

The earliest critical theory of education was closer to mainstream Marxism. The schooling process was seen as a part of the process of the general social formation of human beings – a materially-mediated historical process of the formation of both individuals and the institutions in which they lived.[15] The addressee of critique was the proletariat which had an existential interest in freeing itself from oppression and, in particular, from ideological blindness. The one-sidedness, false sense of necessity, and inversion of the dominant ideology had to be shown as contingent creations of the human mind. Mass culture was one of the main sources by which this false consciousness was propagated.[16]

The task of critical theory of education was to develop a critique of this from the educational perspective, drawing upon the western marxist tradition – a critique with practical, i.e. educational, intent. But it drew on the tradition only selectively. As Keckeisen has shown,[17] the intellectual background of many of the early theorists constituted it as a movement of self-criticism within humanistic educational thought

(*Geisteswissenschaftliche Pädagogik*).[18] Conceptions of contradiction, of Hegelian origin, played a major role in this thinking. The educational problem was defined in terms of a gap between reality and possibility, ideal and real.[19] While this kind of neo-Marxist thinking had considerable impact in Germany during the turbulent years of the 1960s, its tendency to abstract polemic and dogmatism assured it of a speedy decline once the flood-tide of the student movement had subsided.

In response to perceived inadequacies of earlier thought, the emphasis shifted. The rigid functionalism of most Marxist analyses and the failures of 1968 led to a pervasive pessimism. Many theorists turned back to basic philosophical questions, and, in particular, methodological ones. This new emphasis reached its height during and following the dispute over the philosophy of the social sciences (the 1966 *Positivismusstreit*).[20] The concern with method was so strong that practical issues were pushed to one side. Nevertheless, this period produced an awareness of the value of hermeneutical methods in educational research,[21] of the inadequacies of technicist forms of action,[22] of the problems surrounding the role of the educational research community in the politics of educational change and of the inadequacies of technicist–bureaucratic forms of educational administration. Forms of co-operative research with practical intent, such as critical action research, were developed to provide an alternative model to the dominant positivist research paradigm.[23] The influence of positivist epistemology on the constitution of curriculum was also criticised (behavioural objectives). Except, perhaps, in special cases, or when used very judiciously, the constitution of the curriculum in this way blocks the development of creative learning, confining the classroom to a technocratically managed recapitulation of predecided content. It also supports a manipulative pedagogy in which children are treated as educational objects rather than as subjects. Much of this methodological critique was necessary, but it remained incomplete and predominantly negative. Indeed, it was argued that critical theory of education could only proceed negatively.[24] A positive moment was needed. This began to emerge in the next phase of development under the influence of Habermas' meta-normative emphasis on the role of democratic publics and in reaction to the political excesses of the Left.

Habermas' ideas were first applied to education by Klaus Mollenhauer. Mollenhauer attempted to open up a more positive phase in critical theory of education by emphasising the interplay between internal, individual and external, social limitations on education. The leitmotif of this dual freedom for the critical theory of education as it developed in Germany was *Emanzipation*. This concept was taken directly from the classical–humanist tradition and given a critical turn, through the addition of the ideas of ideology critique and critical reflection. Klaus Mollenhauer defined it as follows: 'Emancipation means the freeing of the subject – in our case those growing up in our society – from conditions which limit their rationality and the social actions connected with it' (*Erziehung und Emanzipation*: 11*).

In his pioneering analysis of teachers' roles and ideological aspects of curriculum, Mollenhauer argued that it is through the specific forms of critique that we are able to identify the limitations and constraints on the expression of reason and of rational participation in a democratic public domain – the chains which must be shaken off. The first of these forms of critique is the critique of political economy. Although this stands in need of great modification since Marx's formulation of it, it permits an examination of the way the economic institutions of a nation limit the rational development of particular classes of its people. This critique also requires an international dimension. At its best, liberal critique achieves insights of this kind in its own more fragmented critique of political economy. The appropriate form such critique should take today is exemplified by Habermas' critique of capitalist legitimation and Offe's class analysis of late capitalism and the state. The need for such analysis to be a part of critical theory of education was strongly advocated by Moser.[25]

The second form is ideology critique, which attacks the forces which constrain rationality more directly, or rather, it attacks the immediate, cultural constraints on rationality and rational conduct. For Lempert, emancipation through knowledge meant essentially ideology critique.[26] For most critical theorists of education in the 1970s, the basic form of ideology critique was Horkheimer's immanent critique, which confronts our society's liberal democratic ideals with the reality of the way power and influence is wielded by the Citizen Kanes and Senator McCarthys. There is abundant evidence in the new social movements, in reforms of industrial relations within some industries and in declining trust in authoritarian institutions, that the mass of the people in western democracies are already making this kind of critique for themselves, at least in partial and fragmentary ways. This was seen to be a cause for cautious optimism.

Social psychological critique, as a special form of ideology critique, identifies the interpersonal and intrapersonal forces at work to prevent the development of mature and reasonable conduct. Adorno's critique of the 'authoritarian personality' is an early example of this.[27] Educational thought developed a specifically pedagogical form of this critique focused on the contradictions of the teacher's role and the psychological dimensions of classroom authority. Under the impact of these more specific analyses, the idea that criticism was fixed in a 'circle of consequenceless criticism' was increasingly rejected as more positive and clear cut implications began to emerge.[28] Attempts were made to develop 'constructive'[29] forms of critical theory of education at the school level[30] and even, in one case, at the level of curriculum planning for a whole state, Hessen.[31] However, critical theory of education still remained vulnerable to the charge that it lacked a vision of a complete alternative.

Meanwhile, developments within general critical theory were crucial for the development of its educational extension. The virtual abandonment of the idea of the proletariat as the sole addressee of critique in favour of the idea that the whole coming generation laboured under ideology meant that the addressee became universal.[32] This permitted the linking up of educational critique with the general discussion of authoritarianism and democracy which had been especially intense in Germany since the 1950s. The lack of a clear normative basis for educational construction was finally overcome when Habermas' later work on language and validity, including normative validity, pointed the way to a procedural resolution of the normative problem.[33] Mollenhauer expressed this in educational terms: 'the goal of [education] lies in the establishment of a communication structure [in the classroom] which makes the acquisition of a capacity for free and open discussion (*diskurs*) possible' (*Erziehung und Emanzipation*: 64*).

However, a crucial aspect of the classical conception of emancipation must not be forgotten – the only relatively reliable interest in an individual's emancipation is that of the individual him- or herself – self-affirmation is the ground of critique. A dogmatic critical method, presenting only its own critique of economy, ideology, etc., can only lead to the kind of left authoritarianism whose solution to the problem of modernity is simply another version of asserting the system imperatives over against the individual's development. A growing recognition of this led educators to return to the earlier work of Adorno and Horkheimer, and to reassert themes of emotion, will and aesthetic response.

While educators develop critique and may quite properly advance it at an appropriate stage of young people's development, they must do so only in a pedagogical climate that offers the necessary protections against indoctrination. Dogmatic and manipulative teaching methods would be doubly contradictory for a critical educational practice because the analysis of the obstacles to rational critique and reconstruction reveals that the domination of manipulative forms of knowledge and practice is a central part of the problem of modernity. In education, the manipulative form of pedagogy is implicitly promoted by left authoritarianism, but it is *explicitly* espoused by the behavioural science of instruction. However well-meaning, the manipulation by teachers of children as if they were objects can only reinforce other tendencies in the overt curriculum, and in the messages of mass culture, towards a making of people into things.

This reification was one of Adorno's greatest concerns. Adorno was one of the few original members of the Frankfurt School to pay attention to education. Despite the very limited and aphoristic character of his essays and talks, they have retained their influence and power to illuminate. Adorno's famous essay, 'Education after Auschwitz' in *EZM*, written in 1966, has formed the almost unnoticed Greek chorus which has counterpointed all German thinking on education, authority and emancipation: 'First, men become the kind of persons who make themselves in some degree the same as a thing. Then, if it is possible, they make others into things, too' (*Erziehung zur Mündigkeit (EZM)*: 98*).

This process is accompanied by a calculated 'coldness', so characteristic of many classrooms, which is rooted in the tendency to 'follow one's own interests against the interests of all others' (*EZM*: 101), a way of acting promoted by the competitive consumer culture and by classrooms characterised by competitive modes of learning.[34]

But, Adorno argues, we must also set our face against both traditional and radical authoritarianism,[35] which promote collective values at the expense of the individual's freedom: 'The most important thing we must do if we want to prevent Auschwitz happening again is to work against the blind strength of the collectivity' (*EZM*: 95*).

Educators must work in such a way as to make educators unnecessary.[36] They must aim at promoting in their students the mature capacity to speak up for themselves and not only have the capacity, but the courage to claim their political and epistemic autonomy.[37] In doing this, Adorno argues, they should recognise the historical and social circumstances which limit the possible.[38] In addition, they should not attempt to proceed with no reliance at all on authority,[39] despite the fact that authoritarian teaching is destructive – a balance is required – between adaptation and contradiction, between helping students to become 'well-adjusted' persons, so-called, and rebels without recognition.[40] But in the final analysis:

> Democracy rests on the will-formation of each individual who comes together with others in the institution of the election of representatives. If an irrational result is not to occur it demands the capability and courage of each individual to follow his or her own understanding. (*EZM*: 133*)

It is that capability and courage which is summed up in the word *mündigkeit* – a term taken from legal theory, which refers to the capacity and right of adults to speak up and take responsibility for the witness they bear, to represent their own interests but also to be held accountable for the claims they make.

The process we call education is one which should lead to *mündigkeit* –

it is first and foremost a process of reflection, for Adorno, especially self-reflection on the psychic and social processes which, even in a formal democracy, limit people's capacity to speak and participate in a manner true to themselves. However, for Adorno, the only basis of this reflective process was the inherent contradiction of the social reality itself. The process is thus perpetual. In it, critique is relentless, and perhaps the only mind that could be comfortable in it would be the restless, even homeless mind, of which Nietzsche's Zarathustra spoke, grasping emptiness with an eagle's heartless talons.

Adorno's idea of critique encompassed and extended the idea of critique in Kant and Schleiermacher. However, despite his *substantive* intuitions about the limits of critique, and the positive elements in his discussions of education, these were never *methodologically* integrated with the rest of Adorno's work. Despite Habermas' increasing influence, the suspicion of negativeness due to Adorno's early influence lingered. As of today, the positive implications of Habermas' turn towards language have not been fully worked through in German critical theory of education. Still less has his more recent consolidation of this in his fundamental 'paradigm change' to the theory of communicative action, and his effective critique and appropriation of Foucault been absorbed. Until very recently it was still relatively easy for critics in Germany to make the case that critical theory of education lacked a positive programme.

GERMAN CRITICS

The central charge made by German critics of critical theory of education is the charge that emancipation is an inappropriate goal for education and that attempts to pursue it are empty and destructive. These criticisms were summed up by Spaemann in the charges that emancipatory pedagogy creates a school for suspicion, and that truly effective critique cannot result from it because it fails to recognise the need to master a profession or skill before attempting to improve it.[41] He also argued that the curriculum is weakened if only those forms of knowledge in which everyone can perform equally are taught. Finally, he accused critical pedagogy of being dogmatic and authoritarian – of being a pedagogy in the interest of domination by pedagogues.

These are charges aimed at the very heart of a pedagogy with emancipatory pretensions but they may tell against only a proportion of writers who identified themselves with critical theory. Some writers did lend an inflated meaning to the term *emanzipation*, often when pursuing polemical purposes. This inflation was under trenchant attack from within critical theory of education as early as 1972.[42] The focus of the present discussion is on the mainstream of *Kritische Erziehungswissenschaft*, and particularly those writers who draw to a considerable degree on the work of Jürgen Habermas. Perhaps Spaemann's criticisms apply more readily to the more Marxist analyses, such as Gamm's 'materialistic pedagogy'[43] or to the romanticism of Heydorn's 'left Hegelianism'.[44] Again, we must distinguish between those who, especially in the early period of the development of critical theory of education (1950–70), dealt with issues in such an abstract and impressionistic way that any attempt to apply their ideas in the classroom could well have resulted in the negative consequences lamented by the critics and those who have tried, at least in principle, to be more concrete. However, even when the list of contributors to the critical theory of education is reduced to a core of thinkers who have shown a sophisticated awareness of critical theory and who have produced analyses open to concrete interpretation, the force of Spaemann's criticisms is not entirely dissipated. Even pioneers like Blankertz and Mollenhauer, who were well aware of the dangers of abstraction and negativity were infected by a degree of utopian optimism in the heady days of the 1960s.[45] Work by Schaller and later Schäfer, on communicative pedagogy, was a considerable advance in concreteness but still fell short of offering clear guidance to teachers in the prevailing political climate as far as the avoiding of excesses was concerned.[46]

Similar work by Klafki, on curriculum development, was also characterised by an awareness of its own limitations, but by his own admission still overestimated the susceptibility of German society to change.[47] The degree of decentralisation, local freedom and curricular openness his scheme encompassed soon proved unacceptable to state governments intent on the wishes of voting parents motivated by familial privatism.

Political developments in Germany were also important. However unjustly, the excesses of the student movement of the late 1960s were laid at the door of critical theorists, as was some of the responsibility for the later activity of terrorist groups.[48] Habermas, too, was accused of inciting the students, despite the fact that, from the beginning, he was a critic of the imprudent overextension and idealistic employment of critical ideas, and broke early with the student movement because of its authoritarian and reckless spirit. Habermas speaks scathingly about the inflated use of the term *emanzipation* by educators.[49] He argues that the idealistic application of the ideal speech situation can only lead to 'theoretical despotism and practical terror'.

When we turn to Habermas' own writing on education, largely untranslated, we see a different picture, despite the fact that most of Habermas' educational writing is in the form of responses to specific educational proposals in the German context, and that most of it was written before 1969, it displays a keen awareness of the dangers of historically empty and utopian critique.

HABERMAS AND THE DEMOCRATISATION OF THE UNIVERSITY

Habermas' 1967 discussion of the attempt by the Council on Education and Culture (*Wissenschaftsrat*) to move the still traditionally humanistic German universities toward greater co-ordination with industry and the technological needs of the economy is still highly relevant.[50] (Today we are witness to a further push in the same direction, although starting from a higher base of technologically-oriented courses. It is no surprise that Habermas reiterated these ideas in his 1986 commencement address to the students at Heidelberg.) In his earlier discussion, Habermas recommended a strategy which would have allowed the goal of expansion of technological courses to be reached without at the same time diminishing the non-technical aspects of the education of doctors, engineers, etc. These non-technical goals concern development of professionally-related personal qualities, the development and interpretation of the general cultural tradition, and the formation of the moral and political consciousness of students. He argued that these can be preserved while the universities turn towards greater integration with the economy only if, at the same time, there is a heightening of concern with these issues in the university and greater attention to the social significance of these issues. He opposed the introduction of a more technicist managerial structure in universities because he saw that such a management style would mean that the shift towards technology-based courses would be unlikely to be accompanied by a fruitful increase in social awareness of the problems of technology. The best way to guarantee that the new technological studies became humanised was simultaneously to achieve a further democratisation of the universities. For Habermas, there is an 'affinity and inner relation' of the 'enterprise of knowledge at the university level and the democratic form of decision-making' (*TRS*: 6).

But Habermas did not advocate a mixing up of values and research. He accepted the usefulness of Hume's separation of fact and value, at least at the level of substantive theory, arguing instead for a consideration of the role of values at a meta-theoretical level – in considerations of the expediency of particular research strategies, the implicit assumption of methodologies, the fruitfulness of lines of enquiry, etc. In such matters one must argue about a choice of 'standards'; even if such argument cannot be simply deductive, he claimed, it can be reasoned and reasonable. The more the university gives itself over to technological studies, the more there is a need to emphasise the social and moral impact of technology. There is no technological means of deciding such issues, nor can technocratic styles of management resolve such issues. There is only one form of co-ordination in which such issues can be satisfactorily resolved and that is the democratic form. In a democratic process the principle of public discourse is supposed to eliminate all force other than that of the better argument, and majority decisions are held to be only a substitute for the uncompelled consensus that would finally have resulted if discussion did not always have to be broken off due to the need for a decision. (*TRS*: 7)

Such reflection, where, say, doctors reflect on the social aetiology of a disease, and so moderate the tendency of their profession towards a biological overemphasis, is potentially a critical reflection, which can lead to the release of creative power and innovation in the professions and technologies, as well as to greater social responsibility. This has implications for the role of philosophy or, at least, philosophising, in technical and professional courses of studies. Habermas chooses critical participation in technological structures over futile marginalisation. He makes quite specific and positive suggestions about university governance and the curriculum of professional studies. Habermas also warns of the dangers of too idealistic a conception of the potential of university democracy, and, in particular, the failure to realise that universities are, after all, only a small part of the social whole. The university community must participate in wider affairs responsibly and, ideally, as a united community, since it only enjoys a qualified privilege as an arena of free speech rather than an absolute privilege as a political actor.

CONCLUDING REMARKS

The problem of negativity and the self-marginalisation of critical theory is addressed both by the communicative turn and by Habermas' developmental reconstruction of the idea of levels of development. This reconstruction provides a language in which we can speak of 'better', rather than simply the 'best', of the ideal and the shortcomings of the existing state of affairs when compared with it. As mentioned above, critical theory of education is only now absorbing the implications of these later developments. Discussion of this is deferred until Chapter 6.

Most recent developments in Habermas' work (e.g. his discussions of modernity and the colonisation of the life–world) have led to a call for a further development of phenomenological aspects of educational analysis, bringing the wheel full circle to the humanistic themes which Schaller has long advocated should occupy more of our attention, and providing a basis for a return to fundamental questions concerning the relation between education, the individual and the state in a democratic society. These themes are taken up in the next chapter.

Perhaps the central theme we can draw from this briefest of reviews is that the historical self-relation of theory points to an ever present danger of constructing the interest in emancipation in too idealistic a form – in such a form it cannot be actually understood and practically carried out by real historical subjects. The result is a 'self-marginalisation' of critical theory and those intellectuals who have been responsible for its idealisation.[51] While ideals are an important part of theory, they must be applied to practical circumstances by those actually involved in them.[52] The aim of critique is a relative historical improvement rather than a great leap to perfection. It is too easy for intellectuals to scorn the slow progress of practitioners rather than recognise that the crucial role of ideals is to help us to be sure of our direction. As Lempert has argued, if we can be sure of our direction we can afford to be patient enough to take little steps (*schrittweise*).[53] It is not the understanding or intellectuals which will carry forward actual changes, but the democratic process of many voices and practical problem-solving on a day to day basis.

NOTES

1. F. Nietzsche, *Thus Spake Zarathustra*, The Collected Works, Vol. 4, O. Levy (ed.) New York: Gordon Press, 1974: 73, section 4.
2. I. Kant, *Education*, Ann Arbor: University of Michigan Press, 1964. See also A. Hearnden, *Education, Culture and Politics in West Germany*, London: Pergamon Press, 1976, for a discussion of the background to educational issues in Germany. Habermas, *T & P*: 257 'the critical dissolution of the existing untruth . . . requires . . . even more than rational insight. Above all, it requires the cardinal virtue of courage . . . the *sapere audere* [of] Kant'.
3. F. D. Schleiermacher, 'Erziehungslehre', in C. Platz (ed.) *Friedrich Schleiermacher's sämtliche Werke*, Vol. III, Section 9, Berlin: 1849.
4. D. Misgeld, 'Emancipation, enlightenment and liberation: An approach toward foundational enquiry in education', *Interchange*, **6** (3), 1975, 23–37.
5. J. Dewey, *Democracy and Education*, New York: The Free Press, 1916, 1944, 87.
6. For an accessible discussion of Hegel see M. Inwood, *Hegel*, Oxford: Oxford University Press, 1985.
7. See discussion in A. Hearnden *op. cit.* on Von Humboldt.
8. See also J. Dewey, 'The democratic faith and education', 1–9 in *The Authoritarian Attempt to Capture Education*, New York: King's Crown Press, 1945. [*Plus ça change!*] Also from Adorno/Horkheimer's standpoint H. Giroux, 'Radical pedagogy and student voice', *Interchange*, **17** (1), 1986: 62–70; H. Giroux and J. McLaren, 'Teacher education and the politics of engagement: The case for democratic schooling', *Harvard Education Review*, **56** (3), 1986: 213–38.
9. *LC*: Chapter 7.
10. C. Offe, 'Ungovernability: On the Renaissance of conservative theories of crisis', 67–88 in J. Habermas (ed.) *Observations on 'The Spiritual Situation of the Age' (OSSA)*, London: MIT Press, 1984 (original German version 1979).
11. B. Bloom, *The Closing of the American Mind*, Chicago: University of Chicago Press, 1987, and many other similar works footnoted in H. Giroux and J. McLaren, *op. cit.*
12. S. Castles and W. Wüstenberg, *The Education of the Future: An Introduction to the Theory and Practice of Socialist Education*, London: Pluto Press, 1979.
13. Largely following W. Keckeisen, 'Kritische Erziehungswissenschaft', 117–38 in D. Lenzen and K. Mollenhauer (eds) *Enzyklopädie Erziehung*, Vol. 1, Stuttgart: Kohlhammer, 1983, but also indebted to H. Paffrath (ed.) *Kritische Theorie und Pädagogik der Gegenwart*, Weinheim: Deutscher Studien Verlag, 1987, Introduction.

14. Cf. K. Mollenhauer, *Erziehung und Emanzipation*, München: Juventa, 1968: 22 *et passim*.
15. T. Feuerstein, 'Methodologische Schwierigkeiten einer kritische Erziehungswissenschaft und Perspektiven ihrer Uberwindung', *Pädagogische Rundschau*, **29**, 1975: 165 *et passim*.
16. W. Klafki, 'Ideologie Kritik', in L. Roth (ed.) *Methoden Erz. Forschung*, Stuttgart, 1978.
17. W. Keckeisen, *op. cit.*
18. B. Bühner and A. Birnmeyer, *Ideologie und Diskurs: Zur Theorie von Jürgen Habermas und ihrer Rezeption in der Pädagogik*, Frankfurt: Haag und Herchen, 1982.
19. T. Adorno, *Stichworte*, Frankfurt: Suhrkamp, 1969, 47, and K. Mollenhauer, *op. cit.*, 1968: 65 and 'Sechs Widersprüche': 102–18.
20. See W. Keckeisen: *op. cit.*, 126–8. D. Hoffmann, *Kritische Erziehungswissenschaft*, Stuttgart: Kohlhammer, 1978.
21. See T. Feuerstein, *op. cit.*, K. Mollenhauer, *op. cit.*, 1968: 64, K. Horn (ed.) *Aktionsforschung: Balanzakt oder Netz*, Frankfurt: Campus, 1979.
22. See K. H. Schäfer and K. Schaller, *Kritische Erz. und kommunikativer Didaktik*, Heidelberg: Quelle und Mayer, 1976, and D. Hoffmann, *op. cit.*
23. See K. Horn, *op. cit.*, H. Moser, *Aktionforschung als kritische Theorie der Sozialwissenschaft*, München, 1975. W. Klafki, 'Grundzuge kritisch-konstruktiver Didaktik', *Pädagogische Rundschau*, **39** (1), 1985: 3–28, and 'Pedagogy: A theory of practice', *Suid-Afrikaanse Tydskrif vir die Pedagogiek*, **4** (1), 1970: 23–9, and 'Decentralised curriculum development in the form of action research', *Information Bulletin* (Council of Europe), **1**, 1975: 13–22.
24. E. König, *Theorie der Erz.*, Vols. 1–2, München, 1975, D. Benner, *Hauptströmungen in der Erz.*, München, 1973, K. Mollenhauer, *op. cit.*, 1968: 69, C. Wulf, *Theorien und Konzepte der Erziehungswissenschaft*, München, 1977, 148 *et passim*.
25. H. Moser, 'Programmatik eine kritischen erz.', *Zeitschrift für Pädagogik*, **18**, 1972 : 639–46, 652.
26. W. Lempert, 'Bildungsforschung und Emanzipation', in W. Lempert *Leistungsprinzip und Emanzipation*, Frankfurt, 1971, 320.
27. T. Adorno, E. Frenkel-Brunswick, D. Levinson and R. Sanford, *The Authoritarian Personality*, New York: Harper Bros, 1950, H. Giesecke, *Didaktik der politischen Bildung*, München: 1965, 1971, K. Mollenhauer, *op. cit.*: 75–96, D. Hoffmann, *op. cit.*: 63–6.
28. D. Benner, *op. cit.*: 317.
29. W. Klafki, *op. cit.*
30. S. Miedema and E. Heimans, 'The Marburg elementary school project: the weal and woe of an action research programme', *Curriculum Perspectives*, **6** (2), 1986: 47–50.
31. W. Klafki, *op. cit.*
32. W. Keckeisen, 132–3, and C. Wulf, *op cit.*: 139.
33. For a sceptical view see J. Ruhloff, *Das unqelöste Normproblem der Pädagogik*, Heidelberg: Quelle and Meyer, 1980.
34. T. Adorno, *Erziehung zur Mündigkeit (EZM)*. Frankfurt: Suhrkamp, 1971, 25. See also J. Habermas in a prescient 1978 interview in P. Dews (ed.) *Habermas: Autonomy and Solidarity: Interviews*, London: Verso, 1986, 58: 'there is a rehabilitation of competitive behaviour, pursuit of gain, and exaltation of virtues conducive to a high mobility of labour. For it is necessary to induce people to accept work they would not otherwise perform of their own free will . . . the accent is thus placed upon an acquisitve ethic and instrumental virtues. This orientation penetrates deeply into the first years of schooling, to the point of dominating whole education systems.'
35. T. Adorno, *EZM*: 117, 131.
36. *Ibid.*: 140.
37. *Ibid.*: 90, 107, 136 *et passim*.
38. *Ibid.*: 47, 108.

39. *Ibid*: 139.
40. *Ibid.*: 109.
41. R. Spaemann, 'Emanzipation: ein Bildungsziel?', *Merkur*, **29** (320), 1975: 11–24.
42. W. Lempert, 'Zum Begriff der Emanzipation', *Neue Sammlung*, **13**, 1973: 62–70.
43. H. J. Gamm, 'Die materialistische Pädagogik', in H. Gudjons *et al.* (eds) *Erziehungswissenshaftliche Theorien*, Hamburg: George Westermann Verlag, 1980, 41–50.
44. H. J. Heydorn, *Uber den Widersprüch von Bildung und Herrschaft*, **2**, Frankfurt: Suhrkamp, 1979.
45. H. Blankertz, 'Kritische Erziehungswissenschaft', in K. Schaller (ed.) *Erziehungswissenschaft der Gegenwart . . .*, Bochum, 1979, 28–40, K. Mollenhauer, *op. cit.*, 1968: 27 *et passim*, W. Lempert, discussed in L. Kerstiens, *Modelle emanzipatorische Erziehung*, Bad Heilbrunn, 1975: 62–3.
46. K. H. Schäfer and K. Schaller, *op. cit.*, K. Schaller, 'Kritische Erziehungswissenschaft am Ausgang ihrer Epoche?', *Bildung und Erziehung*, **38** (3), 1985: 357–78.
47. W. Klafki, *op. cit.*
48. H. H. Groothof, 'Zur Bedeutung der Diskursethik von Jürgen Habermas für die Pädagogik, *Pädagogische Rundschau*, **39** (3), 1985: 275–98, and A. Wellmer, 'Terrorism and the critique of society', 283–308 in *OSSA* and Habermas in P. Dews (ed.) *op. cit.*: 40.
49. Personal communication, Starnberg, 1980. See also H. H. Groothof, *op. cit.*: 284.
50. J. Habermas, 'Universität in der Demokratie: Demokratisierung der Universität', *Merkur*, **21** (230), 1967: 416–33, 'Die Idee der Universität: Lernprozesse', 71–100 in J. Habermas, *Eine Art Schadensabwicklung*, Frankfurt: Suhrkamp, 1987.
51. H. Dubiel, *Wissenschaftsorganisation und politische Erfahrung*, Frankfurt, 1978, 129. See also T. Adorno, *op. cit.* 1969, 176.
52. *T & P*: 'Decisions for the political struggle cannot at the outset be justified theoretically and then be carried out organisationally. The sole possible justification at this level is consensus, aimed at in practical discourse, among the participants, who, in the consciousness of their common interests and their knowledge of the circumstances, of the unpredictable consequences and secondary consequences, are the only ones who can know what risk they are willing to undergo, and with what expectations.'

In P. Dews, (ed.) *op. cit.*: 68, he argues for a gradual transformation of decision-making processes through both cultural change and growth in devolution of power and participation; he goes on to say: 'There cannot be any socialism without a radical and coherent appropriation of the gains of the movements of bourgeois civil rights.'
53. These themes were taken up by critical theorists of education, who broke from the authoritarian left in the late 1960s: e.g. W. Lempert, in L. Kerstiens (see note 45).

CHAPTER 4

TRADITIONAL SCHOOLING AND RESPONSIBLE CRITIQUE

> If, then, I am asked why I have spent so much time on expounding a rather abstract philosophy, it is because practical attempts to develop schools based upon the idea that education is found in life-experience are bound to exhibit inconsistencies and confusions unless they are guided by some conception of what experience is, and what marks off educative experience from non-educative and mis-educative experience.
>
> (John Dewey)[1]

With the wisdom of hindsight, it is clear that it is necessary to reconsider earlier understandings of the programme of critical theory of education. In the unpromising political terrain of the present it is absolutely necessary to be quite clear what marks off critical educational experience from simply education in critical theory's name. Despite the pleas for moderation and prudence already mentioned, and criticisms of the inflation of concepts like critique, emancipation and mature articulateness (*Mündigkeit*) into empty utopianisms, there has been a tendency on the part of some to ignore all warnings.[2] The weakness of the practical accomplishments of critical theory have left it, at least in Germany, in such a state of disarray that its critics are already announcing its demise.[3] With the characteristic irony of history, it is at precisely this time that the critical theory of education is attracting increased attention in the English-speaking world. What must be avoided is the tendency, already evident in some of this newer work, to repeat the idealist errors of earlier German thought.

In a recent discussion of the significance of Habermas' discourse ethic for pedagogy, Hans-Hermann Groothof warns against any tendency to idealism.[4] In the ideal of discourse

> we have only seemingly achieved an objective standard against which we can measure the practical rationality of individuals and society. In reality, it would be an illusion to believe we can emancipate ourselves from the, as it were, normatively loaded facticity of our historical situation with its

current norms and criteria of rationality. An attempt of this kind could only end in 'theoretical despotism and practical terror'. (Groothoff, 1985: 285*)

Habermas' position on this question is that the ideal of discourse 'does not provide a process to create norms but only a process to examine them'.

A second kind of idealism is also evident, both in German and in more recent work written in English. The fact that many of the scholars who have turned to critical theory, then and now, have come to it from a background in the humanities (or *Geisteswissenschaften* in Germany) has led to a very negative view of the value of empirical research, particularly quantitative research.[5] This, in turn, has diminished the concreteness of their analyses somewhat. It is allied to a general characteristic of those who are attracted by the systematic scope of critical theory – a tendency to keep analysis at a highly abstract level.

Taken together, these weaknesses suggest that the programme of critical theory of education should incline towards analysis that maximises the significance of the historical and social situation of critique, and relates the necessary process of more abstract reconstructions of general features of pedagogy to the concrete details of the life–world of participants.

The tendency to theoretical despotism noted by Groothof, and by less sympathetic critics such as Spaemann,[6] may be described in terms of Habermas' recent discussion of the colonisation of the life–world.

THE LIFE–WORLD AND ITS MODERN FATE

For Habermas, the life–world is both the background of beliefs and feelings against which human action takes place and it is at the same time, the product of those beliefs and feelings. In other words, when one is following a cultural rule, one at the very least keeps the cultural rule alive. If we follow an old rule in new circumstances, we are adapting and developing the rule. All this can happen quite non-consciously. Normally this world of assumptions, rules, etc. is taken for granted. It is 'co-assumed' or 'co-given' but for it to work it cannot be called into question as a whole – if it were, all daily life would be frozen, even speech temporarily rendered impossible, while we attempted to rebuild some common round for communication.[7] And because this world is normally unquestioned, it is difficult to discover it just from listening to and watching participants.

But it is one thing to have a general idea about this world's existence and how people remake it even as they draw upon it, and quite another to criticise aspects of it.

> Even from this vantage point, [general theory] only formal pragmatic statements are possible, statements related to the structures of the life–world in general, and not to determinate life–worlds in their concrete historical configuration. (Habermas, *PDM*: 299)

The life–world reproduces itself to the extent that actors are socialised, learn sets of norms, absorb cultural traditions and act in terms of them. But if we consider the life–world solely from the point of view of its reproduction, there is no room for actors actively to produce it and in producing it, change it – they are seen as products of the traditions in which they stand.

To get beyond this generalised, rather fixed view, we must depart from the reconstructive approach and engage in specific biographical and historical study, followed by critique (in the manner, say, of psychotherapy). This analytical and critical process cannot bring the whole life–world into question but only single, thematised aspects of it. The general theory of the life–world can only be a *guide* for actual critique through reflection, neither construction nor specific critique can grasp the life–world in its totality. Nor can either reject it in its totality.[8] We must remember that critique is always limited, fragmentary and unsure. Anything else is a utopian fantasy.

But the life–world can change in ways other than through individual rejection or even more systematic criticism. It can change through penetration of it, in which parts of it break down, are disturbed, and suffer colonisation by the exotic flora of bureaucratic rules and money relationships.[9] However, there is an alternative to this colonisation. Those parts of the life–world under threat can be reconstituted through communicative consensus as a new, (initially) conscious set of norms and assumptions. This process must be a product of the recipients themselves, who can harmonise or reconcile this rebuilding with the rest of the general background.

Too often, critical educators have brought the whole of the life–world under a general rhetoric of criticism, causing an unspecified and free-floating fear to permeate even the most innocent of aspects of daily life. In their more concrete pedagogical actions they have often attacked specific sections of the life–world, such as children's general assumptions about gender, religion, or social worth, without, at the same time, providing the opportunity, in dialogue and solidarity, for the children to reconstitute the definition of their biological sexuality, ultimate beliefs or sense of social valuing. There is methodological justification for neither the criticism of a whole form of life nor for rejection of large segments of it. Critical teachers have fostered free-floating fear and an amorphous guilt, especially in white males, a fear and guilt which, unresolved, has now turned on its creators.

Such attacks on the life–world serve only to penetrate it, cause it to break down, and open up its ecology to colonisation by the more dangerous exotic plants of one-sided rational domination or nihilism.[10] It is not the main function of critical educators to attack the life–world of students – to 'make trouble'. Rather, it should be to assist students to make an effective job of reconstructing the already problematic parts of their life–world through communicative, problem-solving learning. In conjunction with this, some limited degree of gentle reconstitution of connected, but not yet questioned, aspects of the life–world may be necessary. Anything else is an idealist form of educational praxis.

The approach that is required would seem to resemble Dewey's problem-solving method. This will be discussed further in Chapter 6. The essential point at this stage of the analysis is that the relation between critical teacher and learner should not be one of hostile critic of everything that belongs to the learner's identity. At the same time, the alternative, more traditional relationship of benevolent manipulation, through behavioural conditioning or through communication, is not acceptable either, since it is also incompatible with the goal of mature, self-confident articulateness. The traditional pedagogy rests on the view that the teacher exerts authority over the learner, and leads the learner through experiences, etc., as an expression not of the teacher's self-interest, but of the teacher's judgement of what is in the learner's best interest. This view is allied to a traditional theory of knowledge.

Ira Shor's *Critical Teaching and Everyday Life* is, in many ways, a valuable book.[11] But the main model of teaching in it is only critical in a one-dimensional way. It proposes a pedagogy based on experiences constructed specifically to disturb the life–world of students. As such, it partakes of the character of traditional pedagogy (at its most experientially skilful, perhaps). The teacher knows what is in students' best interests. It is to challenge them with stimulus materials to rethink basic aspects of the life–world. For example, students are encouraged to explore husband–wife relationships through consideration of the idea of the husband's relationship with a lover rather than his wife. The students then formulate the demands the wife might make on her husband when she discovers his infidelity. These demands are cast in the form of 'marriage contracts'. The students are then encouraged to go home and surprise their real-life spouses or lovers with them! The issue is not whether the substantive aspects of the critique of the sexual double-standard are valid or not but one of what the validity of critique consists in.

Traditional theory of knowledge separates critique from knowledge since it presents knowledge as a matter of fact and valuing as a non-cognitive activity by which knowers can relate to their knowledge from the outside of it, as it were. Ira Shor's *curriculum* may present knowledge as value-laden rather than value-free, and thus be non-traditional, but his *pedagogy* often fails to take into account the internal relationships of his students to the curriculum knowledge he has selected. In this way, it is traditional, because one of the differences between traditional theory of knowledge and critical theory is that the former fails to recognise the internal relation between historical subjects and their knowledge which is constituted by the fact that their knowledge reflexively defines them as historical subjects. Our way of knowing is a part of our way of being and an expression of our culture and our time; it is not a separated history and subject-free product to which we can relate from the outside.

The distinction between traditional and critical theory is crucial if we are to be able to separate educative experiences from non-educative and even mis-educative experiences, even where the latter are produced in critical theory's name.

TRADITIONAL AND CRITICAL THEORIES OF KNOWLEDGE

Horkheimer's distinction between the two kinds of theory[12] may be grafted onto Habermas' discussion, in *K & HI*, of different kinds of knowledge constitutive interests or, at least, onto a selective reconstruction of that argument, for Habermas has since made a paradigm change that attempts to cover the same ground by a different philosophical strategy. For Horkheimer, the self-understanding of traditional theory comprehended it as an activity in the minds of individual historical subjects, through which their experience of the facts was compared with hypotheses about relationships between facts, to build up a body of tested hypotheses, which could now be seen as historically independent and forming a logically inter-linked system. But critical theory 'has for its object men as producers of their own historical way of life in its totality'. He goes on to argue that:

> The real situations which are the starting points of science are not regarded simply as data to be verified and to be predicted according to . . . laws. . . . Every datum depends not on nature alone but also on the power man has over it. Objects, the kind of perception, the question asked and the meaning of the answers all bear witness to human activity and the degree of man's power. (Horkheimer, 1976: 222)

In a way, Horkheimer is drawing out the radical implications of a view of science that has become quite commonplace among post-empiricist philosophers of science since he wrote the words above in 1937. He is calling for a recognition that data and theory are locked in a two-way process, not a one-way process where data are used as the decisive court of appeal against theory, and for a recognition that theory, and indeed the whole process, is imbedded in human history, *is* human history – the history of a self-knowing species. One of the critical corollaries of this view is that the social and communicative circumstances of the concrete historical appearance of knowledge within scientific communities must be recognised as the royal road of critique. Another corollary derives from the recognition that critical theory is concerned: 'not only with goals already imposed by existent ways of life, but with men in all their potentialities' (Horkheimer, 1976: 224). This point is made clearer in Adorno's essay on 'Sociology and sociological research'[13]; in which he points out that surveys of public opinion or 'attitudinal' type may be carried out in a theoretical context which mistakes the appearance for the potential, 'the epiphenomenon – what the world has made of us – with the thing itself'.

> The thing-like [reifying] method postulates a reified consciousness of those whom it subjects to its experiments. If a questionnaire asking members of the public about their musical tastes gives them a choice of the categories 'classical' and 'popular' it is with the justifiable certainty that the people concerned listen according to these categories. . . . But as long as the social determinants of this sort of reaction are omitted from the survey [it] suggests that the division of musical experience into 'classical' and 'popular' is a final one, somehow part of the natural order of things.
> (Adorno, 'Sociology and social research': 244)

Both the empirical–analytical sciences (including behavioural science) and the hermeneutic sciences, are traditional sciences in this sense. Critique of them does not suggest that their methods are without value or their findings without any use, but it does suggest that they are one-sided and inclined to a surface analysis, which tends to accept things as they are.

In the *Positivismusstreit* (the fight about positivism) in Germany sociology, Habermas accused Popper's critical rationalism of much the same faults that Horkheimer had earlier identified in the traditional theory of knowledge. Despite Popper's rejection of the notion that scientific generalisation was built up from collections of facts, in favour of a notion of bold hypotheses which should be subject to vigorous attempts at falsification, Habermas argued that Popper had not overcome the problem of taking the surface phenomena for the underlying reality. Even vigorous tests of theory might remain tied to the present background ideas and assumptions of the common life–world of scientists and their society, if the conventions of method remained as Horkheimer had described them. Although Popper recognised the fact that the critical community of science set up these conventions, and formed hypotheses and decided upon research directions, he did not see that this required cultural and social self-criticism by that community if it was not to remain trapped in the circle of its own culturally-conditioned level of theoretical perception. This was particularly important for the social sciences.

But it is important to understand that Habermas' critique of the positivists, which built on and extended that of Horkheimer and Adorno, did not involve a sweeping rejection of all empirical methods, but a critique of their overextension, unreflexive self-understanding, and of the consequences of this for the application of the sciences. As long as empirical science is pursued, this critique should continue. It is a necessary part of being aware of the very limited predictive power of such methods in the human studies, of the capacity for research to adopt conceptual frameworks and take on directions with ideological implications in a given society, and for practice bound to such methods to substitute domination for a genuine practical capacity.

The excessive claims of analytical-empirical science may be offset by a recognition of the complementary claims of the interpretive or hermeneutic sciences. While they do not yield predictive control of physical processes, they do yield understanding of systems of meaning and of the way individual acts, utterances and practices are given meaning within them, including normative and ethical meaning.

Interpretive science is often *coupled with* critique, but it is not the same thing. Critique always goes beyond interpretation. However, this science can help us understand the way in which the use of behavioural technology to affect human beings can change the traditional meaning of being human – of being first and foremost a subject for others and only secondarily, an object. In this way, the meaning systems of daily life, in which the activities of scientists are themselves embedded, become a basis for an understanding of the doing and applying of science. But only the critical sciences permit us to go further, and raise questions about the circumstances under which it is, or is not, morally acceptable to treat people as things to be manipulated. As long as the analytical-empirical and hermeneutic sciences continue, this critique should continue, because it is the basis upon which these sciences may be made to serve rather than dominate human interests.

It is in a careful examination of the basis of this critical capacity – in the nature of human speech communication – that we are also to find guidance for critical educational method. Where classroom knowledge is seen as a finished product, as in the positivist view, rather than a communicative culture among scientists, it can be seen as something to which students must be made to adapt. But where its historically created character is clear, the fact that students will individually and collectively *make* the knowledge of the future places a great emphasis on their freedom to form their own views.[14]

Where hermeneutic views are stressed, but no critical methodology is developed, it is possible for a generalised and utopian critical programme to be introduced as an imperialistic culture overcoming all that is old, fusty and traditional. Either that, or a studious cultural relativism is adopted. But both of these options are simply tantamount to imposing the currently fashionable agenda of left (or right) intellectuals on the life–world of students. While the surface of things, things as they are today, must not be accepted as an adequate vision of things as they might be for all time, the dogmatic imposition of new systems of meaning or experental manipulation of the life–world does not constitute a justifiable critical method. Freire's name is often mentioned in connection with 'consciousness raising' but Freire's method did not involve themes foreign to his students' perceptions. (In any case, the political–economic circumstances in Brazil may well be seen to justify forms of pedagogy which cannot be justified at a different level of socially institutionalised learning.[15])

Perhaps the most recent version of relativism is that created by post-modernists, such as Foucault, who overestimate the totality of the influence of power structures on the creation of systems of meaning. This leads to a pessimistic cynicism. It is beyond the scope of this book to examine Habermas' detailed response to post-modernism but in *PDM* he demonstrates that the analysis trades in the very coins of the hope for truth and method that it seeks to devalue.

THE IDEAL SPEECH SITUATION (ISS) AND ITS JOURNEY

Habermas' methodological standard for critique, including critical reconstitution of segments of the life–world, is found in his conception of communicative action and the ideal speech situation (ISS). It is in this that the possibility of a critique that is not merely dogmatic assertion of one set of values over others rests.

The idea of the ISS is a critical reconstruction of the assumptions of everyday speech communication. It is argued that these assumptions underlie the possibility of speech communication and are universal. Since they are universal, they are transcendental with respect to historical and cultural differences in the species. Another way of saying this is to say that when we speak we normally act as if a certain situation existed, even though, in fact, it does not. The assumptions we make are counter-factual but we must all make them if speech communication is to provide the normal, everyday means of inter-action, for without these assumptions there would be chaos.[16] The assumptions are:

(i)   that what we are saying or hearing is intelligible, i.e. is coded according to the usual rules, etc.;

(ii) that what we are saying or hearing is true in so far as it implies the existence of states of affairs, etc.;

(iii) that the persons speaking are being truthful or sincere;

(iv)   and that the things said are normatively appropriate considering the relationships among the people and between them and the situation they are in.[17]

Even telling lies depends on these assumptions because deceptive speech cannot be successful unless the hearer assumes it is truthful and true and it is spoken in a context of relationships between speaker and hearer in which such speech is appropriate. In later discussions, Habermas identified speech characterised by these assumptions with a general form or sphere of human action – communicative action – which he contrasted with goal-oriented, manipulative action, which he calls 'strategic' action.[18]

In early formulations, Habermas seemed to many to be saying that the ideal speech situation could be used as a *measure* of actual speech situations.[19] Since the speech roles, the kinds of things categories of participants had a right or an obligation to say, are symmetrical in the ISS, with each person having the same rights, etc., it was argued that the degree of asymmetry could be a measure of the oppressive character of communication situations, and the areas of speech rights and obligations in which asymmetry occurred could tell us about the type of oppression involved. This argument was applied to critical pedagogy.[20] But Habermas soon corrected earlier impressions. The ISS was a tool to think with, not a measure. One could use it to identify the type and degree of asymmetry in concrete speech situations, but this asymmetry required a rational historical reconstruction in which one imagined the parties in a rational discourse, their differences of interest being directly expressed rather than hidden in tacit rules for speaking.[21]

Some of these differences may be unavoidable, they may lie in areas of life which 'do not permit an approximation of ideal limit values' (*TCA*: 73). Even if a concrete consensus is reached in a given instance, we can never be completely sure it is a genuine consensus. Some party to the dialogue may have subordinated their true opinion to another 'to avoid trouble' or because they were tired of arguing, etc. We have to rely, ultimately, on the self-interest of individuals in emancipation, and in their courage, their capacity to 'stick to their guns'.[22] While there is no guarantee that speakers are not trapped by the very concepts with which the power structures of history and life-experience have equipped them, the case against the possibility of creative dissent has not been proven.

In addition, many concrete situations exist in which a degree of asymmetry of speech roles is entirely rational and appropriate. The division of labour in society (e.g. specialisation) means that the physician may ask more questions of the patient than the patient does of the physician, or at any rate, questions of a different kind. If one were to find a situation where the patient did not get a chance to ask any questions at all, or even the questions he or she wanted to have answered, one might, if one had specific and concrete information on the state of medical knowledge, the patient, the illness, etc., be able to conclude that a given situation was asymmetrical in a way or in a degree which did manifest oppression. This conclusion could not be validly reached in the abstract, as it were, through the ideal of total symmetry of Foucault's implicit appeal to the notion that power is totally incompatible with truth.

Much the same might be said about the need, in large social formations, to co-ordinate the activities of large numbers of people.[23] We may soon be forced by environmental disaster to achieve such co-ordination on a global scale. In such circumstances there may be a need for specific types and degrees of asymmetry. The issue is whether the asymmetry present in a given situation is functionally justified and whether some safeguarding apparatus or process (such as an electoral process) is present. Post-modernism's genealogical anthropology, properly used, can assist in the analysis and uncovering of this asymmetry, but not in its evaluation.

Most recently, partly under the impact of criticism by the post-modernists and others, Habermas has suggested that the ISS as a critical device, is limited in other ways. It cannot be used to criticise large-scale communication structures, but only face-to-face ones. Thus it cannot be the sole basis of a rational form of life. It is better adapted to generating critique in some areas than others. It cannot address all aspects or dimensions of life, aesthetic considerations are also important as is some more general sense of restraint or balance – a feel for the overall 'healthiness' of a state of affairs. In other words, Habermas has moved away from the view that the ISS is a sufficient basis for critique, to the view that it offers a limited and partial, if still centrally important, basis of transcendence.[24] Habermas' present view of the ISS is that its

> standards of procedural rationality hold only for dealing with questions
> that are sorted out according to some one universal aspect, for example
> justice or normative rightness; and that the corresponding learning
> processes can be understood in the light of these standards as an
> approximation . . . to ideal limit values.

He goes on to argue that

> But we cannot undertake to appraise forms of life centred on communica-
> tive action [such as pedagogy] simply by applying the standards of
> procedural rationality. These forms of life comprise not only institutions
> that come under the aspect of justice, but 'language games', historical
> configurations of habitual practices, group memberships, cultural patterns
> of interpretation, forms of generalisation, competitiveness, attitudes, and

so forth. It would make no sense to want to judge these syndromes as a whole, the totality of a form of life, from the standpoint of individual forms of rationality . . . perhaps we should speak of a balance among moments incomplete in themselves. (*RTC*: 262)

Thus, while communicative action may be judged in terms of justice, rightness, authenticity and opportunities for the truth of statements to be tested, all of which involve universal criteria, the relation among these issues and between them and other practical problems, must be judged according to less formalisable criteria.

The danger in classroom social criticism is that ideals are applied abstractly to the life–world, in the light of plausible critical theories (about gender, class, etc.) without the kind of concrete analysis and the representation of interests that can only occur in the life–world contexts concerned. Reflexively, there is a similar danger in expecting the ISS to be approximated in every classroom lesson. In his critique of the use by teachers and others, of qualitative methods to comprehend students' subjectivity and the concept of life–world colonisation, Brumlik speaks of the need for 'pedagogical tact'.[25] The privacy and personal 'space' of students can be invaded and problematised too easily in the name of 'openness' of communication. However, outside the teacher/learner or therapist/patient relationships other considerations may prevail. In the institutionalised debate of academia and of science, there is a presumption of equality. This is not to suggest that it is a case of no holds barred, norms of tact, trust and the like still apply, but in the absence of the marked asymmetry of power and knowledge characteristic of the school classroom, the debate can be more vigorous. It is in a careful examination of the basis of this critical capacity – in the nature of human speech communication – that we also find guidance for critical method.

THE METHOD OF CRITIQUE

Habermas' original formulation of the critique of knowledge was based on a Kantian reconstruction of the general possibility of human knowledge in which the concept of universal, anthropologically-based interests in knowledge formation played a key role. By a progression through a series of partial and historically limited accounts of knowledge by Kant, Hegel, Comte, Mach, Marx, Peirce, Dilthey, Freud and Nietzsche, Habermas attempted to [re]construct a general overview in which the connection between theory and practice was stressed at the level of the interests which underlie knowledge formation itself. As we have seen in the foregoing discussion of the ISS, he has since attempted to secure much the same territory by another line of argument, acknowledging some of the weaknesses in *Knowledge and Human Interests* without at the same time abandoning its views entirely.

This is not the place to review the very extensive literature concerning Habermas' epistemological position, or to defend it.[26] Debate about the issues raised is not closed, but the very existence among intellectuals of divergent views about the nature of the physical (and social) sciences, and the fact that these are not clearly aligned with any simple model of the personal politics of the philosophers concerned, suggests that at least some process of critique which goes beyond the surface forms of research is a necessary part of giving that research an ethical direction. At the very least, critical science is 'a result of reflection upon and critique of' the other two forms of science (Hesse, 1982: 111).[27] From the standpoint of much modern philosophy of science it is possible to take a different view of knowledge from that taken by Habermas, but as Mary Hesse has pointed out, the need for a community of critique which deals with the processes and findings of the empirical sciences remains (1982). Even if one retreats from Habermas' early claims to found this critique in the postulation of a counter-factual process of reaching uncoerced consensus among inquirers, to a more modest Kantian 'regulative idea' or norm of science, as Ottmann wishes to do, the need for a reflective, open, critical process remains.[28] Accordingly, a great deal of critical theory's critique of mainstream educational research, whether of a behavioural or a 'qualitative' kind, may retain some of its validity, even were more transcendental claims for it given up. It may also be easy to underestimate the value of a continuing, reflexive and rational *internal* critique of the natural sciences and technology. The receptivity of many to such a critique may become heightened as the environmental consequences of unbridled technological expansion and limited holistic biological understandings become evident on a global scale.

The identification of internal conflict or contradictions in a body of thought, or between the claims of a community of practitioners and their conduct, has always been regarded as an act with critical implications. In somewhat the same way, the discovery of gaps (*aporias*) in the story told, or of connections between different branches of epistemologically complementary forms of knowledge, such as economics, history or sociology, has always been regarded as a discovery with critical import. Horkheimer's method of internal criticism, or *immanent critique*, employed at times by Habermas, is a development of these views. It cannot, of itself, *methodologically* transcend the present, but its identification of the contradictions in it, particularly, for Adorno, the contradictions between the ideal of the good life and the practices which most clearly fall short of it, can prepare the way for transcending change, since such ideals can function transcendentally, whatever their epistemic status. Ultimately however, the willingness to listen to such arguments, particularly where moral issues are involved, can only be secured by processes of educational development.

> The same holds for the new interpretations that allow our needs and interests to appear in another light and thereby open new opportunities for consensus. However these innovations arise, it is not through discourse that they gain the power to convince and are spread abroad; this happens only in social movements. (Habermas, *RTC*: 253)

Where Habermas parts company with those who would limit critique to immanent critique, is his rejection of the view that critique can only proceed effectively as a critique located in tradition or spread only through processes of political and social organisation, however important these may be. While critique must remain in touch with the actual contexts of its application, it must also be driven by a transcending sense of direction. In Habermas' case, the counter-factual ideal of free and open processes of argumentation is one of the things that plays this role. Only when *both* components are present and there is also a crucial element of uncoerced rational conviction can critique be freed from the nexus with power. It is the burden of most post-modernist arguments, such as Foucault's, that no basis for a universally acceptable transcending idea is possible.[29] If Foucault is right critique would be reduced to a state where it would become as much a claim to power as to truth. The claim of critical theory is that it is possible to go beyond power.

The essential point which both proponents and opponents of the critical theory of education sometimes miss is this: the methodology of critique is a product of the reconstruction of our understanding of the way our species comes to know – it is thus necessarily a method which has some power to transcend cultural differences – but the actual process of critique with practical intent is immanent. It is immanent in two ways; it proceeds by internal criticism of the existing state of affairs and it must be incorporated in social movements and organisational forms if it is to be effective.

Critique cannot afford to remain merely contemplatively immanent, as it were. An immanent theoretical focus and logic is not enough to make critique historically immanent as well. For this to happen, it has to be reflected in changed persons and changed lives, and ultimately, changed practices and culture. Critique which remains merely notionally or contemplatively immanent is still idealist critique. It is not merely ineffectual, it is dangerous. In the case of science, or the educational research community, it is insufficient to confine such critique to theoretical papers delivered largely to like-minded people and polemical papers flying in the teeth of those with whom one disagrees. In the case of the classroom, no amount of shouting it from the podium or the blackboard will do anything more than further break down the structures of the life–world on behalf of the expansion of power and money.

The manner of critique's historical immanence must be consistent with its critical principle. Unlike mainstream Marxist critique, in one version at least, whose verification could be found in the revolutionary creation of a dictatorship of the proletariat, at the present stage of social evolution in the West, critical theory can only proceed by actions which either organise further enlightenment, through communication, or develop greater democracy, through organisational changes to communicative opportunities which institutionalise more open communicative participation in humanity's self-formation. While at a given historical moment forms of action may be justified which involve strategic actions, expressions of (democratic) political power, and negotiations towards compromises of groups disposing of certain numbers of votes etc., it should be recognised that these, in turn, fall short of the mode of action in resolving political differences which critical theory seeks eventually to reach in practice. The ideal mode of action is rational persuasion. The onus of proof falls on those who want to depart from such means, to demonstrate that the form of action at least does not fall back below the historical learning level already generally reached (i.e. the usages of democratic politics) and that it brings about a situation where future decisions may be more dialogically reached. Rational persuasion, of course, is dependent on the rational capacity of the hearer as well as the speaker and on the interchangeability of these roles. In the pedagogical relationship the same self-limiting features of critical methodology apply. If a hearer is unable, for reasons of emotional state or limited maturity, to respond rationally to a particular validity claim, the question as to whether it is appropriate to make such a claim (at that time) must at least be asked. However justified by intersubjective consensus among another circle of interlocutors (such as educators) such a claim may be, the circumstances surrounding its advancement to, say, children, must themselves justify the making of it in terms of the possibility of their rational response to it. The principle that gives critique the ability to transcend relations of power, namely that it must rest in the uncoerced rational acceptance of the better argument must be reflexively immanent in the historical process of the social relationships of critics.

THE METHOD FOR AN EDUCATIONAL CRITIQUE OF SCHOOLING

That schools are not necessarily educational is more than a mere cliché, it is the basis of critique of schooling. It points to the transcendental basis of the *educational ideal* that we critically reconstruct. This reconstruction has already been developed to a high degree by Mollenhauer, Blankertz and others. The goals of education are rational emancipation, and mature articulateness. In a similar way we can produce a more specific critical reconstruction of teaching and learning, curriculum processes, educational research, the course of studies for teachers, and the ideal organisational processes for education. On the basis of these reconstructions we can produce a specific critique, sometimes in the form of ideology critique, of the present historical forms of schooling, pedagogy, curriculum development, administration, research, and so on. This critique consists essentially in an immanent critique of the ways in which schools fail to be educational or even are anti-educational.

Finally, in a complex and diversified way, as well as at higher levels of organisational complexity, it is necessary to find organisational forms and practices which offer the possibility of transcending existing inadequacies and permit a vision of a concretely realisable state of affairs which represents an *improvement* on the existing state of affairs. At this level, there is no substitute for detailed concrete analyses, creative invention or appropriation of new practices, shrewd political judgements concerning what is achievable, organisational skill and political action of organisations and social movements, and solidarity among democratically inclined progressive forces. At this level, the social holism which must in some degree characterise even specialist or sectoral forms of ideology critique, must retreat into the background a little, to allow the specific context of the critically informed practitioner to be taken into account, as well as the nature of his or her opportunities.[30]

What happens when the curriculum is based on a traditional theory of knowledge? The main features of traditional theory may be summarised as a set of tendencies towards an ahistorical, value-free view of knowledge as a finished product, towards a mistaking of the contemporary surface of things for their full range of possible states and towards a view that critique is not a matter of method, but of personal and non-rational decision. These features are also present, but in a tacit and inverted way in traditional theories of the Left as well as the Right. All of these tendencies are reflected in the selection of what is to be taught and in the attitude of teachers towards this content. In turn, this finds an echo in the choice of teachers' methods.

TRADITIONAL THEORY OF EDUCATION AND RATIONAL SOCIAL DEVELOPMENT

Traditional theories of education are incapable of assisting processes of rational social development. Such theories are characterised by traditional theories of knowledge. In the traditional curriculum:

1. Knowledge is presented as a given, as either a collection of previously tested and now at least corroborated (if not proven) propositions, lacking an internal historical dimension, or as the product of a previously completed 'scientific' critique.

2. Either the possible contradictions, limitations and other *aporias* are glossed over under a general rubric of the progress of knowledge, in which the history of science is depicted as a history of transitions from tentative hypotheses to permanent additions to collections of known propositions, or the validity of critique is presented in terms of a distant utopia of classlessness which is to be achieved by the improbable means of a revolution or revolutionary change in the social order.

3. The finished product forms a system of propositions which exists prior to the student and, independently of any human agency, including the student's own – a fixed system to be acquired as such. Where this system of propositions is socially critical, the student may be expected to validate this system in his or her own experience of oppression, but the method of this validation is the crucial issue.

4. The systems of knowledge or parts of them chosen for discussion or the aspects of social life chosen for problematisation are selected by teachers largely for utilitarian reasons, as an instrument of a larger collective purpose. They are either objectified and dealt with as if they were not the expression of the historically situated, value-creating life of individuals and groups, or if this is formally recognised, are not treated with full acceptance that they are ways of being rather than attributes or possessions.[31]

In the neoconservative form of traditional theory, the needs of the existing crisis-ridden state are the basis of an instrumental view of education; in the old-left form, it is the putative needs of a state as yet uncreated – the proletarian state. The possibility of the development of surprising, as yet untheorised lines of progressive development through the thematisation of the needs of individuals and groups in the existing contradictory situation, requires, respectively, too much and too little hope for Procrustes of the Right and Left. Both willingly commit themselves to their own theory of the needs of the collectivity. In both the socialist and neoconservative versions of the two tendencies this takes the form of an orientation to the national state. Neither group is willing to commit itself to a widening of the democratic process, because both groups accept (at least tacitly) a pessimistic anthropology in which there is no room for the possibility of widespread achievement of higher learning levels.

But any strengthening of the social whole not produced *through* greater individual freedom and maturity, and thus through greater awareness of the communal good, is an historical–developmental regression. It is merely a strengthening of the hold that the mire of blind history exerts on humankind, whereas the story of emancipation has been one of attempts to free humankind from history.

The middle road passes between the horns of the individual/collectivity dilemma. At the appropriate learning level self-affirmation may be conceived of only as the affirmation of a self committed to justice towards others. The whole can be stronger and better only if the parts are also developed. Navigating this middle road requires great balance, balance between the strength, the motivating force, of neoconservatism's individualistic liberalism, since it recognises that the source of freedom is self-affirmation, and the agility, the co-ordinating awareness, of the Old Left's analysis of the collective and structural effects of individual actions.

These two forms of awareness are concretely brought together *only* in a view of validity which requires the free assent of all individuals in a *universal* discourse.

NOTES

1. J. Dewey, *Experience and Education*, New York: Collier Books, 1938, 1969: 51.
2. Habermas, in *T & P*: 37–39, clearly rejects utopianism. See also *TCA*: 73: 'A complementary error of modernity is the *utopianism* which thinks it possible to derive the "ideal of a completely rational form of life" directly from the concepts of a decentred world understanding and of procedural rationality.'

   Warnings were also given by K. Mollenhauer, *Erziehung und Emanzipation*, Frankfurt, 1969, by W. Lempert, 'Zum Begriff der Emanzipation', *Neue Sammlung*, **13**, 1973: 62–70*: 'Lately, since the beginning of the student movement, we in Germany have frequently spoken of "emancipation", especially among teachers. In the meantime the word has become fashionable . . . and its inflationary broadening has given its opponents cause to diffame (it)' and, of course, Habermas' own writing on the issues of school reform and the democratisation of the university discussed in Chapter 3 should also have acted as a warning.
3. See R. Spaemann, 'Emanzipation: ein Bildungziel?', *Merkur*, **29** (320), 1975: 357–78, and D. Rustemeyer, 'Wirkliche Schatten der Vernunft: Grundprobleme "kritische Theorie" als ungewolltes Erbe kritische Erziehungswissenschaft', 97–118 in F. Baumgart *et al.* (eds) *Emendio Rerum Humanarum: Erziehung für eine demokratische Gesellschaft: Festschrift für Klaus Schaller*, Frankfurt: 1985. But cf. K. Schaller, 'Kritische Erziehungswissenschaft am Ausgang ihrer Epoche?', *Bildung und Erziehung*, **38** (3), 1985: 357–78, and J. Ruhloff, 'Ist Pädagogik heute ohne "kritische Theorie" möglich?', *Zeitschrift für Pädagogik*, **30** (2), 1983: 219–332.
4. H. H. Groothof, 'Zur Bedeutung der Diskursethik von Jürgen Habermas für die Pädagogik', *Pädagogische Rundschau*, **39** (3), 1985: 275–98, also A. Wellmer, 'Terrorism and the critique of society', 283–308 in J. Habermas (ed.) *OSSA*.
5. On the influence of the *Geisteswissenschaften* see the historical treatment by Schaller in the opening sections of K. H. Schäfer and K. Schaller, *Kritische Erziehungswissenschaft und kommunikative Didaktik*, Heidelberg: Quelle und Meyer, 1976, and H. Gassen, *Geisteswissenschafliche Pädagogik auf der Wege zu kritischer Theorie*, Weinheim/Basel, 1978, also D. Hoffmann, *Kritische Erziehungswissenschaft*, Frankfurt: Kohlhammer, 1978.
6. R. Spaemann, *op. cit.*
7. J. Habermas, 'Communicative versus subject-centred reason', 294–326 in *PDM*: 299, A. Brand, 'The colonisation of the lifeworld and the disappearance of politics: Arendt

and Habermas', *Thesis Eleven*, **13**, 1986: 39–53. See also K. Schaller, *op. cit.* and M. Brumlik, 'Verstehen oder kolonisieren: Uberlegung zu einem aktuellen Thema', 31–62 in S. Müller and H. U. Otto (eds) *Verstehen oder Kolonisieren?* Bonn: Deutschen Gesellschaft für Erziehungswissenschaft, 1985.

8. *PDM*: 300.
9. For an early statement of the damage that can be done by overenthusiastic educational reformers see H. Giesecke, *Ist die bürgerliche Erziehung am Ende?*, München: 1977, 165.
10. On the danger of nihilism see C. Bowers, 'The dialectic of nihilism and the state: Implications for an emancipatory theory of education', *Educational Theory*, **36** (3), 1986, 225–32.
11. I. Shor, *Critical Teaching and Everyday Life*, Boston: South End Press, 1980: 220–33.
12. M. Horkheimer, 'On traditional and critical theory', 206–24 in P. Connerton (ed.) *Critidcal Sociology*, Harmondsworth: Penguin, 1976.
13. T. Adorno, 'Sociology and empirical research', in P. Connerton (ed.) *Critical Sociology*, Harmondsworth: Penguin, 1976, 244.
14. *T & P*: 37–9: 'The theoretical interpretation in terms of which the subjects come to know themselves and their situation are retrospective: they bring to consciousness an educative process [my translation of *Bildungsprozess*]. Thus the theory that creates consciousness can bring about the conditions under which systematic distortions of communication are dissolved and a practical discourse can then be conducted; but it does not contain any information which prejudges the future action of those concerned.'
15. P. Friere, *Pedogogy of the Oppressed*, Harmondsworth: Penguin, 1972. See also Bühner/Birnmeyer's discussion of Friere's approach as a practical illumination for critical pedagogy, *Ideologie und Diskurs: Zur Theorie von Jürgen Habermas und ihre Rezeption in der Pädagogik*, Frankfurt: Haag und Herchen, 1982, 247–53.
16. *T & P*: 19.
17. *C & ES*: 2 and Chapter 1 *et passim*.
18. *TCA*: 282–95 on types of action. On 'communicative action', see J. Habermas, 'Remarks on the concept of communicative action', 151–78 in G. Seebass and R. Tuomela (eds) *Social Action*, Dordrecht and Boston: Reidel, 1985.
19. See the discussion by T. McCarthy, *The Critical Theory of Jürgen Habermas*, London: Hutchison, 1978, 305–10, which makes Habermas' position quite clear.
20. Most recently V. Robinson, 'The nature and conduct of a critical dialogue', paper presented to the Joint Australian Association for Research in Education and New Zealand Association for Research in Education Conference, Christchurch, New Zealand, 1987.
21. D. Ingram, *Habermas and the Dialectic of Reason*, London: Yale University Press, 1987, 174–5, 238 ff, and Habermas, *K & HI*: 315.
22. *T & P*: 257 also *TCA*: 73: 'Winch is right to insist that forms of life represent concrete "language games", historical configurations of customary practices . . . cultural patterns of interpretation . . . attitudes and so forth. It would be senseless to want to judge such a conglomeration as a whole, *the totality of a form of life*, under individual aspects of rationality. If we do not want altogether to relinquish standards by which a form of life might be judged to be more or less failed, deformed . . . we can look if need be to the model of sickness and health. We tacitly judge life forms and life histories according to standards of normality that do not permit approximation to ideal limit values. Perhaps we should talk instead of a balance among non self-sufficient moments, an equilibrated interplay of the cognitive with the moral and the aesthetic-practical.'
23. See C. Offe, *Industry and Inequality*, London: Edward Arnold, 1979, and J. W. Murphy, 'Critical theory and social organisation', *Diogenes*, **117**, 1982: 93–111, but cf.

R. Jehenson, 'Effectiveness, expertise and excellence as ideological fictions, etc.', *Human Studies*, **7**, 1984: 3–21.

24. *TCA*: 73, 50 ff, 412; *RTC*: 255, 263.
25. See Note 29 in Chapter 2.
26. Apart from the discussion in J. Thompson and D. Held (eds) *Habermas: Critical Debates*, London: Macmillan, 1982, see F. Dallmayr, 'Critical theory criticised: Habermas' *Knowledge and Human Interests* and its aftermath', *Philosophy of Social Science*, **2**, 1972: 211–29, N. Lobkowicz, 'Interest and objectivity', *Philosophy of Social Science*, **2**, 1972: 193–210, and other articles in that issue.
27. M. Hesse, 'Science and objectivity', 98–115 in J. Thompson and D. Held (eds) *op. cit.*, 1982: 111, but see Chapter 2, Note 14.
28. H. Ottmann, 'Cognitive interests and self-reflection', 79–97 in J. Thompson and D. Held (eds) *op. cit.*
29. Habermas on Foucault in *PDN et passim*.
30. See *T & P*: 33 and quotation in Note 51 to Chapter 3.
31. See W. Keckeisen, '*Kritische Erziehungswissenschaft*', in D. Lenzen and K. Mollenhauer (eds) *Enzyklopädie Erziehung*, Vol.1, Stuttgart: Kohlhammer, 1983: 125.

CHAPTER 5

TRADITIONAL TEACHING AND LEARNING

The main purpose or objective [of traditional education] is to prepare the young for future responsibilities and for success in life, by means of acquisition of the organised bodies of information and prepared forms of skill which comprehend the material of instruction. Since the subject matter as well as the standards of proper conduct are handed down from the past, the attitude of pupils must, on the whole, be one of docility, receptivity and obedience.

(John Dewey)[1]

When education becomes an instrument of a collective purpose without at the same time being an expression of individual interest it loses its capacity for rationality, since rational social participation must rest on the communicative autonomy of the participants rather than upon some pre-decided and believed-to-be incontrovertible foundational knowledge. Yet the classical conception of the education of children has always embodied a model which is both instrumental and communicative.[2] The educational intention is not oriented towards the educator's own interests but towards the interests of the child – to influence the child for the child's own good. Oelkers argues that this is a risky and uncertain process which must proceed by means of influence rather than genuinely complete communication, but which has the state of communicative equality as its ultimate goal. When fully reciprocal communication is achieved it is no longer appropriate to speak of teaching but only of mutual learning.[3] Oelkers argues that Habermas has no appropriate concept to deal with this form of pedagogical action in which the teacher selflessly 'not serving his own, egoistic interests, but pursuing goals which are of no personal advantage, is simply of help to others in their (own) processes of educational formation' (Oelkers, 1983: 277*).

However, Oelkers does not make it clear whether the transition from teaching [influencing] to [mutual] understanding of which he speaks is meant to occur over the whole of the years of schooling, or from moment to moment in a lesson or series of lessons. Indeed, his connecting of this issue with processes of socialisation seems to indicate the former. The latter, the notion of a strategic moment in an interaction which culminates in understanding, has already been discussed by Habermas, and, as will become clear in subsequent discussion, presents no problem for a critical educational intuition. If, however, Oelkers means the former, a long-term process of transition to the achievement of the good of the other, a number of problems arise for Oelkers, at least, in so far as he subscribes, as he seems to do, to *Mündigkeit* as the goal of education.

The problem with the classical conception of teaching is that it is difficult to see how the intention of the good of the other can be safeguarded. If the goal of education is a capacity for mature self-representation (*Mündigkeit*), there may be a contradiction between the goal and the means. How can the teacher who manipulates the child, that is, who deals with the child as capable of less than full communicative understanding, guarantee that this manipulation is in the service of the autonomy necessary to genuinely reciprocal communication and not the installation of the teacher's views or the views considered acceptable in society at large. At this point, the problems raised by Oelker's critique intersect with English language discussions of the problem of autonomy in education, and, in particular with the dichotomy between the exercising of autonomy and the educational conditions considered necessary for its development. This dichotomy is characteristic of the work of Peters.[4] The intention of seeking the good of the other rather than one's own good may be a necessary part of the 'educational attitude' but it may not be a sufficient condition for its success. Without some further consideration of how this intention may be realised – of pedagogical method – it may remain uncritical. Without further safeguards, the classical or traditional conception of the educational intention of the teacher may be allied to an uncritical, traditional pedagogy and, at the same time, function as a justification of it.

Here, in a nutshell, is the educational dilemma. The teacher, on behalf of society, indeed, the state, attempts to teach a pre-decided curriculum which, it has been determined, is in the child's interest. One set of educational goals concerns the acquisition of knowledge regarded as socially useful and necessary to the child's eventual full participation in adult society, the political process, the economy, etc. Another goal of education is the formation of democratic citizens, capable of autonomous political judgement in the exercise of their democratic franchise. Still another goal, considered to be subsumed in both of the foregoing, is the goal of truth. It is considered that the child will acquire knowledge that is true (because if not true, not useful) and will acquire the skill to discern the truth (necessary for citizens in a democracy to play their role).

At this point it becomes clear that the common ground in all approaches to education, whatever their other emphases, is the assumption that what is to be taught should be true. In addition, some assumption of rational autonomy in adulthood as an educational goal is common to both neoconservative and democratic socialist views of education. At least in the long run, across the whole educational process, there is a rejection of processes which do not seek to achieve this. Such processes are called 'indoctrinational'.

INDOCTRINATION: THE CLASSICAL DOCTRINE

There is widespread agreement that indoctrination involves students' coming to believe a proposition or viewpoint otherwise than on the basis of their understanding of the grounds for warranting its belief and their uncoerced assent to these. A slightly weaker version of this view involves the concession that it is not necessary actually to examine the grounds for *every* belief providing beliefs are held in such a way that they are open to such assessment.[5] However, disagreement begins when it comes to the question of whether this openness is required of all teaching and learning or, in the case of schooling, only of its culmination. There is a corresponding diversity of views when it comes to the specification of those aspects of teaching and learning which are indoctrinational.

Accounts differ in respect of the criteria which would permit an unequivocal identification of instances of indoctrination. Attempts to define these in terms of the teacher's intentions, teaching methods or the selection of content have all met with exceptions. Nor is the attempt to displace the problem to the level of outcomes any more successful. The problem of defining outcomes in which beliefs come to be held in 'a manner open to rational assessment' remains. Is openness to assessment to be defined in terms of an intention to assess beliefs, or a method of assessing them, or in terms of choosing those beliefs whose content renders them susceptible to questioning, etc.?

At a time when many philosophers have adopted a fallibilist and socially influenced understanding of the process of the growth of scientific knowledge, it may be appropriate to recast the indoctrination debate in similar terms. After all, the key issue is that students should acquire true ideas and a capacity to enquire critically into new ideas they will meet in later life, rather than false ideas held unquestioningly, and an unquestioning attitude to new ideas.

In this less absolutist view of knowledge, the search for a completely secure foundation has been abandoned in favour of a recognition that all theories are the product of communities of historically located theorists. As Lakatos argued, there is no 'instant rationality'. It may be more appropriate to suggest that judgements about such theories may be judgements about whether a particular theory (or series of modifications around a core of central ideas in a theory) is progressing or degenerating.[6] It may be appropriate, then, to revisit intentions, teaching methods and the like, not with a view to constructing watertight definitions, but with a view to identifying processes that are more or less likely to lead to an attitude of inquiry and a recognition of human fallibility, while at the same time, avoiding an empty relativism.

But can teachers teach in such a way that 'knowledge' can be acquired, built on and used by growing children and still remain open to reassessment (or to rational assessment for the first time when children attain maturity)? We will examine doubts about this in the next chapter, but what is clear, though, is that research on the prevailing pattern of teaching in schools permits us to conclude that there is very little evidence of learner autonomy along the road to maturity. The most common patterns of teaching revealed by research may properly be called traditional teaching, for reasons of their documented persistence over a long period of time, as well as their associated theory of knowledge.

TRADITIONAL CLASSROOM COMMUNICATION

Classroom communication research over more than 80 years has identified a dominant pattern or group of patterns of communication with which educators are now quite familiar. The following discussion is confined to just one structural component of teacher/pupil communication: the question/answer cycle. Across a number of samples of classroom talk this component appears to constitute around 60 per cent of total 'official talk'. It has been named the 'teaching exchange' because, apart from teacher monologue, which typically constitutes only 10 per cent or so of talk, it is the component in which more than three-quarters of active teaching occurs.

Of course, reading textbooks, carrying out exercises and writing to order are also communicative activities that take up a lot of classroom time, but in most cases the structure of these activities is analogous to the question/answer cycle. The textbook or teacher sets the 'question' or exercise, the student carries it out, and the textbook or teacher provides the criteria of evaluation and models the correct forms for the answer.

Although, obviously enough, many researchers who have described the nature of the question/answer cycle have not done so with the subject of indoctrination explicitly in mind, it is interesting to note that their descriptions of this component of classroom talk have been remarkably stable over the years. The picture they have drawn for us is more consistent with indoctrination than with education. As early as 1912 the first verbatim transcript of official classroom talk was collected. It was found that a pattern of rapid question/answer exchanges characterised most classrooms observed, as had been anecdotally reported by earlier observers. This pattern was criticised because teachers asked nearly all the questions (90 per cent) and the type of questions stressed verbal memory and 'superficial judgement' rather than the development of 'self-reliant and independent' thinking. Later behavioural research confirmed these observations many times. Typically 80 per cent or more of classroom questions are shallow. Even when a question is worded in an apparently open way, the teacher's reaction to the student's answer often indicates that a genuinely thoughtful reply is not being sought.[7]

THE STRUCTURE OF THE QUESTION/ANSWER CYCLE

The question/answer cycle has been analysed as a structure of three parts, initiate/respond/feedback, following the non-linguistic category system of behavioural theory. This analysis is unsatisfactory for three reasons. First, it does not divide the structure into functionally differentiated units. A categorisation based on a theory of human linguistic communication, such as that which can be derived from functional linguistics,[8] does this, as does conversational analysis.[9]

For instance, the term 'feedback' is inappropriate because a functional analysis shows that feedback and its associated concept of reinforcement is appropriate to only a minority of teacher 'reactions' (to employ another, more neutral label for the same structural component).[10] Second, a number of functionally differentiated and distinctively different communicative moves can be identified within each of the three components of the behavioural analysis.[11] Third, the structural relations between the three behavioural components are not simply a chain of relations, $1 - 2 - 3$, but, as Streeck[12] has shown, are an imbedded set of relations with the first adjacency pair $1 - 2$ becoming the first component in a new adjacency pair:

$$(\text{Note: } 1-2 = A)$$
$$1 - 2$$
$$|$$
$$A - B$$

That is to say, the conditional relationship set up between question and answer becomes the basis for the relationship set up between the question/answer accomplishment as a whole and the teacher's reaction.

In simpler language, the teacher's reaction is conditional on the relationship between the student's answer and the original question. The crucial issue centres on the nature of the conditions involved.

Let us focus for a moment on this latter pairing and on the conditions governing the teacher's reaction. This reaction itself may be deemed to have a micro-structure, e.g.:

Evaluation:	Ownership marker:	**Formulation**:	Confirmation invitation
'**Good,**	You're saying	**the Nile has a delta**	aren't you?'

Evaluations, either explicit or implicit appear near universal.[13] Formulations are perhaps less frequent, but are still extremely common, the other moves illustrated and certain moves which sometimes appear in the formulating slot are relatively or very rare.[14].

Formulating practices are those practices in which speech becomes reflexive and constitutes itself as speech of a certain kind by announcing, for instance, 'what is being said'. If a speaker is talking about something he or she saw, another speaker may need to formulate aspects of what is being talked about, e.g. where the events happened, by saying something like 'that was the southern entrance'. In other words, formulations are glossing practices which gloss what the talk is about. Heritage provides an example:

A: Isn't it nice that there is such a crowd of you in the office.
B: You're asking us to leave, not telling us to leave, right? (formulation of gist)[15]

There are many kinds of formulating but the kind that occurs most often in classrooms is that which glosses the knowledge content of student answers considered relevant by the teacher, the 'school knowledge' or 'lesson knowledge' content of the students' talk (answers to teacher questions constitute about 80 per cent of official student talk).

In classrooms the teacher formulates the lesson as outcome by means of monologue and by formulating student answers (and/or by rejecting them in whole or part). The contribution of individual students is formulated as lesson-relevant knowledge, in an appropriate terminology, and as intersubjective or common knowledge, as *our* knowledge or 'what everyone knows'.[16]

(Year 6: science lesson)
T: So what happens to the air?
P1: It gets warm.
T: Yes, it gets warm and what happens to it then?
P2: It rises.
T: So what happens?
All: Hot air rises!
T: Right. So our conclusion is that hot air rises.

The crucial point here is not simply that an official version of lesson knowledge replaces student talk but that this version is not formulated as authoritative telling but as a mutual product of shared reasons or grounds.

However, unlike epistemic formulations in everyday talk, there is usually no opportunity in classrooms for students to confirm or disconfirm the formulations of their talk made by teachers. In other contexts such as news interviews this is not so.[17] In more than 70 transcripts and lesson tapes available to the author, and in the literature, such opportunities are rare.

Two moves which are often present in talk where disconfirmation is likely are ownership markers and confirmation invitations: 'so you are saying . . . is that right?' But ownership of the total structure of the Q/A cycle in classrooms is vested in the teacher:

> The teacher provides a framework into which pupil talk is fitted, and that talk is assessed according to the closeness of fit. Brief pupil contributions are taken as being representative of the group and the interaction proceeds *as though* the other pupils knew already, or shared the same and now corrected inadequacies of those who spoke. In its orderliness, and in the shaping of meanings, the interaction can be seen as the managed product of one of the participants.[18]

One of the differences between the present analysis and that of Edwards and Furlong is that it isolates the specific talk practices by which this is accomplished and places a greater stress on the significance of the apparent mutuality of the accomplishment. Classroom talk is often managed as if it were a dialogue. At one level it is, but at the next highest structural level implicit constraints operate to constitute it as perlocutionary (i.e. strategic) rather than illocutionary (i.e. communicative) action. While the discourse takes on a cumulative content which reflects the strategic intention of one of the participants, the teacher, it proceeds by a process of active student (illocutionary) co-operation[19] in which the 'accumulation of a common, available corpus of information' (Streeck, 1979: 249 my translation) appears as an accumulation of the *students'* statements about the world as much as, and sometimes more than the teachers'.

In terms of language act theory, the illocutionary force of the students' statements about the world is weakened and subordinated to the teachers' discourse. In his analysis of the evaluative component of these reactions, Streeck has shown that the teachers' evaluations, no less than the formulating practices just discussed, weaken the students' capacity to control the cognitive agenda of the lesson:

> The evaluation thereby takes over a part of the illocutionary force of the constative. An answer alone is only a tentative statement, until, working

backwards, the ratification transforms it into an intersubjectively recognised statement. (Streeck, 1979: 250*)

In other words, the individual illocutionary claims inherent in the teacher's question and the student's answer are subordinated to the constraints of a perlocutionary structure which is created through tacit rules for speaking which specify that student answers should be 'what the teacher wants' and that teacher questions should be read as in some sense closed questions no matter how open in form. Thus the Q/A cycle can be seen as a specifically pedagogical form of strategic action.

In turn, each cycle in the teaching exchange is linked to its successor in chains of Q/As which, with teacher monologue, make up the greater part of 'on task talk' in classrooms. The mechanisms of linkage are the 'rule' that the teacher will be every other speaker and the specific strategic goal expressed in the cognitive progression of teacher questions – the usually tacit something that the teacher's series of questions is 'driving at'.[20]

RECONTEXTUALISATION AND COLONISATION

Perhaps a useful way to think of one of the major functions usually served by the third component in the Q/A cycle, the teacher's 'reaction', is to see it as a recontextualisation device, at least as far as the work done by the evaluation–formulation sections of it is concerned. The child's answer is typically treated as inadequate in some way, since it is altered, corrected or undergoes changes of emphasis more often than not.[21] But the inadequacies in it are often partial. It is not often a case of rejecting it out of hand, but of changing vocabulary from lay to technical, or from personal to textbook, of paraphrasing and shifting emphasis, so that the child's response, cast in terms of the marginal connections the child is beginning to make between the new knowledge and some part of its existing schema or frame of reference, which is based on its own experience, is recontextualised into the teacher/textbook's existing 'complete' or 'correct' frame of reference. That is, it is *formulated* as a statement in that new context. For example, in a discussion of the virtues of rational discussion to solve problems, a point of view not dissimilar to that being advocated by the present author, a teacher constantly censors out students' references to conflict:

(Year 9: English)
P: (Critically) The unions are always fighting!
T: Right (Evaluation) So you're going to have lots of discussions, aren't you?
P: Yes.
T: . . . with people having lots of ideas.

and

P: That's an argument when you're fighting back.
T: No, it doesn't have to be an argument. A discussion can be just where you *talk* about things.

and

T: What do you do in a discussion?
P: Sometimes you've got to be careful what you *say* (pause) about people.
T: All right. You've got to think about what you're going to say.

The implicit criticism of the child's frame of reference in this process, precisely because it is implicit, places a premium on the child's capacity to read the special contextual demands 'between the lines'. As has been argued elsewhere, the capacity to deal with decontextualised specialised knowledge in the classroom and to be aware of the contextual requirements of communication aimed at recontextualising it, is a capacity which varies systematically with socio-economic class.[22] However, in the above example it is the child's personal knowledge that is being recontextualised. The ideological function of recontextualisation has been examined recently by Bernstein.[23] When the present considerations are taken together with Bernstein's analysis, it is clear that the structure of the cycle may well be more deeply involved in both the colonisation of the life–world and in the reproduction of ideology than first meets the eye. The typical structure of teacher reactions is not merely evidence of a perlocutionary instructional intent which prevents the lesson proceeding by way of rational assent by pupils, but it is an active form of colonisation, since it seeks to replace the frameworks of learners with other frameworks, while mimicking the surface forms of genuine dialogue.

TEACHERS' THINKING

Not surprisingly, the pattern of classroom communication is often mirrored in teachers' beliefs about knowledge. Teachers typically view knowledge in terms of individual thinkers weighing the evidence for or against the truth of propositions or statements rather than in terms of communities of enquiry, research traditions, cultures or other social influences. In the first study of teacher epistemologies which explored these questions, about 85 per cent of secondary teachers from two separate samples possessed a monological view of knowledge rather than a social or dialogical one.[24] Within this monological approach, teachers are divided between logical–empirical and hermeneutic views of knowledge, both views being characterised by a degree of objectivism, with little awareness of questions of reflectivity and problems of the social independence or dependence of knowledge formation. Some teachers had reached the level of awareness at which the genuinely personal character of knowledge was recognised, à la Polanyi, but few of these recognised that the social imbeddedness of the person might lead to *collectively shared* personal knowledge. A traditional view of knowledge presents it as something which can be codified into a restricted set of statements and communicated. It is believed that, while the empirical or hermeneutic experience which warrants the truth of propositions cannot be communicated, it can be communicated *about* or, in some cases, replicated. The assumption of the interchangeability of experience between all individuals supports the view that the textbook's account of the evidence is almost as good as the individual's experience. Knowledge is a standard commodity which you can come to possess, it can be bought and sold, and it is possible to assess and certify possession of it.

Teaching as we have traditionally found it displays a traditional theory of knowledge and a traditional pedagogy. Both research on classroom communication and research on teacher beliefs reveals a set of intersecting factors which lock teaching into an indoctrinatory style. Can we still hope that learners will reach a stage at the end of this formal education or afterwards where they will suddenly be able to respond autonomously to what they have been taught?

TRADITIONAL PEDAGOGY

The tug of war between autonomous learning, which is commensurate with the end or goal of education for both liberal and critical educators, and the need of society to ensure that certain things are taught, which leads to non-autonomous learning, has usually been resolved in favour of the goals of the collectivity.

Traditional pedagogy resolves the dilemma in favour of teaching a pre-decided curriculum in a manner which does not stress students' own validity-judgements but rather proceeds by constant evaluation and correction against imposed models of valid responses. Whether this curriculum is the curriculum of the establishment or a subversive curriculum, its pedagogical structure is the same. It displays teaching methods which:

1. Tend either towards what Freire has called a 'banking' concept of learning, in which a knowledge store is built up like a bank account, by many small deposits or to a demolition concept of learning where the destruction of tradition is the goal.[25]
2. Demand from teachers an active role of either knowledge 'transmission' or pre-decided critique of existing institutions which tends reciprocally to define the learner role as passive knowledge reception.

3.   Do not pay a great deal of attention to the relationship between the life–world of the learner and the knowledge and attitudes selected for the curriculum.
4.   Base the organisation of curricular knowledge on either the existing disciplines as repositories or stores of knowledge or on a pre-decided 'critical' agenda rather than upon the relationship between these and the problem context of the students.
5.   Employ assessment as a process of verifying the level of acquisition of the pre-decided system of knowledge and attitudes or, perhaps, reject assessment, appraisal and evaluation altogether.
6.   Allow no real space for critique, because this has been already carried out by the knowledge producing community of experts or the intellectual vanguard of the revolution, who are quite separate from the learning community. In the first view, the learners will only be able to contribute to critique when they have mastered (i.e. recapitulated the historical development of) the knowledge storehouse. In the other, they can only parrot critique rather than make it.
7.   Either conceive of the world from the standpoint of a dominant culture or dogmatically reject the possibility of evaluative comparison of cultures altogether, that is, they embrace either cultural imperialism or relativism.

What traditional views of education fail to realise is that there is a big difference between setting out to teach a pre-decided curriculum and succeeding, in the sense that students not only come to know what the teacher is trying to teach but also to accept it. There remains the question of truth, especially at the level of the student's own experience. When students are told there is no shortage of meat in their country, yet they cannot buy meat, or when they are told there is one law for both rich and poor and they see how useful (and expensive) a top lawyer may be, they may be excused for a certain cynicism.

The question of truth, then, may enter the discussion of who decides on what is taught, regardless of collective objectives. The mere fact of society's choosing a certain curriculum does not make it an efficient curriculum or an accepted one. Traditional theories of education in their pursuit of politically acceptable or economically valuable knowledge fail to recognise the irrepressible and perennial presence of individual interests, including an interest in emancipation from dogma. The fact that traditional pedagogy is a source of destruction and colonisation of the life–world may not excuse a utopian critical pedagogy when it fosters the same process, but it does suggest that the choice of a traditional pedagogy is not the recipe for immunity from change conservative educators take it to be.

NOTES

1. J. Dewey, *Experience and Education*, New York: Collier Books, 1938, 1966: 18.
2. J. Oelkers, 'Pädagogische Anmerkungen zu Habermas' Theorie kommunikativen Handelns', *Zeitschrift für Pädagogik*, **30** (2), 1983: 271–80.
3. J. Oelkers, *op. cit.*: 277.
4. R. Peters, 'Reason and habit: The paradox of moral education', W. Niblett (ed.) *Moral Education in a Changing Society*, London: Faber & Faber, 1963, 271, R. G. Oliver, 'Through the doors of reason: Dissolving four paradoxes of education', *Educational Theory*, **35** (1), 1985: 15–32.
5. J. Kleinig, *Philosophical Issues in Education*, London: Croom Helm, 1982.
6. I. Lakatos, 'Falsification and the methodology of scientific research programmes', in I. Lakatos and A. Musgrave (eds) *Criticism and the Growth of Knowledge*, Cambridge: Cambridge University Press, 1971. Of course, this was only the beginning of a long argument.
7. R. E. Young, K. Watson and R. Arnold, 'Linguistic models of teaching and learning' in *International Encyclopedia of Education*, London: Pergamon Press, 1985. Much of this chapter is taken from R. E. Young, 'Critical theory and classroom questioning', *Language and Education*, **1** (2), 1987: 125–34.
8. J. Sinclair and M. Coulthard, *Towards an Analysis of Discourse: The English used by Teachers and Pupils*, Oxford: Oxford University Press, 1975.
9. R. E. Young, 'Teaching equals indoctrination: The dominant epistemic practices of our schools', *British Journal of Educational Studies*, **22** (3), 1984: 220–38.
10. J. Streeck, 'Zur Pragmatischen und Konversationellen Analyse von Bewertungen im Institutionellen Diskurs der Schule', in J. Dittmann (ed.) *Arbeiten zur Konversationanalyse*, Tübingen: Max Niemeyer, 1979.
11. J. Sinclair and M. Coulthard, *op. cit.*, P. Griffin and F. Humphrey, *Talk and Task at Lesson Time*, New York: Carnegie Corporation, 1980.
12. J. Streeck, *op. cit.*: 244.
13. P. Griffin and F. Humphrey, *op. cit.*
14. K. Watson and R. E. Young, 'Teacher reformulations of student discourse', *Australian Review of Applied Linguistics*, **3** (2) 1980: 37–47.
15. J. Heritage, 'Formulating the news', paper delivered to the International Institute of Ethnomethodology and Conversational Analysis, Boston University, 1977.
16. D. Barnes, J. Britton and H. Rosen, *Language, the Learner and the School*, Harmondsworth: Penguin, 1969.
17. J. Heritage, *op. cit.*
18. A. Edwards and V. Furlong, *The Language of Teaching*, London: Heinemann, 1978.
19. P. Griffin and F. Humphrey, *op. cit.*, R. E. Young, 1984.
20. A. McHoul, 'The organisation of turns at formal talk in the classroom', *Language in Society*, **7**, 1978: 183–213.
21. K. Watson and R. E. Young, 'Discourse for learning in the classroom', *Language Arts*, **63** (2), 1986: 126–33.
22. R. E. Young, 'A school-communication deficit hypothesis of educational disadvantage', *Australian Journal of Education*, **27** (1), 1983: 3–16.
23. B. Bernstein, 'On pedagogic discourse' in J. Richardson (ed.) *Handbook on Research in the Sociology of Education*, London: Greenwood Press, 1985.
24. R. E. Young, 'Teachers' epistemologies', 5048–51 in *International Encyclopedia of Education*, London: Pergamon Press, 1985.
25. P. Freire, *Pedagogy of the Oppressed*, Harmondsworth: Penguin, 1972. See also list of characteristics in W. Keckeisen 'Kritische Erziehungswissenschaften', in D. Lenzen and K. Mollenhauer (eds) *Enzyklopädie Erziehung*, **1**, Stuttgart: Kohlhammer, 1983: 125.

CHAPTER 6

CRITICAL TEACHING AND LEARNING

> Insofar as the teacher is teaching, he is, in any event, risking his own particular truth judgements, for he is exposing them to the . . . general critique . . . and to the free critical judgement of the student's mind.
>
> (Israel Scheffler)[1]

We have already seen the outline of an ideology critique of the current structure of classroom communication. In this chapter I wish to present a rational reconstruction of the ideal pedagogical speech situation. The reader should be warned that there is no easy way to represent Habermas' quite philosophically technical argument here. This is followed by a developmental reconstruction of the teaching/learning relationship, which provides a moral agenda for curriculum. In conclusion, this chapter recognises the need for a movement for critical reform, focused on an enabling administrative structure for schooling. Only a movement of this kind can provide the impetus for the organisation of enlightenment necessary to the resolution of the modern educational crisis.

THE IDEAL PEDAGOGICAL SPEECH SITUATION

The theory of communicative action

Habermas' theory of language action is really a theory of communication as action. Setting out from Frege's theory of meaning, he develops it in a pragmatic direction. This means that instead of looking at the meaning of sentences in isolation from their social context, they are looked at in the situations in which they are used. The context in which many sentences are examined in philosophy is oversimplified when compared to daily life, where many things are going on simultaneously. Sentences which might have 'originally' been uttered to achieve some result are taken into the philosopher's 'laboratory' and dissected. The philosopher starts, as it were, with the naked sentence, a string of mere words, and notionally adds back the context. The sentence 'Joe won't be coming tonight', can be shown to have a kind of dictionary meaning 'There is a "Joe" such that at a future time, viz. tonight, Joe will not be arriving', or some such. Then the philosopher can hypothesise that prior to the utterance of this sentence it was expected that Joe *would* be coming and so on. Gradually, a set of multiple layers of meaning of the *utterance* builds up. Utterance meaning is multilayered. A theory of *real* sentences, that is sentences uttered by people in the midst of life, must be extended to include much that previous theories of meaning tended to leave out. They must be extended laterally, to include meanings other than those which relate to the truth of propositions, and vertically, to include the speaker and hearer's reactions to the validity claims of speech in and during the process of understanding. Habermas does this and then (following Austin and Searle) uses the result to distinguish between general types of action or interaction on the basis of the dominant intention of speakers and hearers.

But Habermas sets out by rejecting those semantic theories which begin from an analysis of speakers' subjective intentions. He argues that 'only those analytic theories of meaning are instructive that start from the structure of linguistic expressions' (*TCA*: 275). Sentences and the signs that make them up are not isolated elements but take their meaning, in some sense, from a publicly available and shared language system. At least at one level, meaning is 'objectively' linguistic. But he then goes on to look at the way intentions structure whole exchanges, and the way in which context makes meaning. Let us start with a look at single language acts.

Following the line of development in truth-conditional semantics from Frege, through the later Wittgenstein to Dummett, Habermas takes up the argument that 'speakers and hearers understand the meaning of a sentence when they know under what conditions it is true' (*TCA*: 276). He takes this idea and broadens it. He wants a richer notion of the things surrounding the words; the world must be brought into the philosopher's laboratory. The kind of world that Frege and others admitted was too narrow. There needed to be more in it than the things provided by the 'narrow ontological presuppositions of truth-conditional semantics' (*TCA*: 277). Habermas draws upon his definition of rationality and his earlier identification of three kinds of rational validity and three kinds of valid argumentation to extend these presuppositions to include normative and expressive 'truth':

> Well-grounded assertions and efficient actions are certainly signs of rationality; we do characterise as rational speaking and acting subjects

(those) who, as far as it lies within their power, avoid errors in regard to facts and means–ends relations. But there are obviously *other* types of expressions for which we can have good reasons, even though they are not tied to truth or success claims. In contexts of communicative action, we call someone rational not only if he is able to put forward an assertion and, when criticised, to provide grounds for it by pointing to appropriate evidence, but also if he is following an established norm and is able, when criticised, to justify his action by explicating the given situation in the light of expectations. We even call someone rational if he makes known a desire or an intention, expresses a feeling or a mood, shares a secret, confesses a deed, etc., and is then able to reassure critics in regard to the revealed experience by drawing practical consequences from it and behaving consistently thereafter. (*TCA*: 5)

Next, he rejects the monological view of rationality and meaning which has dominated semantic theory since Descartes (*cogito ergo sum*) and beyond. This rejection is consistent with earlier critical theorists' rejection of 'subjective reason' – the theory of reason (and meaning) that starts out from the armchair of a single, knowing subject, and seeks to establish 'what I can know'. In a dialogical view, meaning must be understood as something created between people, 'the literal meaning of a sentence cannot be explained at all independently of the standard conditions of its employment' (*TCA*: 297). The philosophical abstraction of utterances from context, while it may have analytical uses, can cause a distortion if the whole of a theory of meaning is based on it. Human languages mean in context. Thus, language utterances may faithfully be seen as language acts or action. He turns to Austin's language act theory to illuminate the consequences of this.

Austin's distinction between locutionary, illocutionary and perlocutionary functions of speech acts is taken up. 'Locutionary' refers to the propositional content of speech acts, roughly, what is said; 'illocutionary' to the action performed in saying what is said, again, roughly speaking, this refers to the immediate addressee of the speech act and focuses on the saying of what is said, i.e. telling someone something; and 'perlocutionary' refers to the effect on the hearer that the speaker seeks to bring about, roughly, that through coming to understand what has been said the addressee should perhaps do something else. But, in accordance with his earlier argument, Habermas develops this analysis broadening it from constative (statement-making) speech acts, whose surface form accentuates propositional content, telling and coming to know, to interpersonal speech acts which concern the normative regulation of conduct, and expressive speech acts, which concern the communication of the internal attitudes or states of feeling of speakers. However, following Searle, he asserts that all three functions are present, at least latently, in all utterances, even though normally one will dominate the surface form. For instance, the warning 'Look out!' does not actually make a statement, but it implies, when spoken in some contexts, that 'there is something to look out for'.

Habermas distinguishes sharply between action oriented to reaching understanding and strategic action – often goal-directed action, oriented to bringing about some state of affairs a speaker may desire other than the state of *reaching an understanding itself*. Habermas means rather more than is usually understood by the phrase 'reaching an understanding'. As we will see below, it includes something rather more like 'reaching an agreement'.

Perlocutions differ from illocutions in two ways. First, some perlocutions may involve self-concealment or, at least, non-revelation. Such perlocutions as 'giving a fright to', 'plunge into doubt', 'annoy', 'mislead', 'humiliate' or 'offend' or even 'win over', 'cause to agree' or 'allay fears of', may all involve speech acts which try to bring about a result not obvious to the hearer. This is related to the second property of these particular acts. As Habermas says:

> Perlocutionary acts are an indication of the integration of speech acts into contexts of strategic action. They belong to the intended consequence or results of a teleological action which an actor undertakes with the intention of influencing a hearer in a certain way by means of illocutionary successes. Naturally, speech acts can serve this nonillocutionary aim of influencing hearers only if they are suited to achieve illocutionary aims . . . what we initially designated as 'the use of language with an orientation to consequences' is not an original use of language but the subsumption of speech acts that serve illocutionary aims under conditions of action oriented to success. (*TCA*: 292–3)

In other words, perlocutions are a special class of strategic interaction where the aim is brought about through illocutions. A speaker has to achieve his or her illocutionary aim in order to achieve the further perlocutionary aim. For instance, a hearer has to believe a false truth claim, even an implied one like that in the 'look out!' example, if someone with the intention to mislead is to succeed in doing so. Normally, too, that person will have to give the appearance of sincerity. The distinction strikes deep. In contrast with perlocutions, Habermas says,

> Illocutionary aims are different from those purposes that can be achieved *under* the description *of something to be brought about in the world* . . . illocutionary results are achieved at the level of interpersonal relations in which participants in communication come to an understanding with one another about something in the world. In this sense they are not inner-worldly [i.e. in the world] but extra-mundane. . . . A teleologically [strategically] acting speaker has to achieve his illocutionary aim – that the hearer understand what is said and undertake the obligations

connected with the acceptance of the offer contained in the speech act – without betraying his perlocutionary aim. This proviso lends to perlocutions the peculiarly asymmetrical character of concealed, strategic action. These are interactions in which at least one of the participants is acting strategically while he deceives other participants regarding the fact that he is not satisfying the conditions under which illocutionary aims can normally be achieved. (*TCA*: 293–4)

Thus Habermas distinguishes between two kinds of action or interaction, 'strategic action' and 'communicative action'. In communicative action, participants may harmonise their individual plans of action with each other – that is, they may co-ordinate their action plans – but one individual or class of participants does not simply seek to get another to conform their action plans to their own. Here, we are again brought up quite sharply against the validity question. When individuals seek to co-ordinate their action plans through reaching understanding – remember, in factual, interpersonal and expressive ways – the sole force for co-ordination is validity. Only through reaching a common truth can plans be co-ordinated. Thus Habermas is distinguishing here between, on the one hand, co-ordination of human action through, say, increased agreement about the validity of norms or rules for just or fair conduct, an agreement reached through communicative understanding, and agreement reached through the coercion of minor psychological distortions, fear, rewards and punishments, or factors other than assent to reasons or grounds.

As remarked above, Habermas' concept of reaching understanding must be clearly understood. Habermas argues that meaning cannot be separated from validity. The argument he presents runs something like this:

1. Meaning is tied to the truth conditions of statements.
2. 'Truth' or validity is broader than matters of fact. Normative and expressive utterances can be adjudged valid in rational ways. [Both 1 and 2 we have already discussed].

This leads to the most philosophically radical step in Habermas' argument

3. Validity judgements are not merely virtual they are *actual*. Actual truth judgements – judgements about the presence or absence of the conditions under which an utterance is true – are normally made by speakers and hearers as part of communication. [I will ask the reader to bear with the constant switching from talk of validity as truth about the world, to talk of normative rightness or about sincerity.] All speech acts make an offer and we 'accept the speech act offer or decline it'. (*TCA*: 297)

The acceptability of a speech act depends on the addressee's being able to take a positive position on its claims. If its claims are normative, this involves acceptance of the validity (legitimacy) of the norms involved. Habermas is arguing that 'the concept of the validity of a sentence *cannot* be explicated independently of . . . the concept of redeeming the validity claims raised through the utterance of the sentence' (*TCA*: 316).

But he is also arguing that 'an interpreter cannot, therefore, interpret expressions . . . without taking a position on them' (*TCA*: 116) because to understand the conditions under which one would judge an *utterance* valid or invalid one must understand the reasons or grounds upon which it could call. And it is in the nature of reasons, that they do not count *as reasons* unless you understand why they are sound or unsound. 'One can understand reasons only to the extent that one understands *why* they are sound or not sound' (*TCA*: 116). 'The interpreter absolutely cannot present reasons to himself without judging them, without taking a positive or a negative position on them' (*TCA*: 132) or at the least, leaving them undecided while wishing for more information. For instance, to understand a normative claim, of the kind, say, that is implicit in someone speaking to you in a certain way in a given context (e.g. about a sexual topic in church), you need to know quite a lot about the customs and rules of the speaker's culture. But knowing this, say, you cannot really help realising that the speaker is not behaving in the way normally considered to be following the rules of the culture. As a part of understanding the claim, because you understand 'the rules' and what counts as following them, you also immediately recognise whether or not a claim is valid. The main underpinning of Habermas' argument is a detailed analysis of the phenomenology of responses to claims by speakers and the presuppositions of observer/interpreters. Basically, his argument boils down to the claim that there is a kind of communication – the kind that is fully illocutionary – in which the hearer cannot 'dodge' the claims made by moving to another frame of reference. At the level of communicative action, speakers and hearers share frames of reference (worlds), and responses to claims must be at a level open in principle to the speaker too. Thus, in communicative action, the claim made in a speech act may be called acceptable if it fulfils the conditions which permit the hearer to take a 'yes' position on the claim raised. 'However these conditions cannot be satisfied one-sidedly, either relative to the speaker or the hearer. They are conditions for the *intersubjective recognition* of a linguistic claim' (*TCA*: 298).

Universal and empirical pragmatics

But these broad, general conditions are only a guide to understanding actual speech. As Habermas asserts,

The three general pragmatic functions – with the help of a sentence, to represent something in the world, to express the speaker's intentions, and to establish legitimate interpersonal relations – are the basis of all the particular functions that an utterance can assume in specific contexts. (*C & ES*: 33)

But it remains necessary to develop an empirical pragmatics that can recognise these functions in concrete situations.

As argued in Chapter 4, the theory of universal pragmatics (the ideal speech situation, ISS) is an abstract or general theory developed against the background of an undifferentiated and notional social context. It is intended only as a guide for empirical developments. Empirical pragmatics is the study of actual utterances in specific, differentiated social contexts. Habermas enunciates the steps whereby his formal (universal) pragmatics might be connected with empirical pragmatics. He argues that an empirical pragmatics unguided by formal pragmatics would lead to confusion and a failure adequately to locate the problem of rationality in modern society.

A first step towards an empirical pragmatics is the development of a typology of six basic speech acts. For reasons of simplicity, the following discussion will be limited largely to constative speech acts (assertions and statements), with occasional reference to expressive (avowals and disclosures) or regulative acts (promises, oath taking, etc.) to keep alive the notion of breadth. Imperative, communicative and operative acts will not be discussed.

Habermas goes on to argue that these basic types of act, and, in particular, constative, expressive and regulative acts 'constitute corresponding types of linguistically mediated interaction' (*TCA*: 327), that is, the overall communication structures can be dominated by one kind of communicative purpose and can be typed accordingly, e.g. an elaborate warning would occur through an interpersonal speech structure. The latter two of the types, expressive and regulative, correspond with the forms of action he discusses elsewhere under the titles 'dramaturgical' and 'normatively regulated', respectively. He points out that constative speech acts establish a context of action, too, but not one primarily oriented to the communicative harmonisation of action. Constative speech establishes, in its pure type, a form of interaction where the goal of reaching an understanding is an end in and of itself. Habermas calls this type of interaction a 'conversation'. It is this type of interaction which involves or can involve seeking the better argument, the truth, for its own sake.

As we take this typology into the empirical setting, we begin to see a number of influences at work. We must extend our analysis in a variety of complex ways. Among them are:

1. To enlarge our focus 'from isolated acts of communication (and

yes/no responses) to sequences of speech acts, to texts or conversations, so that conversational implications can come into view' (*TCA*: 330).
2.   An inclusion of 'analysis of the resources of the background knowledge (that is, life–worlds) from which participants feed their interpretations' (*TCA*: 336).

These two steps are the subject of work in progress. The work of Kress, Hodges, Kreckel, Bernstein, Edwards and Furlong, and many others might be brought to mind in this respect. Generally speaking, ethnomethodology focuses very strongly on the second of these steps. The third step is the most significant from the point of view of critical theory, since it is the heart of critique.

3.   A recognition of the specific distortions of communication which occur in the relationships of specific institutional settings.

On systematically distorted communication

At the formal level, it is possible to identify several types of distortion in communication. This will permit us to extend the ideology critique of the structure of classroom communication begun in Chapter 5. Perlocutionary action involves a special class of strategic interaction – that in which illocutions are employed as a means to ends other than reaching understanding and freely co-ordinating action plans in the light of validity claims (e.g. normative claims about right conduct). However, this characterisation of perlocution must be qualified by the recognition that imperative utterances, which are usually seen as the epitome of perlocutions, form only one class of perlocutions. This class admits of two subdivisions. Imperatives which appeal to known positive or negative sanctions which the person in power can control (type 2) and imperatives which appeal to a known normative context of legitimate authority (type 1).[2] The latter contains a criticisable validity claim and can be a part of a process of communicative action; the former does not and cannot.

But, as discussed above, there exists another general class of perlocutions which might be called 'deceptions' or 'ulterior purposes' (type 3). In these, as Strawson has shown, a speaker has to succeed in getting a hearer to accept an illocutionary claim in order to succeed in some further purpose, which must remain concealed. Thus, a car salesman might praise a (faulty) car, and give every evidence of claims to sincerity in his or her manner, in order, strategically, by getting the customer to accept his claims, to effect a further goal – the sale of the car. Again, a physician might resassure a patient, despite the presence of a grave illness, in the belief that the patient will have a worse time of it if he or she worries about the outcome of the illness. In regard to perlocution in the sense of types 2 and 3, Habermas points out that:

> when a speaker is pursuing undeclared ends with perlocutionary acts – ends on which the hearer can take no position at all [because they are unknown] – or when a speaker is pursuing illocutionary aims on which hearers cannot take a grounded position – as in relation to imperatives [of the sanction type 2] – the potential for the binding (or bonding) force of good reasons remains unexploited. (*TCA*: 305)

And, moreover, it is possible to characterise a range of types of systematically distorted communication of the kinds that are found in attempts at perlocutionary manipulation (the car salesman) or neurotically disordered communication:

> Such communication pathologies can be conceived of as the result of a confusion between actions oriented to reaching understanding and actions oriented to success. In situations of concealed strategic action, at least one of the parties behaves with an orientation to success, but leaves others to believe that all the presuppositions of communicative action are satisfied. (*TCA*: 305)

If the ideal pedagogical speech situation (IPSS) is one in which the student is able rationally to assess views or, at least, come to hold them in 'a manner open to rational assessment', then only those speech acts which are illocutionary but not perlocutionary (in senses 2 and 3) can characterise the form of action we would want to call 'educational' rather than 'indoctrinatory'.

The central distinction between illocutionary and perlocutionary is an intentional one. As Habermas argues, following Austin, 'the intention of the agent is constitutive for teleological actions' of the kind involved in strategic action and perlocution. However this will be little comfort to those philosophers who have espoused an intentional basis for the distinction between 'indoctrination' and 'education' since they focus on the content of the teacher's intention rather than its *structural* relation to the participants in discourse as interlocutors.[3] In a critical theory approach the difficulties which Kleinig notes for the content-oriented view of an indoctrinational intention are overcome.[4] Similarly, the discussion of just what methods might be likely to be indoctrinatory is bypassed, since, in respect of the validity questions associated with the perlocutionary (senses 2 and 3) intentions of a speaker, and therefore, in respect of the reasons by which validity might be judged, the adoption of a method of communication which involves concealed strategic action provides no possibility, of itself, for non-indoctrinatory teaching because it provides no access to reasons at all – that is, it is non-illocutionary in respect of the goals of perlocution.

At the empirical pragmatic level, in regard to any single speech act, it may not be possible to distinguish reliably between an illocutionary and a perlocutionary intention, but it is possible to do so in an empirical pragmatics which extends its scope to the analysis of whole interactively produced texts. In other words, we are not left in the difficulties of trying to identify inner-mental states. The argument that can be made concerning the presence of an indoctrinatory method, as is the case for all ideology critique, is one that can be made more or less strongly, rather than absolutely, but it can be made by examining the course of interaction. Perlocutionary intentions show themselves in the structure of interaction over time, particularly in those features of communication which reflectively shape its course. However, while our theoretical identifications may be clear, as always, in empirical cases we must be content with a more or less likely structural and/or causal analysis, at least, until someone comes along with an absolute, and therefore, acontextual criterion for indoctrination (or a perfect empirical method).

I have several times used the somewhat tedious locution of 'teaching/ learning', for a reason. It is quite clear in Habermas' theory that validity is an intersubjective affair. First, the conditions that a claim (utterance) must satisfy

> cannot be satisfied one-sidedly, either relative to the speaker or hearer. They are rather conditions for the *intersubjective recognition* of a linguistic claim, which, in a *way typical of* a given class of speech acts, grounds a specified agreement covering obligations relevant to the sequel of interactions. (*TCA*: 298)

In other words, as has just been argued, if the agreement were not mutual, it would soon or eventually become evident – we are talking here about social beings who have to live together – concealed strategic action will out (for students, perhaps in their exams!). In addition, because teachers are not the only ones who can and do pursue perlocutionary agendas, one aspect of the characteristic structure of distortions which can be found in some classrooms is that there exists two discourses not one.

Under the perlocutionary structure of strategic instructional action of this kind, the student is unable to respond to the perlocutionary 'claim' except through the mobilisation of resources gained elsewhere (background knowledge, cultural capital and/or successful guessing).[5] Yet this perlocutionary aim is the aim of the lesson. It is precisely this which is hidden, *typically* hidden, as the analysis in Chapter 5 shows, while at the same time students are expected to accept the illocutionary claims of each of the building blocks of the lesson as they are introduced, one by one, by the teacher.

Such a structure is formally indoctrinatory since a rational response to the perlocutionary intention is not possible. That is, it is indoctrinatory at the level of the aim of the teacher's 'lesson plan'.

The point being made here is not that teachers are pursuing sinister purposes or that they are 'cultural fools'. The aims they pursue, the goals of their lessons (the validity claims inherent in them) may be unobjectionable. The point is that they are pursuing them in a manner which tends to result in students accepting these claims on grounds other than those which seem valid to them in their own frameworks of relevance. This results in a shallow knowledge, unconnected with students' deepest beliefs, which is soon forgotten after leaving school. Ultimately, the perlocutionary pedagogy, however well-intentioned, is self-defeating – its content goals are not reached in any sustained way and it fails to provide opportunities for students to develop the critical interlocutory capacities that would enable them to develop a mature ability to continue to learn. In addition, when we turn our attention to the overall structure of lessons, it can be seen that the cognitive work which leads towards the lesson's goal is typically a hidden or implicit work – it is non-reflexive. Non-reflexive learning is defined as learning 'which takes place in action contexts in which implicity raised theoretical and practical validity claims are naively taken for granted and accepted or rejected without discursive consideration' (*LC*: 15).

In Chapter 5, it was noted that talk in the dominant classroom type was characterised by a low degree of reflexiveness. Methodological work was simply done, often without any announcement or identification that it had occurred. For instance, if a student gave an answer characterised by misplaced specificity (from the teacher's viewpoint) the answer would simply be made more general in its (re)formulation [F]:

> (Year 9: English)
> T(Q): How long could a discussion go on for?
> P(A): For five minutes or even longer.
> T(F): Yes. You talk . . . (Pause) . . . for a *while* about something.

The work of weighing evidence, testing logic, generalising, inferring, hypothesising was simply done, by the teacher in the moments *between* the utterances.

Expressive functions

The analysis to this point has been unbalanced towards the constative functions of language. The talk has been mainly of propositional knowledge and learning in interplay with regulative processes – the classic interplay of control and cognitive learning commented on by so many observers of the classroom.[6] Our discussion has also been conducted in the 'as-if' world of mature students rather than say, that of seven-year-olds, and so may be more relevant to the later stages of education – education's telos. But perhaps the most important source of the one-sidedness of the account given here is that it has mimicked the classroom's own bracketing of the expressive or emotional dimension of life.

There is an indissoluble bond between the idea of education as something other than mere instruction, adopted earlier, and the modern situation or modernity. It was argued that the notion of rationality, as understood by Habermas, implied a particular view of meaning and interaction. The rise of institutions that concern themselves, at least in principle, with the spread of rational learning levels to the mass of the population, is, of course, a distinctly modern phenomenon. Such institutions are part of the problem of modernity and, perhaps, also, many educators hope, part of the solution.

Such institutions, if non-indoctrinatory, and to the extent that they are, demand development of maturity and ego autonomy in the learner, for without such autonomy 'the learner is incapable of transcending the cognitive framework of his immediate milieu. Ego autonomy, in its full sense, implies both freedom from repression and from complete immersion in the normative world of one's own culture of origin.'[7]

At the highest level of purely, or one-sidedly, cognitive development lies 'formal operational problem solving' – but those who attain this level may confine themselves to working to solve puzzles within paradigms developed by others, cognitive technicians without a trace of critique. Without ego development the emergence of critical practical reason seems even less likely than cognitive critique. For instance, when we take into account the full social and communicative context of theoretical innovation in, say, the natural sciences, the relevance of ego autonomy and courage for creative activity within the communicative and power structures of scientific communities must also be asserted.

A DEVELOPMENTAL RECONSTRUCTION

Children and autonomy

The ideal of uncoerced, open dialogue is a counterfactual construct. As discussed earlier, it is not simply a measure to be applied mechanically to existing states of affairs. Its application to real, historical situations through immanent critique, especially ideology critique, is a complex, fallible historical process of self-emancipation by the species. One of the reasons why the ISS cannot be directly applied to real life situations is the absence in its construction of differentiation in knowledge, power and status between its hypothetical interlocutors. To the extent that any analysis of such differentiation must be an historically concrete analysis, it belongs not to the realm of the reconstruction of universal features of human communication but to the more relative field of historical endeavour. However, it is possible to address at least some of the differences in power, status and knowledge in a reconstructive way. The generalisation of Kohlberg's stages of individual moral development to the social level, and the analysis of the institutional development of western democracies in terms of the emergence of partial institutional-isation of discursive methods of problem solving (e.g. in the sciences), represents an attempt by Habermas to produce just such a reconstruction. This reconstruction has implications for the general role of education in democracies. But the direct application of developmental ideas to children may provide a reconstruction of universal possibilities for human development which has a pedagogical significance.

No doubt both of these reconstructions face many difficulties, but the point about rational reconstructions is that they are open to the influence of evidence. The jury of science is still out as far as the Kohlbergian project and Habermas' appropriation of it are concerned. However, even if these constructions were to be accepted in principle, one might still want to express doubts about their relevance for education, particularly the education of the young – schooling. After all, J. S. Mill argued that it was legitimate for adults to abridge the liberty of children because they were 'not capable of free and equal discussion'.[8] Other philosophers, such as Peters and Dearden have argued along similar lines. 'The brute facts of child development reveal that at the most formative years of a child's development he is incapable of [a rational] form of life.'[9] In another place, Peters rejects progressive schools, saying: 'Progressive schools therefore, which insist *from the start* on children making their own decisions and running their own affairs, ignore the crucial role which the stage of conventional morality plays in moral development.'[10] Peters fears that if children are encouraged to criticise moral principles while still at this conventional stage, i.e. at elementary school age, they will suffer from a loss of 'ontological security'.[11]

If these philosophers are right, discourse cannot function as a regulative ideal for pedagogy because it makes no sense to judge classroom communication between adult teachers and child pupils in terms of the differences from the ideal it exhibits if one category of participants is simply incapable of the ideal. Nor can the perlocutionary character of typical classroom communication revealed by research be regarded as a distortion of the proper form of pedagogy.[12] But the views of these philosophers about children's capacity for rational discourse are expressed in all or nothing terms and, as Dewey suggested, the development of children's capacity to enter into discourse may not be like that: 'Any power, whether of child or adult, is indulged when it is taken on its given and present level in consciousness. Its genuine meaning is in the propulsion it affords toward a higher level.'[13]

In critical theory, the counter-factual role of the concept of ideal openness in discourse was always intended to encompass the analysis of specific limitations on the extent and kind of discourse participation by categories of participants. Although Habermas himself does not deal with the problem of child/adult communication, he does deal with a number of analogous cases. I will review these cases first, then examine relevant features of the development of children's capacity to enter into rational argumentation, and finally, examine the significance of this for a critical theory of schooling.

Institutionally bound and distorted communication

Habermas discusses two forms of communicative distortion, neurotic and strategic. Neurotic communication is that which may be involved in the communication of a single, neurotic subject, and which is manifested in disjunctions between speech and gesture, in compulsive behaviours and in the employment of speech governed by other than the normal linguistic rules. 'The usual congruency between linguistic symbols, actions and accompanying gesture has disintegrated.'[14]

Strategic distortion is a form of distortion which manifests itself when there is a 'confusion between actions oriented to reaching understanding [illocutionary structures] and actions oriented to success [perlocutionary structures]' (*TCA*: 332). A common form of this distortion occurs in processes of conscious manipulation, as in the case where a salesperson attempts to get a customer to make certain commitments in order to be able to place him or her in a position where it is difficult to refuse to buy a product:

> So you are not just looking. You're ready to buy a car today if you see the right one?
> Sure.
> O.K. you want a Chevy. A convertible.
> Right.
> I've got just the right car for you!

However, there is an area of common ground between the two forms of distortion. In this third, composite form, manipulation is unconscious, as in the case of interpersonal speech pathologies, where at least one individual in, say, a family can be seen by an outsider as manipulative but does not see him- or herself in this way.

In the case of neurotic communication, including communication which is unconsciously manipulative, it is possible for a learning process to be initiated in which the distortion is overcome. This may involve the intervention of an outsider, often a psychoanalytical professional, who engages in a particular kind of communication oriented to learning through recognition of the fact of distortion and discovery of its origins – this is called 'analysis'. Now, the point which is relevant to the present argument is simply that it may be possible, through further communication, in which there is a progressive shift in communicative roles, to create recognition of the sources of distortion in communication and through the promotion of learning to overcome the distortion.

In an empirical pragmatics, which takes formal pragmatics as a guide, while taking into account the contextual features of language, and, in particular, the 'rules for speaking' governing the dialogue of particular categories of participants in recognised and regularly structured (institutionalised) social settings, we must recognise that manipulation is one common means of domination.[15] Of course, the exercise of normatively authorised imperatives (even in the soft form of 'suggestions') is not a form of manipulation, but modern society is replete with situations where lines of authority are not all that clear, and where, in any case, persons in authority may wish to legitimate their control by avoiding recourse to legally recognised authority to issue imperatives and by giving the appearance of consultative and even democratic processes (e.g. presidents or vice-chancellors of universities, business leaders who believe in 'teamwork').

Such manipulation may be institutionalised in dialogue roles through tacit rather than legally recognised or formalised constraints on communication. Few students fail to feel some trepidation at flatly contradicting their professors even when they know their professors are wrong. Junior members of faculty, and junior executives in business are considered to 'know their place' when they speak less often and more tentatively at meetings than senior faculty or corporation presidents.

Studies of classroom communication reveal strong regularities governed by tacit 'rules' as in, say, the regulation of turn-taking[16] or the roles of pupil and teacher in the Q/A cycle.[17] But further speech can make this speaking process 'topical'. By speaking about the speech roles of participants and about how breaches of protocol are recognised, felt and dealt with, it is possible to recognise and change these patterns. Specific limitations on the dialogue roles of students, such as the 'rule' which states that students should give the answer to teacher' questions that the teacher wants, or the 'rule' which states that teachers should always evaluate the adequacy of student answers to teachers' questions but that students should *never* evaluate teacher answers to (the few) students' questions can be identified and overcome by the introduction of specific structures designed to implement new 'rules' (e.g. structured debates, student question time, time for student critique of teachers' arguments).

Similarly, by entering into a risky reflexive communication about the form communication is taking it is sometimes possible for subordinates to confront the democratic pretensions of administrators with the actual structures of their communicative practices. This can result in changed procedures, widened consultation and review and the like.

To sum up, the account in Habermas of distorted communication, and specifically, of institutionalised forms of distortion, is one which anticipates a process of 'analysis' and learning, which uncovers manipulative and other forms of distortion by examining the ways in which these specifically depart from an ideal speech situation. The essential difference between the situations sketched above and child pedagogy is that the limitations on the participation of children are not basically neurotic in origin and that the 'cure' for them consists in fostering a developmental learning process in which these limitations may be overcome rather than a critical process resulting in immediate recognition of distortions and their origins. The limitations of children's participation cannot be overcome by their own acts of recognition and reconstruction in the absence of developmental progress, but the process of learning and development and the role played in it by teachers is nonetheless analogous to the process of analysis and the role of the analyst.

This was also Dewey's insight:

> Such and such are the capacities, the fulfilment, in truth, and beauty and behavior, open to these children. Now see to it that day by day the conditions are such that *their own activities* move inevitably in this direction, toward such culmination of themselves.[18]

In the process of analysis, analysts must adapt their communication to the appropriate stage of the analysis, changing their communicative role and their level and kind of communicative participation as their patients undergo or pass through stages of analysis such as transference. Specific stages of the process of analysis 'enable' specific kinds of communicative relationship. School teaching involves a similar kind of progression. We must turn to empirical studies of the development of children's capacity to enter into argumentation to understand the nature of this progression.

The development of communicative competence

An early discussion of the developmental process underlying the emergence of a capacity for moral judgement is found in Habermas' 1979 discussion of 'moral development and ego identity' (*C & ES*).

The normative and expressive dimensions of teaching and learning are often ignored in favour of a more cognitive emphasis. The fact that much of the relevant analysis has been developed by Habermas and others outside the cognitive 'domain' may be accidental as far as educational analysis is concerned, but if so, it is a happy accident, since it permits the analysis to deal more directly with motivations and practices and with the obstacles to more autonomous teaching and learning, which lie primarily in the affective area.

Habermas identifies three phases of development:

1. For the pre-school child, who is cognitively still at the stage of pre-operational thought, the sector of his symbolic universe relevant to [social] action consists only of individual, concrete, behavioral expectations and actions, as well as consequences of action that can be understood as gratifications or sanctions.
2. As soon as the child has learned to play social roles his symbolic universe [can now include] actions as the fulfillment of temporally generalized behavioral expectations [norms].
3. When, finally, the youth has learned to question the validity of social rules and norms of action . . . there . . . appear principles in accordance with which opposing norms can be judged. (*C & ES*: 84)

At the first level children cannot be responded to as subjects who can be 'held responsible for actions with a view to generalized behavioral expectations' (*C & ES*: 85). At the second level the child associates norms of roles of family members and others, and group norms. Conventional responsibility emerges. Finally, at the third level, actors can 'assert their identities independent of concrete roles and particular systems of norms' (*C & ES*: 85). They become capable of a critique of norms on the basis of principles. As we move through the levels, actors' symbolic capacity becomes less context dependent, more reflexive, abstract, individually differentiated and generalised.

In later developments of this work, Habermas and his co-workers widened Kohlberg's model to include the development of a capacity to enter into argumentation. Unlike the development of a capacity for moral judgement, the development of a capacity for argumentation, as conceptualised by Miller, one of Habermas' co-workers, encorporates the social capacity for *entering into* argumentation, as well as the mere cognitive capacity to generate or criticise arguments in some formal sense, as children might do when confronted by an experimenter describing argument scripts. 'Because interpersonal reasoning is pervasively contextual in character, it is more likely to "fit" a situation and thus reveal its possibilities for resolving action.'[19]

Miller, following a generally Piagetian methodology, but working with groups of children, has theorised a stage-like developmental process in respect of a capacity to enter into moral argumentation at various moral argument levels.[20] In observation of group problem-solving argument among children, Miller identifies the stages of argumentation in terms of the kind of problems which children can collectively solve in resolving a moral dilemma situation. At the first level, among children aged 5 years, the problem of justification is recognised and solved. At succeeding levels, problems of coherence, circularity, and language arise. All four levels are identifiable in the argumentation of older children, with, typically, a recapitulation of the developmental sequence in a series of contextual switches during the process of argument.

Miller employed Kohlberg's Heinz dilemma story in his research. This story concerns a man, Heinz, who stole from a drug store owned by another man, because his wife was sick and he had no money to buy the life-saving drug concerned. The problem of justification is solved by either a pre-existing agreement on right and wrong among members of the group, or by a process of joint argument which can be traced back to a collectively valid set of views of right and wrong. The remaining problems are sub-problems of justification. The problem of coherency emerges when the detailed moral criteria for evaluating the action of stealing the drug are not shared. Miller illustrates the remaining types of problem by a dialogue something like this:

Heinz: [In justifying his theft.]
         Everyone has a right to live.
         (A potential justification.)

Owner: Nonsense! It's the same for me. After all, I live by selling medicine and not by having it stolen.
         (At this point the problem of social coherency of proposed justification arises.)

Heinz: If I hadn't stolen from you my wife would have died, whereas all you lost was your property, not your life. (Heinz attempts to solve the problem of coherency by this argument, which essentially draws the distinction between the two meanings of 'live'.)

Owner: That's precisely the point. You should have respected my property. You could have taken a lottery ticket to get the money for the drug.

Heinz: That's a bad joke. By my breaking into your store I achieved the best all round result. We all live. But if I hadn't stolen the drug my wife would almost certainly have died.
         (Here, the problem of circularity emerges. Any possibility of a joint argument is threatened unless this problem is overcome. Each protagonist is presenting different criteria as key criteria. The argument goes in circles.)

Owner: Are you crazy? My life is not in question. What you say is completely beside the point.

Heinz: (Attempting to solve the problem of circularity.) Well, we seem to be proposing different contexts for judging what I did. I maintain I had no choice if I was to save my wife's life. But you maintain I have alternatives, such as gambling. Let's put this aside for the moment and let me ask, if in fact I didn't have any alternatives, would you agree that saving a life was more important than saving property. (Here Heinz is trying, through a meta-argumentative move to get a resolution of the circulatory problem.)

Owner: No way! For me what is morally justified is keeping to the law. The law says you can't steal but it doesn't say you must commit burglary to save someone's life. (Now the problem of language emerges. What does the owner mean by 'morally justified'? It doesn't seem the same as Heinz's view but rather a formal and narrow idea. Further argument can't be productive until the most basic terms of the debate are clarified.)

(Miller, 1986: 437–47)

Miller argues that recognition of these problems and a capacity to solve them 'ontogenetically develop in a . . . sequence' (Miller, 1986: 447). He argues that the first stage, of justification, manifests itself as early as 2 years, and presents evidence, albeit somewhat sketchy evidence, that the remaining 'stages' manifest themselves successively as children grow and develop.

If Miller is right, even in a most approximate way (and that is a question for further research), it suggests that children do have a capacity to engage in moral argumentation from an early age, certainly pre-school age, but that the nature of the problems of moral argumentation that they are able to resolve form a developmental sequence. Provided there are appropriate constraints on the problem situation, a three-year-old child can argue just as validly about a problem of justification (i.e. the relationships between an action and a norm) as you or I. Indeed, Miller's argument details the logical structure of such arguments in such a way as to show there is no formal logical difference between a rational adult and the three-year-old child in this respect.

At this point it seems possible to enter an important qualification against the views of Mill and Peters – provided situational constraints limit problem types to those with which children are developmentally able to deal, it is possible for teachers to enter rational dialogue with children.

Within the limits of the problemlevel, the child, in principle, could as easily demonstrate the invalidity of the teacher's validity claim as vice versa. What Peters apparently failed to take into account is that rationality is situation specific. Not only is it a matter of degree (as Dearden recognised)[21] but it is a matter of circumstance. This line of analysis also suggests that the management of an appropriate succession of problemlevels should be a major concern of pedagogy.

Recent developments in empirical research are of interest in this context, despite any methodological reservations one might have about the empiricist paradigm. Several lines of research converge on a model of teaching and learning not dissimilar from that being presented here. First, studies of pupil error have produced a 'constructivist' rather than behavioural model of learning, in which the construction and reconstruction of learners' schema or frameworks plays a central role. Problem-solving learning seems to be related to a better and more useful organisation of knowledge in the learner's schema, but only where the student has adequate support (e.g. 'scaffolding') and the problemlevel is not higher than the student's problem threshold. The only resource from which this fine-tuning can come is, with the teacher's assistance, the learners themselves. Co-operative learning with high levels of learner control can provide the support necessary for a problem solving approach and it can do so in a manner which helps learners to want to learn. However, it would be a mistake to assume that this communicative, progressive problem-solving style of learning could be co-operative in some coerced fashion. It must take place in such a way as to maintain the individuals' perceptions of themselves as being independent, autonomous and critical learners.[22]

Questions for curriculum

A number of issues are opened up by the notion of a progressive, problem-solving pedagogy. For instance, under what circumstances can we justify the introduction into the classroom of problemlevels beyond the argumentative capacity of children if this inevitably leads to forms of rational heteronomy? This question raises a number of curriculum issues.

To put the same question in another way: If it is possible to devise a curriculum which does not simply ignore the problemlevels at which children are capable of operating, but moves approximately with them in their development, allowing for respect for and preservation of children's rational autonomy, can we justify not doing so, or settling for a curriculum based on heteronomy? More practically, what is to encourage teachers and pupils to change their communicative practices so that they operate at the appropriate problemlevels in autonomy-creating teaching and learning? Put in this way, the issue of moral performance rather than the more restricted notion of moral capacity is thrust into the spotlight. The act of entering into argumentation in such a way as to pursue the end of a common truth, or, as Habermas says, to reach an understanding, is an act of a rational subject linking and exposing his or her own rational processes with and to those of others. It is an act of assertion of one's own rational identity or rational being but as a member of a social world. It requires an appropriate emotional and motivational climate and a courage for rational participation, with its risks for one's own cherished beliefs. The teacher's role is much closer to that of psychoanalyst and requires more of the qualities of character and communicative constraint of the successful analyst that might have appeared obvious at first sight.

The approach adopted here bears a strong resemblance to Dewey's problem solving method of pedagogy:

> From the side of the studies [the disciplines of knowledge], it is a question of interpreting them as outgrowths of forces operating in the child's life, and of discovering the steps that intervene between the child's present experience and their richer maturity.

and

> the problem . . . is just to get rid of the prejudicial notion that there is some kind of gap in kind (as distinct from degree) between the child's experience and the various forms of subject matter that make up the course of study.[23]

Ego autonomy and rational autonomy in communication

Armed with the foregoing it may be possible to throw some light on an argument that is often presented as a natural extension of Mill's exclusion of children from participation in rational argumentation – the argument that, in any case, it is not necessary to exercise rational autonomy in order to be able to develop it. We have already seen that any absolute exclusion of children from rational dialogue by reason of incapacity may be based on false premises.

In constrained problem situations or, to adopt a more specific vocabulary, at particular problemlevels, children are capable of formally equivalent reasoning to that of adults. While it has been suggested that problemlevels might be artificially constrained, as a part of the art of pedagogy, it is also true that such constraints can occur 'naturally' in the social environment. Providing children are not faced with problemlevels beyond their capacity under conditions of emotional pressure, there would seem to be no reason why critical dialogue would be incompatible with the creation of an environment conducive to that 'ontological security' which Peters considers necessary for the development of mental health. If so, it would not be necessary, as Peters would have it, for children 'to enter the Palace of Reason through the courtyard of Habit and Tradition' (Peters 1963: 275), or, at least, to stretch the utility of the architectural metaphor, they could enter some rooms of the Palace of Reason directly, even if they had to pass into the courtyard to get to the rest. Various other, weaker reasons are also given for the construction of heteronymous teaching/learning, arguments which canvas issues of social necessity, practicality or economy of teacher/ pupil ratios and the like. We will come to them in the next chapter of the present work. For the moment let us be distracted one last time by the rose-coloured argument that usually accompanies these utilitarian arguments, drawing critical attention away from them – the argument that all will be well in the end because it is still possible to develop (the desirable) rational autonomy even though it is not exercised.

While Peters tries to avoid specific pedagogical and curricular recommendations, it appears that the methods available for the development (without exercise) of rational autonomy are rather limited. They must consist in some practices which are initiated and motivated by the teacher, such as, the setting of exercises in skills or content knowledge deemed a part or a necessary but not sufficient condition of autonomy, training in the recognition of logically valid arguments, the learning of past critiques or the modelling of critique by the teacher. The teacher tells the students an argument, or reads out an account of the reasoning of say, a great scientist, or sets exercises in logical analysis of arguments, demonstrates a law by conducting a demonstration experiment and so on. The student picks up the skills of logic, of structuring argument, recognises reasons given by teachers for accepting or rejecting evidence and so on. In short, the practice of skills in set exercises and experience of the arguments held valid by others is supposed to create rational development which can then manifest itself in the actual exercise of rational participation in argumentation when the circumstances are appropriate.

However, such an account would be one-sidedly cognitive. It ignores the interpersonal reality of argumentation, and the element of risk and engagement. From the standpoint of Habermas' approach to meaning and validity, it is an account which is simultaneously monological and narrow. It is monological because it fails to recognise that the resolution of validity claims is ultimately a social (i.e. dialogical) rather than an individual process and that validity only emerges in social engagement, engagement which, in turn, is only made possible by appropriate normative and emotional conditions. One gets the impression that many who learn about argumentation in the way suggested above would never dare to argue.

It is narrow because it fails to recognise, with Habermas and with modern linguists that each and every utterance, even in the most abstract arguments, is multi-functional.[24] Interpersonal relationships and personal feelings are always communicated at the same time as statements about the world, even in primarily constative speech. It is in the normative and expressive relations of speaker and hearer that many of the institutionalised incapacities to explore validity questions in a rationally open way are located.

Much dialogue can take place within accepted norms and under some expressive constraints, and cognitive progress of a limited kind might still be made. But sometimes cognitive dissonance, normative disagreement (e.g. about speaker roles) and the like emerge, and the dialogue may shift to a meta-level where the assumptions and procedures underlying the previous level of dialogue may themselves be directly discussed. Such shifts of level are normal parts of the process of argumentation as Miller's analysis also shows, and a necessary part of the expression of rational autonomy (conceived of as rational participation). Given that all actual dialogues take place in social and historical conditions of constraint, the capacity to make such shifts becomes crucial to the likelihood of cognitive progress. The modelling of argumentative processes by teachers in a monological and narrowly cognitivist way is no preparation for the real hurly-burly of argument.

A capacity for recognising logical contradictions, conceptual confusions, statements unsupported by evidence and so on, however valuable, does not add up to a capacity for intellectual autonomy. Whatever the problems with 'capacity' as a concept, it is clear that the idea of a capacity for autonomy is vacuous unless it is a capacity for its exercise in the form of participation in forming validity judgements in actual social situations of unequal power and authority. Here, Habermas' distinction between linguistic competence and communicative competence is important. The former may be fully engaged in silent recognition but the latter only in participation.

Teaching and critical development

It is fairly clear that the developmental structure of pedagogy which emerges from the foregoing considerations produces a different model of the school from that implicit in some progressive schools. The idea of children being required to create their own moral principles, or to criticise conventional principles in, say, school meetings, while still at the conventional level of moral development, is one which finds no place in a critical pedagogy. However, the idea of 'reflexive participation' by children in setting the conditions for their own learning, and in deciding the specific and *concrete* forms in which such principles might be realised, *is* potentially important. The production of an orderly learning environment is crucial to the educational effectiveness of schooling. This is not the same thing as teacher control. In most discussions of teacher control, the teacher is seen as producing the rules as well as enforcing them. In a discourse model of pedagogy, the teacher and the pupils produce and reproduce the rules in discourse, within a framework of constraints. There is a close relationship between the normative conditions for learning, which these rules define and the constative discourse that takes place under their aegis. It has often been remarked by classroom researchers that there is a negative relationship between teachers' attempts at control and their attempts to promote cognitive learning. In the process of involving children in responding to the normative and expressive validity claims of classroom organisation and practices, for the purpose of allowing their cognitive discourse to be heard and taken seriously, this relationship can be turned into a positive one.

At least in principle, critical schooling would not be characterised by a curriculum enslaved to the limited vision and interests of children and adolescents. Its disciplinary standards would not be those of the blackboard jungle nor would its academic standards be less rigorous than those of today. In such schools, teachers' claims on students' conduct would be strong, but their strength would be drawn partly from students' claims on teachers' conduct. Similarly, parents' and the community's claims on the curriculum, the knowledge considered worth learning, would be respected, but they would have to compete with the growing capacity of children to challenge them critically, that is to challenge them with reasons and reasoning. The very emergence of this capacity, which is not the same as a simple capacity to reject or say no, would be prima facie evidence for the view that pedagogy should adapt to it in that particular case.

The acceptance of the normative authority of the teacher in some areas of school organisation and conduct, and the presence of imperative language acts in teacher talk, is not necessarily incompatible with educational validity. What is incompatible with it is the situation at present so common in our schools, where the scope of the teacher's authority ranges over all aspects of validity or truth judgements as well as the normative appropriateness of conduct and where this all encompassing extension of authority does not systematically diminish as children's capacity for responsible participation in co-ordination of their conduct and for resolving questions of cognitive validity develops.

Obviously, flexibility, and an openness to children's emergent capacity to take responsibility for the truth of their own beliefs, the justice and authenticity of their own relationships with others, should be the hallmark of our future schools. A picture like this is not so very different from that painted by the finest ideals of traditional educators and, a fortiori, progressive educators, such as Dewey. The difference is in the brush strokes. By its development of a concrete, hermeneutic model of pedagogy, critical theory offers a method for achieving this openness by identifying behaviour that leads away from it. It provides objective[25] criteria where the finest progressive and traditional teaching relied only on the intuitions and sensitivities of teachers. It thus strengthens but does not replace ideals of education whose telos was the independent learner who has learned how to cope with new knowledge and new situations.

The problem of the organisation of critical practice

One might be excused for thinking that the remaining somewhat contingent practical arguments would appear a trifle makeshift were the philosophically much more formidable defences which stood between them and an outbreak of autonomy in teaching/learning to be demolished. Far from it. Such practical issues have probably fuelled the engine which has motivated argument all along. The difficulties of holding rational discussion between one teacher and 30 children are obvious. In addition, many school classrooms may contain children who are developmentally separated by three or more years, providing an additional difficulty if the kind of situationally limited dialogue of problemlevels discussed earlier is to be implemented. Finally, the possibility exists that any limitation of teaching to children's rational problemlevels may prevent the teaching of knowledge deemed socially necessary.

When one starts to unpack these difficulties it becomes clear that they rest on a background of assumptions about the way schools are at present organised and funded. For instance, the one-to-many communication problem assumes whole-class instruction and fixed teacher/student ratios in the teacher/student communication process, but relatively inexpensive means exist for organising teacher time in such a way as to permit lower ratios for at least a proportion of school time. It would be unadventurous, to say the least, to fail to explore the possibilities of a new theory of education simply because it would meet with difficulties in schools organised along the lines of an old theory of education. Clearly, though, a critical theory of education has implications for school organisation and administration. It may also be the case that, as the new theory unfolds, it suggests grounds upon which we might justify quite new arrangements for relations between teachers and learners. Practical difficulties may justify an evolutionary approach to the taking of *practical* steps but can scarcely tell as grounds for avoiding thought about new possibilities leading, eventually perhaps, to new practical arrangements. From a rational reconstruction of an ideal pedagogy and an ideology critique of existing pedagogy it is necessary to move to a historically situated immanent critique of forms of educational organisation and to the risky task of outlining possible strategies for the organisation of educational enlightenment.

NOTES

1. I. Scheffler, *Conditions of Knowledge: An Introduction to Epistemology and Education*, Glenview: Scott, Foresman, 1965: 12–13.
2. *TCA*: 298–303. Most of this chapter is drawn from R. E. Young, 'Critical teaching and learning', *Educational Theory*, **38** (1) 1988: 47–59, and R. E. Young, 'Moral development, ego autonomy and questions of practicality in the critical theory of schooling', *Educational Theory*, **38** (4) 1988: 391–404, with the permission of the editors.
3. I. Snook (ed.), *Concepts of Indoctrination*, London: Routledge and Kegan Paul, 1972.
4. J. Kleinig, *Philosophical Issues in Education*, London: Croom Helm, 1982, 59, 60–1.
5. See R. E. Young, 'A school communication-deficit hypothesis of educational disadvantage', *Australian Journal of Education*, **27** (1), 1983: 3–16.
6. J. Hoetker and W. Ahlbrand, 'The persistence of the recitation', *American Educational Research Journal*, **6** (2), 1969: 145–67.
7. R. E. Young, 'Critical theory, curriculum and teaching', *Discourse*, **3** (1), 1982: 13–14, 22–39.
8. J. S. Mill, *On Liberty*, London: Dent, 1910: 73.
9. R. Peters 'Reason and habit: The paradox of moral education', W. Niblett (ed.) *Moral Education in a Changing Society*, London: Faber & Faber, 1963: 271.
10. R. S. Peters 'Freedom and the development of the free man', in J. Doyle (ed.) *Educational Judgments*, London: Routledge and Kegan Paul, 1973: 135.
11. *Ibid.*: 127–30.
12. R. E. Young 'Classroom questioning and critical theory', *Language and Education*, **1** (2), 1987: 125–34, and Chapter 5.
13. J. Dewey, *The Child and the Curriculum*, Chicago: University of Chicago Press, 1900, 1956:15.
14. J. Habermas, 'Toward a theory of communicative competence', *Inquiry*, **13**, 1970: 205.
15. *Ibid.*: 205–18.
16. *TCA*, Vol. 1, 332. This is a form of communicative language act. A. McHoul, 'The organization of turns at formal talk in the classroom', *Language in Society*, **7**, 1978: 182–213.
17. See Chapter 5.
18. J. Dewey, *op. cit.*: 31.
19. See N. Haan, 'Two moralities in action contexts: Relationships to thought, ego regulation and development', *Journal of Personality and Social psychology*, **3**, 1978: 300.
20. M. Miller, 'Learning how to contradict and still pursue a common end: The ontogenesis of moral argumentation', in J. Cook-Gumperz, W. Corsaro and J. Streeck (eds) *Children's Worlds and Children's Language*, Berlin: Mouton de Gruyter, 1986, and *Kollektive Lernprozesse*, Frankfurt: Suhrkamp, 1986.
    Habermas' use of Kohlberg raises many questions. Habermas himself is well aware of the many difficulties of genetic structuralism, and of the circularity that afflicts the theory–data relationship in this kind of research (e.g. *Moralbewusstsein und kommunikatives Handeln*, Frankfurt: Suhrkamp, 1983: 49–50, 183–200). He notes a number of problems of Kohlbergian theory and discusses the relationship between developmental psychology and his rational reconstruction of universal developmental possibilities. It may be sufficient for the purposes of this discussion to state a caveat concerning the adequacy of expressing development in stage terms.
21. R. Dearden, 'Autonomy as an educational ideal' in S. Brown (ed.) *Philosophers Discuss Education*, London: Macmillan, 1975: 9. But also see R. Peters, 'The development of reason', for a recognition of the situated character of reason and the necessity of

courage, 229–331 in S. Benn and G. Mortimore (eds) *Rationality and the Social Sciences*, London: Routledge and Kegan Paul, 1976.

22. See a recent collection of readings in E. De Corte, R. de Lieuw and C. Leishaut (eds) *Learning and Instruction: European Research in an International Context*, London: Pergamon Press/Leuven University Press, 1987.
23. J. Dewey, *op. cit.*: 11.
24. E.g. M. Halliday and R. Hasan, *Language, Context and Text*, Geelong: Deakin University Press, 1985.
25. Perhaps the use of the term 'objective' here needs some explanation. It is not used in any absolute sense, but in the sense of a partially socially-transcendental method.

CHAPTER 7

CONTEXTS FOR RESEARCH AND ACTION

The sovereigns of the world are old
and they will have no heirs at all.
(Rainer Maria Rilke)[1]

The task of the organisation of enlightenment must be guided by ideology critique, but it must also go beyond the negative. It must take on its own creative and original historical form. But there is no blueprint for this; the ideal speech situation (ISS) provides us, at best, with only a glimpse of God's vast sleeping form. Certainly, professional educators at all levels must participate in this process and traditional separations between academics, administrators and classroom teachers must be overcome. Nevertheless, we must begin from the historical situation where most educational writing and research is done by academic educators, and it is this situation which is assumed in the following discussion. In much of this chapter we are engaged in the relative activity of ideology critique and the claims being made are not intended to be universal claims. That is, they are context-bound and risky sensitising statements, which must be adapted, even rejected, in particular situations, even though some care has been taken to cast the net broadly enough to cover most late capitalist societies. This chapter begins with a reminder of the contingent and fallible nature of historically situated and socially contextualised emancipatory action. A series of hypothetical contexts is then discussed, as an aid to reflection, culminating in a recognition of the need for a greater exercise of professional responsibility by practitioners. In some cases this may take the form of passive resistance and civil disobedience, especially in the face of current attempts to further distort the educative process.

UNIVERSAL IDEALS AND HISTORICAL REALITY

As pointed out earlier, the ISS cannot be contrasted with real situations and the gap between ideal and reality read off like figures from a calculator. In addition, the universal character of speech could not, in principle, provide guidance for the direct analysis of human situations which go beyond the small scale of speech events. Even at the small-scale level, a knowledge of the characteristic validity claims of speech could not provide a complete basis for the critical analysis of real situations, since one must still balance truth against sincerity against appropriateness, and the ISS provides no basis for this. Quite simply, human situations can be ambiguous, and, of course, moral dilemmas in which truth is contrary to justice, etc. are the very stuff of tragic drama and literature. That is why Habermas recently felt it necessary to introduce notions of balance, aesthetics and health into the meta-normative discussion. How then does the ISS provide guidance for situated critique?

It provides guidance for analysis of real speech situations by making issues of truth, truthfulness and appropriateness problematic. Perhaps an extended example will make this clearer. A concrete analysis of, say, doctor/patient talk can show that different speakers have different roles with respect to the truth or referential functions of talk. Some aspects of this difference may be grounded in differences in medical knowledge relevant to the task in hand, e.g. diagnosing an illness, while others may be associated with differences in power or status, rather than knowledge. Now the undifferentiated meta-context of the ISS posits mutual responsibility for the validity of conclusions. Habermas' own example of this is found in the need for psychoanalytic conclusions to be verified by the patient rather than the analyst. But in the presence of an actual one-sided expression of responsibility for a set of conclusions, i.e. in the doctor/patient relationship, the significant question is not simply: Is this situation asymmetrical? but: Is this asymmetry justified?

In an ideal world, perhaps, all individuals would possess equal knowledge or, failing that, complementary knowledge of equal value. In the co-operative task of accurate diagnosis of an illness both doctor and patient have interests. The patient's interests are more immediate and personally engaged than the doctor's, so the patient's interests are likely to provide a better existential guarantee of the justice, etc. of an outcome than the doctor's. And on any logical basis, the patient's information about his or her own symptoms must be more extensive than the doctor's. The task of accurate diagnosis is logically dependent on the sharing of complementary forms of information. But structural influences on doctor patient talk associated with differences in power and status prevent open exchange of information and vest control of the exchange in the party whose interests are less involved in the adequacy of the outcome – the doctor. Only in a fully contextual analysis of the talk in the situation could one reach a defeasible conclusion as to whether the level of cognitive asymmetry in the talk was simply consistent with the differences in knowledge of doctor and patient and with the area of mutuality of interests between doctor and patient, namely, a professionally adequate and accurate diagnosis, or whether this outcome was hindered in some way.

In turn, the analysis of a sample of such speech situations may become a resource for a more macroscopic analysis of the social role of the medical profession which has critical relevance for the medical school curriculum. In this way, the indirect critical role of the ISS at the macroscopic level is illustrated. The critical question raised here is: How do these structures inhibit or enable better speech situations? It is, after all, in the face-to-face situations of life that we live and move, suffer and succeed. They can be a touchstone for the analysis of structure, which, admittedly, proceeds by its own conceptual apparatus (systems analysis, etc.). In the context of medicine, the structural issue becomes the delivery of health services and the administration of hospitals in such a manner that the doctor/patient relationship is effective, just and authentic. In the context of education, the analysis of educational administration, at both system and school levels, becomes the analysis of school and system as 'parapedagogical organisations' – organisations judged on the basis of the kind of pedagogy they inhibit or promote.[2] In educational critique, we must begin with the context of pedagogical action and widen our scope to include the kind of structures that will enable critical pedagogy. The first such context is the learner's problem context. This context must have primacy for the Kantian reason that it is only when the learner's problems are not suppressed that we can find a reasonable guarantee against the interests of the teacher and the system overwhelming the interests of the child and its parents. (I speak of the child and the family in the same breath because the interests of the child and the parents are normally intimately intertwined in the beginning of the child's life, although in later phases of education a separation and individuation of interests gradually emerges.)

In the following pages, after an initial general discussion of some of the various educational contexts, I will focus on the reconstruction of educational research and discourse. Then, in the next chapter, a number of recent practical innovations and developments in critical education will be discussed.

THE CHILD'S PROBLEM CONTEXT

As discussed earlier, there already exist areas of the life–world which are under attack by instrumental rationality. These areas of thought and practice can become the focus of critical attention because they are already 'problematic'. The first task for critical theorists in such circumstances is to 'make' rather than simply accept or 'take' such problems, or rather, the accompanying folk definitions of them, as social givens.[3] Problematic situations are already in a state of flux, so redefinition is possible. Critical interventions, providing they are prudent and guided by appropriate criteria will not necessarily be seen as either creating the problems in the first place or as 'fishing in troubled waters'. Such interventions can draw on existing, socially recognised ideals of justice, democracy and authenticity in a positive rather than negative way. Instead of taking general ideals and simply comparing actual practices with them, which always leads to a negation of the existent, problem-based critique takes such ideals as a way of defining the problem prior to a positive or constructive stage, characterised by a stage where real and feasible improvements in practices are suggested. The aim of critique in such situations is usually to devise problem solutions which fend off bureaucratic and market–economic solutions in favour of those which involve widening the sphere of public discourse and participation.

Problem analysis and resolution will involve the examination of the fragments of the broken life–world revealed by the already existing colonisation process, the pedagogical opportunity to make these thematic (in Freire's sense) and through this to examine the structure of distortions in the taken-for-granted practices of the existing situation which have led to distortions of the communicative construction of reality and to the reification of past constructive practices.

THE PEDAGOGICAL CONTEXT

In the pedagogical relationship, though, the mode of action must not be expected to be as robustly political as it might be in national politics. The pedagogical relationship is under a special set of constraints, since the dogmatic imposition of critical theorems begets dogmatism rather than a mature and emancipated capacity for participation. This is true even for adult/adult relationships. The exercise of autonomy by children, as was argued in Chapter 6, is a necessary condition for its development. Pedagogical tact or restraint is necessary as far as the content of the teacher's own critical theorems is concerned. Critical pedagogy has far more to do with the method of teaching than with the advocacy of a particular set of criticisms concerning racism, sexism, peace or whatever – however valid these may be in another context.

The teacher's role is one which takes place in a series of socially-separated, yet interlocking contexts.[4] The process of a critique which realises itself immanently as changed social practices is one which involves an interaction among intellectual critique (which is the fruit of reflection), educational processes where reflection is shared and criticised, organisational structures of movements for greater public and

democratic participation in discussion and decision-making and processes of personal and inter-personal reflection and critique aimed at
personal development.

Concrete contexts exist for such activities and have their own existing
hierarchical social structures and norms. When one is working within
one such structure, to develop, say, a critical theorem at the intellectual
level about another structure or process, it is necessary to remind
oneself that one's mode of working is conditioned not by the situation
which is the object of critique but by the circumstances in which the
critique is being produced. For example, I am writing this book in a
university, but its subject matter is primarily the schools. The conditions
which govern and limit my activity in advancing the reconstructions
and critical theorems which this book contains are those which pertain
in an Australian university. Quite different conditions will govern the
process of the dissemination of these reflections. Similarly, one's
employment as a teacher in a school provides a context which interlocks
with, say, the context of the local community, in which the teacher may
be active in community movements.

The work of education is carried on at the level of the broad public
domain – the press, etc. – at the level of the institutional structures for
knowledge formation – scientific institutes, universities – at the level of
educational bureaucracies – the ministry of education, the school
district – at the level of the school – school boards, administration – at
the level of the community, and at the level of the classroom and
playground or campus. Any individual educator may operate mainly at
one level, but the state of affairs at the other levels will limit and
condition what is possible at that level.

The process of critique must go on at all levels with related but locally
appropriate strategies. To put it in a nutshell, the mistake of a lot of early
critical educational practice was to import the strategies appropriate to
politics into the classroom.

THE ADMINISTRATIVE CONTEXT

The administrative context of schooling is dominated by bureaucratic
and technicist images of administration. The result of this is the
proliferation of rituals whose function is only indirectly related to the
actual processes of administration but which have a more direct
function at the level of the management of legitimation. As Richard
Bates has pointed out as recently as 1988, 'standard texts in educational
administration adopt, virtually without exception, the rational organisation approach to schools.'[5] Such approaches to administration adopt a
perspective in which systems theory places the interest in system
steering and control above all else. This is not surprising when you

consider that the clients for such views of administration are typically principals or administrators, who have been shown consistently to be obsessed with problems of control. Nor is it surprising to find that the predominant form of knowledge in such approaches is control-oriented knowledge, usually in the behaviourist form.

Now, it has been argued that control-oriented knowledge is not necessarily an inappropriate form of knowledge in human affairs. The crucial questions concern the degree to which the knowledge available to administrators is confined to this form of knowledge, and the degree to which the particular theories employed overreach their validity or contain strongly one-sided and ideological analyses. A concentration on the technical form of action may not necessarily be in the interests of system effectiveness. It may be more in the interests of lowering administrator anxiety than anything else. But the effectiveness of education systems is achieved through what they achieve in classrooms. The penetration of classroom life by system imperatives steered by bureaucratic power and market incentives can only destroy the pedagogical relationship by industrialising it. Just as the individual teacher needs to exercise pedagogical tact and restraint, so the administrator needs to exercise administrative tact and restraint. There is an irreducible field of pedagogical freedom without which the pedagogical relationship is not possible. Indeed, without such freedom there can be no act of teaching as such, and no need for teachers, except as supervisors of ranks of computer consoles and administrators of standardised tests.

Perhaps the idea of decentralisation, and the separation of those functions which need to be performed by administrators from those which do not, might permit a reconciliation between teachers and administrators and, at the same time, lower the anxiety level of administrators. Questions which arise at the school level do not all find their echo at the national level, at least in a society characterised by democratic pluralism. At each level – school, district, nation – the participants have interests in the level above which can be expressed by structures of representation. Decentralised structures of this kind may have other benefits, too. The common belief, that the larger the scale over which a bureaucrat tries to exert control, the less adequate the information available to him or her, is quite valid. The only will-formation processes that will succeed are those forms of administration which devolve processes that are dependent on a flow of detailed local or specialised knowledge to the local or specialised level.

For such democratic flexibility to work, organisations need to be able to learn through critique. As Argyris has shown, it is difficult for organisations to learn.[6] Max Miller's discussion of collective learning processes canvasses some of the limitations of personality and communication structures which block such learning.[7] Administrators are threatened by the new, and by the possibility of fields of action independent of their direct control. They are more comfortable with risk minimisation strategies. They make problems 'undiscussable and then make their undiscussability undiscussable' (Argyris, 1980: 20). Argyris argues that organisations have trouble changing their learning level – that is, learning in ways which require changed administrative arrangements as opposed simply to changing the quantity of existing resource inputs. Miller points to an intolerance of ambiguity, to ethnocentric organisation of the personality, and to collective limitations on discourse as causes of various types of limitation of the rationality of collective learning.

With Miller, Argyris finds that people fear those who criticise existing ways of doing things or suggest new patterns of practice. They are typically labelled 'nuts', 'foolish' or 'abrasive' no matter how carefully they try to avoid these perceptions or how successful their innovations ultimately are.[8] The crime consists in the advocating of change. Even corporation presidents in one of Argyris' groups reported fear of encouraging significant changes in the level of maturity of relationships in their own companies. One of the major problems Argyris found was that the ideology of organisations seldom matched the real motivations and goals of participants (espoused theories versus theories-in-use). Theories-in-use are difficult to deal with because they are usually unacknowledged. In terms of the phenomenological terminology employed in Chapter 4, such theories were a taken-for-granted part of the life–world of organisational participants, while espoused theories often functioned as a smokescreen for real motivations and needs.

One of the most important elements of technicist ideologies of administration is the 'naturalisation' of administrative processes. This is accomplished by the employment of physical metaphors and images to refer to processes which are actually communicative and cultural – 'span of control', information 'flow', 'input', 'output', etc.[9] Education systems, viewed concretely, are largely symbolic systems. Strictly speaking, most of the processes which take place in them could take place in the open air rather than in buildings or with laboratory equipment. They are appropriately analysed in terms of systems of symbolic action.[10] Their forms and structures are symbolic. Their oppressions are symbolically mediated oppressions. Their vulnerability to critique is essentially a vulnerability to ideology critique. In the last few decades such critique has begun to become effective; small wonder we are hearing calls to purge the system of critical voices.

THE CURRICULUM CONTEXT

In curriculum decision-making, it may not be possible for teachers to operate in an unconstrained way, but in every subject there are possibilities for effective, prudent and empowering critique. Every subject has its own internal contradictions and problems. An ideology critique that is guided by social and historical theory can identify central concepts and images of prevailing understandings of national history, science, art, etc. A necessary but not sufficient condition for effective critique is that it focus on logically and conceptually central aspects of forms of knowledge. Indeed, as Habermas has argued, this is the only epistemic road open to critique.[11] Many of the contradictions and *aporias* of existing forms of knowledge are closely related to topical issues and public debates and controversies. Thus, for instance, it would be possible to bring students to a more adequate understanding of science as a fallible, historical human activity if their attention were drawn to scientific controversies and the role of political problem-solving in them. However, conservatives like Spaemann are right in identifying the danger of pursuing critique in such a way as to destroy young people's faith in the possibility of rational learning. While it may not be necessary, as Spaemann holds, to master an existing discipline, complete with ideological distortions, before criticising it, it might, indeed, be worse entirely to dismiss it before mastering it.

Critique should not attempt to negate the form of knowledge by wide-ranging, but vague charges of 'ideology', but should find specific and detailed problems within a body of knowledge, point to alternative findings in some cases, examine and make precise the limits of method and generally contribute towards the development of a more valid and balanced view of the state of the art, free from dogmatism. In this way the student who arrives near the frontiers of the form of knowledge, perhaps at the undergraduate level, does so with a sensibility of the limitations and problems of a historically emerging, fallible and tentative body of knowledge. The problem with Spaemann's view is that uncritical mastery of existing disciplines offers no hope that learners will suddenly undergo a change of attitude, becoming sceptical and analytical about their ideas, or that they will suddenly be able to display the courage to criticise, after having hidden this virtue away for so long.

A mature capacity to deal with doubt and to hold one's beliefs without absolutising them or abandoning all warranted assertion in the face of nihilism and relativism is the aim of critical education. There is a deep, inner connection between maturity in knowledge and ego autonomy, especially in those areas of knowledge which relate to our professional lives, and upon which we are dependent in a day to day way.

Thus, the curriculum context has a number of dimensions; it

interlocks with the child's problem context and the context of pedagogical restraint. The royal road into pedagogically adequate ideology critique is the teacher's social analysis of the background to the problem situations and definitions which the child perceives and presents, either within the context of those parts of the curriculum where children are free to choose their own problems, or the context of the problems the child meets within a pre-decided subject matter. This analysis provides the possibility of redefinition and changed or broadened perceptions of the original problem. Common types of redefinition might include a change in the perception of a problem from seeing it as the outcome of natural and inevitable characteristics of the self or the situation (e.g. because I'm a girl or because that's not a natural way to act) to seeing it as a product of human definition (e.g. the gender role changes historically and cross-culturally or most adolescent boys masturbate). Another common type of redefinition involves broadening perceptions, by showing the connections of a problem with other issues, and by connecting one's experience with the experience of others (e.g. showing correlations between crime and poverty).

No prescription by governments should prevent teachers from answering students' questions honestly, from addressing the concerns which inevitably arise, and arise at precisely those points in their lives connected with the structures of domination with which ideology critique deals. There is no need to go looking for opportunities for critique. If you encourage open communication about perceived problems, such opportunities will emerge and at precisely the theoretically appropriate locations.

THE DEVELOPMENTAL CONTEXT: SELF AND OTHER

One of the most effective safeguards against the dogmatic imposition of critique with its threat of nihilistic personality development is the recognition that the main role of counter-factual ideals is not as models for practice but as aids to analysis. Such ideals, used as models for practice, negate everything in the present state of affairs. But in any historical context they need not negate everything equally, providing the developmental reconstruction is taken seriously at both the personal and social levels. The combination of the two critical reconstructions provides a safeguard against negativity because the ideal of perfectly rational interaction, which is a *teleological* ideal (i.e. an ideal end-state) is tempered by the reconstruction of a series of stages which lead towards it. Certainly, in so far as even the general idea of a developmental progression is preserved, rather than a notion of necessary stages, it is possible to locate an existing situation on such a progression, and confine critique to the obstacles to taking the next step. In such a context, it is possible to be positive about each next step, despite any relative distance from the ideal.

What has been said earlier about the curriculum context must be modified in the light of the developmental context. One must not preach Hegel's logic to ten-year-olds. The student's level of problem perception must not be overridden by the teacher's cognitively or emotionally more mature levels of critique. Rather, the students must gradually broaden their problem perceptions, and develop their critique of false 'naturalism' in accordance with the pace of their own development.

A further safeguard lies in the self-criticism of the professional community. At present this safeguard is at best weak. How often do we find ourselves speaking scathingly about some proposal by educators of good will which is, objectively, as it were, progressive, because it is not well-theorised, or because it is a little naive politically, or simply because we are jealous that they have got a grant we feel should have come to us? How often do we fail to speak out about practices and performances or fail to open up our own classroom practices to student and peer scrutiny?

But perhaps the greatest professional failure in the field of education, outside the school, is the failure of professional discourse in the community of educational researchers. For this to be remedied, there must be a critical re-theorising of the role of the educational academic and of the contribution of educational intellectuals, wherever situated, to reflection in schools and the public domain.

THE CRITICAL RECONSTRUCTION OF EDUCATIONAL RESEARCH

A rational reconstruction of the full range and complexity of issues in educational research is beyond the scope of a single book. All that can be done here is to make a few programmatic suggestions. In any case, the German language literature on critical educational thought has paid a great deal of attention, some would say too much attention, to methodological questions, including those which are asked at a sufficiently universal and transcendental level to be properly called reconstructive.[12]

The following suggestions are confined to two aspects of this reconstruction – the need to re-theorise or reconstruct general methodological understandings in educational research and the need for a reconstruction of the cognitive politics of educational research, particularly through teacher and student involvement.

THE EDUCATIONAL RESEARCH COMMUNITY

The educational research community is characterised by excessive individualism, coupled with a failure by many to engage in a rational debate or contribute towards the development of an informed educational public domain. It is also marked by the adoption of obscurantist and defensive postures by those who have identified themselves with the mainstream (in the English-speaking world) empiricist paradigm of the field. I hasten to add that, in the English-speaking domain, it has not been critical thought which has produced this defensiveness, because by and large the mainstream has not seen fit to enter into any kind of rational engagement with critics, as Bates has recently shown.[13] No, it has been put on the defensive by neoconservatism itself, which has seen the mainly liberal implications of mainstream research as a dangerous product of an unnecessary form of state expenditure.

The excessive individualism of the field is a corollary of non-engagement. Each researcher seems to go his or her own way without reference to anything other than the narrowest conception of the relevant 'literature'. The hypothetico-deductive game of playing twenty questions with nature continues, as ad hoc hypotheses, plucked out of the taken-for-granted consciousness of the land of 'discovery' are sent like forward scouts into the land of 'verification', not usually to be lost without trace, but to come back fatter and richer than when they set out, smiling and confirmed, leaving their generals uncertain whether they have gone over to the enemy – untruth – or not.[14]

Research conferences seldom generate a genuine engagement between very different positions. Factions snipe at each other, but seldom fight it out. In the English-speaking educational domain, one longs for just one *Positivismusstreit*. There is little sense of a common responsibility, across ideological differences, for avoiding the production of so many spurious confirmations of hypotheses. At an international conference of physicists, one would not be surprised at the emergence of a near-consensus that certain lines of research were promising or should be given up (at least temporarily) as a waste of resources until such time as someone devised a new approach to them. Such agreements can be reached in open discussion, across national boundaries, and are often remarkably effective, despite having only moral force. Educational researchers do not seem to talk about such matters. In a not isolated example, it was possible for more than 700, yes, 700, studies of the effects of class size on academic outcomes to be carried out, more than 140 of them on a large scale, and employing quite similar methodologies, without even a near-consensus on the central question. One of the central problems of this wasteful process is non-engagement with critique (such as it is). It is not that some journals in the field do not carry occasional 'exchanges' and so on, but that these do not often add up to an effective engagement and response, and they are often across narrow rather than wide critical distances. I have argued elsewhere that the techniques of empirical meta-analysis within the empiricist paradigm would be better employed in a systematic examination of the co-variation of results and methods than in accumulating dubious estimates of effect size across groups of studies employing similar methods.[15]

Never in the history of science has a research community produced so many 'results' or 'findings' with so little effect as have educational researchers since the advent of the electronic computer – one would have thought that there would, by now, be a thirst for critique, rather than a burgeoning of defensive claims about research's effectiveness.

RECONSTRUCTING METHODOLOGY

Changes within the philosophy of science in the last few decades have produced a very different image of science from that upon which much of the present self-understanding of the educational research mainstream is predicated. The choice of one theory over another, and even the testing of a single hypothesis are no longer to be seen as cut and dried processes. There exists no unequivocal logic of theory choice or hypothesis testing. Talk of 'elegance' or even 'coherence' simply begs the question of how these things are to be specified. While arguments can be mounted in favour of preferred doctrines of, say, coherence, these are not themselves either deductively unassailable or testable empirically – they are in the domain of reasonable belief rather than demonstrable truth. While debate on such questions continues, Habermas has argued that we should take a step back into the scientific community itself – we should take the argumentative activity of Popper's critical community seriously.

For instance, an account of experimental methods has typically played a leading role in methods textbooks. There has been a more or less subtle preference for these methods based on the argument that they allow theoretical precision, by permitting a focus on one or a small number of hypotheses, by allowing control of known interacting variables, and by allowing control over the conditions under which the focal theory is examined. They have generally been seen as superior to other methods as instruments for theory-building.[16] Indeed, a recent review of their role in educational research, after canvassing many of the objections which have been made to experiments having such a key place in the methods repertoire, attempted to resolve the differences in views about this by distinguishing between theory-building and applied research and reserving for experiments a pre-eminent role in the former.[17]

Experiments have also been the preferred methods in educational research both in practice and in the expressed or implied preferences of research fund granting bodies such as the US Office of Education and the Australian Education Research and Development Committee (ERDC, now defunct), as judged by published research and documents containing advice to researchers produced by the agencies.[18]

It is possible to undertake an immanent critique of the prevailing view of the role of the experiment from the standpoint of the recently emerging post-empiricist account of science and scientific method. Such a critique clears the way for a more critical reconstruction. Now the problem for the prevailing view of the role of the experiment is that it rests on an outdated view of both the theory-building process and the logical properties of theory-testing. The inductivist view that theories were built by the accumulation of facts, or even tested hypotheses, has been rejected. The hypothetico-deductive successor to it has also been rejected, even by its founders. While such processes may play a part in theory-building, and theory change, it is widely accepted that it is a far more complex and holistic process than is suggested by the earlier models.

The Quine–Duhem thesis asserts that we can never test a single hypothesis anyway, but always test the whole background of our ontological and methodological assumptions about the world and ourselves.[19] One of the consequences of this is that the usefulness of a method, which allows the degree of focus and control of variables that experiment does, is dependent upon the level of confidence we are justified in having in the background assumptions of the focal theory to which we are attending at any time. In a field of study in which little systematic theory exists, or where there is little scientific agreement, the precision of the experimental method can be a liability. That is, even if the testing of hypotheses were the royal road of science, experiments could not necessarily take us down that road.

This conclusion must be placed in juxtaposition with what we know about the state of the art in educational research in general. There is no agreement that *any* reliable background theory exists in instructional research, as is evident from Cronbach's view, summarised by Gage, that the 'complexities of teaching have been shown to be intractable. Any hope of mastering these complexities is forlorn,' and Gage's only qualified disagreement with Cronbach.[20] Similar remarks have been made more recently by researchers on both sides of the Atlantic.

Perhaps even more serious is the fact that there is no agreed set of understandings about the nature of the interaction which occurs in the educational research process itself, at least, not one that is reflexively based on research. The existing literature theorises the activity of researchers in epistemological terms and not as social agents. That is, for the most part, educational researchers are theorised as privileged epistemological actors within a theoretical model which is *conceptually* quite distinct from the theory in which the behaviour of teachers and pupils is theorised.

However, if experimental research is not to play such a key role, what is to replace it? Perhaps we cannot yet answer this question. The work of re-theorising the repertoire of methods, including experiments, has not yet been completed. One candidate, many have argued, must be some form of field method with a discursive ethnographic intent. While such methods may lack the degree of theoretical focus of experimental approaches they have the advantage of having greater ecological validity in the present state of our theoretical development.[21]

To an extent, the critique of hypothetico–deductive research made by British ethnographic researchers runs parallel to the argument of this chapter, but there is one crucial area of divergence. Much of that critique, while arguing for a shift to naturalistic, field-based methods, remains wedded to an empiricist understanding of ethnographic research.[22] It is beside the purpose of the present argument to become involved in an assessment of the validity of the criticisms of 'interactionist empiricism' or the lack of it.[23] It is sufficient to note that the underlying epistemology of the British approach is empiricist and that we are here exploring the significance of post-empiricist views for educational research. Whatever we may decide concerning the charge that interactionism, because it is empiricist, is weak when it comes to macroscopic social explanations of interaction patterns, the fact remains that this movement is not particularly characterised by theoretical holism or reflexivity, although it has given some attention to the interactive nature of the research process.

Powerful and innovative arguments in favour of the primacy of ethnographic research have also been advanced recently by Australian philosophers Walker and Evers.[24] However, it is enough to say here that before the nature of the problem becomes clear a great deal of development of the social theory of method needs to be carried out. As Walker argues, the social theory of method is closely connected with the epistemological questions we seek to answer, indeed, it is part of the same theory.

Two areas of research method which might seem more central than experiment in the post-empiricist understanding of method are ethnographic research and interviews. Both of these areas of method have been extensively theorised within the empiricist understanding of method, so it might be useful to demonstrate some of the practical implications of a post-empiricist view of method if one of these areas of method were to be taken and reconstructed from a post-empiricist viewpoint. The method selected is the interview, mainly because it provides a more compact and clear cut case than the more difficult case of ethnographic method. In addition, interviews are themselves a key component of ethnographic methods.

One of the main methods of immanent critique of methodology is the location of the research process as a human process, with its own cultural and social aspects. Once Popper's rigid separation of such a historical understanding of the knowing process from all considerations of epistemic questions is rejected, it is possible to confront the epistemological pretension of research with its own biography and history. The research interview must be theorised reflexively, that is, as a social process in the same world as other social processes, if it is also to be theorised epistemologically, that is in terms of its role with regard to the validity of theoretical inference and the truth of theories.

One of the purposes of theorising the research interview is eventually to extract meaning from it more readily, in somewhat the same way as one might extract meaning from any other interactively produced text. To do this, it is necessary to understand how and why the interactants have produced the text which they have produced. For the purposes of illustration it may be useful to take only one aspect of textual structure and examine it in some detail to explore how the research interview might be more completely theorised. The aspect of the interview selected is that of 'coherence'. Coherence refers to the way in which the temporally separated parts of a text are connected to each other in orderly and meaningful ways, including the parts of the texts for which different participants are responsible.

Of course, coherence is not the only feature of an interactively produced text upon which we might focus. But, it is useful to focus on coherence in the texts produced by interviewer/interviewee interaction for much the same reasons that, earlier, we focused on coherence in theory testing – the significance of an interaction must be judged holistically. It is enough to say that coherence is a very general and necessary feature of texts-which-make-sense to participants and that questions of coherence are sufficiently rich and central to permit a wide range of social interaction to be explored.

Coherence in a text is not a simple matter and it has been theorised in different ways. We approach it here from an ethnomethodological standpoint. Coherence can be understood in terms of form – as patterns of rules that interactants follow in order to talk coherently to each other. Alternatively, and in a complementary way, it can be understood as strategy – the structure which emerges from a creative use of rules and standard patterns used as resources to achieve goals. Rules and patterns in talk vary from turn-taking rules, through rules which connect clusters of utterances together by the creation of expectations (e.g. questions can create some expectation of answers), to large-scale structures of interaction such as classroom lessons, conversations, legal trials, and interviews. But rules and patterns may be transformed and used creatively. As in a game, there may remain strategic options, within the limitations of rules, which are not themselves rule-governed. In any case, some situations may permit the evocation of rules or sets of rules which are clearly contradictory.[25]

The particular aspects of coherence on which I wish to focus now has been called 'alignment'.[26] Alignment talk is speaker meta-communication which defines speaker social and communicative roles. It falls into Habermas' category of 'communicative' speech acts. Several species of alignment talk have been identified. Some kinds of alignment talk seem to be aimed at repairing breaches of expectations – disclaimers, justifications, excuses and discussion of motives, for instance. Other kinds appear, more generally, meta-communicatively to manage talk by constituting its ongoing character reflexively as it develops – among these are 'formulations', 'side sequences' and 'my side tellings'.[27] Alignment talk functions meta-communicatively in that it provides a framework for the interpretation of 'the talk in progress' which instructs participants how that talk should be taken. How is research interview talk to be taken by participants? And what meta-communicative devices can be found in that talk to indicate the ways in which such talk should be taken? The answers to these questions are essential for the development of a theory of the research interview. Note that the two questions are not equivalent, because it is not in the devices employed in talk alone that we may seek answers to these questions. Aspects of the expectations and background knowledge participants bring to the research interview are important sources of information concerning the interpretation of such interviews, even if such expectations are never manifested in a specific conversational device or in any specific part of the micro-detail of an interview (as opposed to manifested in its overall structure, direction, import, etc.). What we are engaged in here is an exercise in empirical pragmatics with critical intent.

SOME FUNCTIONS OF ALIGNMENT DEVICES IN JOB INTERVIEWS

In her analysis of job interviews, Sandra Ragan lists seven types of alignment devices – accounts, formulations, meta-talk, side sequences, meta-communicative digressions, qualifiers and 'you knows'.[28] Accounts function to defend and justify behaviour and dispositions which the interviewee judges the interviewer might deem inappropriate. Formulations function to interpret, summarise and recognise the progress of talk. These are used mainly by interviewers to manage the talk of the job applicants. Meta-talk, such as classifications, remediation, direction, requesting and agenda setting is used mainly by interviewers. Side sequences and meta-communicative digressions are also used mainly by interviewers, to achieve consensus, to clarify talk and seek rapport. Finally, the use of qualifiers and 'you knows', particularly by job applicants, appears consistent with previous analyses of the role of such verbal fillers as an indicator of powerlessness.[29] Ragan concluded that:

1. Interviewers use primarily those aligning actions that assert control over talk and thus that typify them as the more powerful communicator.
2. Applicants use those aligning actions that signify tentativeness and powerlessness – markers of low status communicators.

How much do research interviewers, or at least, some research interviewers, resemble Ragan's sample of job interviewers? The point is not so much the power asymmetry of this talk structure as the fact that such asymmetry is both taken for granted and accomplished by talk devices which are also less than deliberate and consciously recognised to be doing the work that they are doing, which leads us to ask to what degree research interviewers, even in supposedly 'non-directive' and 'sensitive' interviews may not be employing similar devices with similar, if less obvious, effect? One of the virtues of an ethnomethodological approach to the analysis of research interviews, rather than an approach from the point of view of any other variety of symbolic interactionism, is that ethnomethodologists have, to date, more fully developed the analysis of the tacit dimensions of discourse than any other group of theorists.

Ethnomethodology, in common with Habermas' theory of communicative action, moves us to ask what dispositions participants might bring to an interaction which could lead them to pursue strategies of the kind manifest in the talk structure. But, parting company with ethnomethodology, we might then ask such a question within a wider social and comparative analysis of job givers and job seekers, across different labour market conditions or labour market locations of job applicants, and be on our way towards a theory of the power relations of the structures of employment opportunity in our kind of society. Under what circumstances, then, do research interviewers and research interviewees come together in our kind of society? Any adequate theory of the research interview must include a social mapping of the research interview – its market conditions, if you like. And, of course, we already know something about the broad features of such a map – most research interviews are carried out by middle- to high-status interviewers upon low-status interviewees. Can goodwill or paternalism on the part of those interviewing 'down' the social structure offset the emergence of the kind of effect noted above in job interviews? Clearly, the task of theorising research interviews must back up into our theory and our interviewees' theories of research-in-society. We cannot escape the fact that our presuppositions about the very enterprise of social research, our assumptions about the usefulness of social science theory, about social literacy and enlightenment, indeed, about the worthwhileness of what we are doing, will all play a part, along with similar or dissimilar assumptions on the part of those with whom we interact in the course of research, in constituting the research process as a constructed outcome. Theoretical links of this kind permit us to raise again, and for the first time in a manner which is not theoretically ad hoc, that complex set of problems associated with the ethics of research and formerly addressed variously in terms of questions of 'ownership' of information, confidentiality and feedback of results to participants. Such matters become much more clearly associated with the very scientificity of our enterprise rather than being viewed, in the positivist manner, as a separate, perhaps optional, moral luxury, associated with the personal and individual ethical sensitivity of particular researchers. What I am arguing is that, seen in this way, such questions are intrinsic to issues of scientific validity rather than separate from them – a conclusion which might be reached from Habermas' analysis of the phenomenology of communicative interaction discussed in Chapter 6, but which has been reached here independently through immanent critique.

Thus, in locating the research interview in a comparative and macroscopic framework we are doing more than create the basis of a useful typology of research interviews which could be employed to 'calibrate' our research interpretations of each type of interview. For the paradox of all critical methodologies is that they systematically raise questions of practice, and normative questions in general, as a part of research practice itself, not as an ethical adjunct to a central cognitive purpose, but as an integrated part of the scientific transformation process characteristic of a theorising species which cannot know without simultaneously transforming itself.

TECHNICAL QUESTIONS

A corollary of what has been argued above is that there are no 'technical' questions in the usual sense. The appropriate model for research is constitutive, that is, all research interaction is a form of action and shares many of the key characteristics of so-called 'action research', whether participants in the research set out consciously to change each other or not. Indeed, while the difference between unintended action in the research situation and the intended action of 'action research' must be noted, we can recognise that the very term 'action research' is a part of a positivist lexicon of research terminology. What is more, it is argued that a failure to recognise that research is of this order of human activity will be associated with a concomitant failure to draw meaningful conclusions in the process of interpreting research experiences. That is, whatever the degree to which we focus on or separate out a theoretical/ cognitive outcome for our research activity, and relegate to the sidelines the outcomes of our research which involve some changes to the consciousness and way of life of researcher and researched, a recognition of the nature of research as action is quite crucial to the achievement of the cognitive objective.

So-called technical questions – how to record the interview, how long to give it, how to analyse the record, how to aggregate or generalise across interviews, how to relate such aggregations to the production of general descriptions or to the modification of pre-existing explanatory theories – must be dealt with with one eye on the purposes and goals, in the research interactions, rather than with both eyes, as is customary, on the researcher's epistemological goals.

Our hitherto non-existent theory of the forms of action available to research subjects in specific opportunities for research interaction and of the strategies which such subjects might be pursuing, will condition, alongside other elements of our total theory of language and interaction, the kinds of research decision we might make in regard to so-called technical questions. As many researchers know from experience, the appearance of a researcher at the door of a house, or in a school, or elsewhere, can be construed as an opportunity – an opportunity to let the makers of a product know what's what, to let head office know what the problems 'out here' are, to let 'them' have an earful – to tap just one quite rich vein of possible strategies for research subjects. Obviously, considerations of this kind have implications for research procedures, which is not to suggest that interviewees will pay the slightest attention to the most elaborate disclaimers and/or preambles to the so-called 'actual' interview. But they also have implications for sampling procedures, for recording the preamble to an interview and the reaction to it as well as the interview proper, and much more. However, the point is not that we can make a definitive list of more and more elaborate procedures to guard against misinterpretation, but that we cannot effectively safeguard a one-sided approach to the research interview at all. The only procedures in which we might find some safe refuge are procedures that let research subjects in on the research 'secrets', that is, procedures which maximise openness and authenticity rather than manipulativeness and instrumentality. In short, what some writers on research method have argued for on ethical and political grounds is being recommended here on scientific grounds.

The implications of this for teachers and students is profound. Social research is, after all, an activity in which the human species looks at itself. It can serve the interest of emancipation in two senses: it can serve in the sense of the general evolution of the species and it can serve in the sense of the emancipation of particular sections or classes of members from domination by others or by structures which operate in the interests of others. This general, knowledge-forming interest in self-understanding is the broadest and most universal interest since it is the only interest which can accord with the individual existential interests of everyone. The knowledge-forming interest in control or even the understanding of human meanings are both capable of a less than universal coincidence with people's existential interests, that is, they can be used one sidedly, whereas universalism is a defining feature of the emancipatory interest. It makes no sense to be emancipated and to dominate another, since, as Hegel has shown, to be dominated or to dominate are both a form of limitation. Let us assume, for a moment, that the narrower goals of instrumental and hermeneutic knowledge are valid in their limited domains, that is, that they permit some control over our relationship with the natural environment and some understanding of cultures with which we must deal. Even so, because the associated research interests are not necessarily serving universalisable existential interests it is possible for them to provide knowledge which can be used by one section of the species to its own advantage or even against the interests of another. Of course, the self-image of such knowledge forms is deficient if limited to a simple mirror image, in which, for instance, instrumental reason takes an instrumental view of itself, etc. Such knowledge is at best incomplete, because it omits those areas in its potential self-understanding which do not serve the interests of the group to which it belongs. It is also biased or distorted because it understands its object from the standpoint of the existential interests sedimented in the consciousness of the researchers who belong to the dominant group.

When research is designed to pursue only technical or hermeneutic goals, it is encumbent upon teachers, whose co-operation is necessary for the research to proceed, to make two judgements. The first is a judgement about whether or not they should co-operate with the researchers. Such research is not necessarily a 'good thing'. Teachers must make an analysis of the politics of the context of research before they can make a strategic judgement whether co-operation would be contrary to their own interests and those of their students. Much the same might be said about 'qualitative research', which can function as a form of market research for administrators, who can then package otherwise objectionable policies in more attractive ways.

But teachers must also make a judgement about the validity of the research, even within its general methodological context. The general cognitive context of an interest in control may determine that the research will try to identify 'behavioural variables' and their relationships, but even within such a paradigm, the interests of a particular funding source, say, administrators, may mean that only certain behaviourable variables are studied, rather than others. In a similar, but more subtle way, the research process itself may be influenced, and, as discussed in respect of the interview example, communicatively distorted so that the understanding of the meaning of research subjects becomes a caricature of the reality.

As far as research in schools is concerned, only teachers can act as guardians of their own and their students' interests. Researchers, by and large, cannot be trusted to do this, since their existential interests lie elsewhere. This does not mean that research should not take place, but it does suggest that it is only when the subjects of research are able to negotiate the research *design* and process that we can be reasonably sure of an outcome which does not harm their interests. The researcher *or the critic's* understanding of him/herself as a person with benevolent intentions towards teachers and students may be valuable, but it is not, in itself, a sufficient safeguard. Only the individual has an internal and fundamental relation to his or her own self interest. Some would say that it is only through the security of this relation that altruism is made possible.

One of the implications of this position is that the 'teachers as researchers' movement may be regarded as advocating a practice that is not merely an optional extra to existing research practices but one which is essential and central to the character of valid collective reflection in the educational research community.[30]

NOTES

1. R. M. Rilke, *Poems from the Book of Hours*, trans. Babette Deutsche, New York: New Directions Press, 1941: 43, reprinted with the permission of New Directions Press.
2. W. Fischer, *Schule als parapädagogische Organisation*, Kastellaun: Henn, 1978.
3. J. Seeley, 'The making and taking of social problems: Toward an ethical stance', *Social Problems*, **14**, 1967: 382–9.
4. K. Mollenhauer, *Erziehung und Emanzipation*, München: Juventa, 1968: 75 *et passim*. See also R. Bates, 'Morale and motivation: Myth and reality in educational administration', *Educational Administration Review*, **1** (1), 1983: 26–52.
5. R. Bates, 'Is there a new paradigm in educational administration?', paper presented to the Annual Conference of the American Educational Research Association, 1988, C. Argyris, 'Making the undiscussable and its undiscussability discussable', *Public Administration Review*, May/June, 1980: 205–13, 'Theories of action that inhibit

learning', *American Psychologist*, **31** (9), 1976: 638–54.

6. C. Argyris, *op. cit.*

7. M. Miller, 'Kollektive Erinnerungen und Gesellschaftliche Lernprozesse', Colloquium über Nachkreigantisemitismus der Reimerstiftung, Bad Homburg, March, 1988.

8. C. Argyris, *op. cit.*

9. C. Offe, *Industry and Inequality*, London: Edward Arnold, 1979. J. Nias and S. Groundwater-Smith (eds) *The Enquiring Teacher: Supporting and sustaining teacher research*, London: Falmer Press, 1988.

10. P. Gronn, 'On studying administrators at work', *Educational Administration Quarterly*, **20** (1), 1984: 115–29.

11. *K & HI*: 69: 'Objectivism deludes the sciences . . . it thus conceals the a priori constitution of the facts. It can no longer be effectively overcome from without, from the position of a repurified epistemology, but only by a methodology that transcends its own boundaries.'

12. B. Bühner and A. Birnmeyer, *Ideologie und Diskurs: Zur Theorie von Jürgen Habermas und ihrer Rezeption in der Pädagogik*, Frankfurt: Haag und Herchen, 1982.

13. R. Bates, 1988.

14. See D. F. Hamilton, 'Educational research and the shadow of J. S. Mill', in J. V. Smith and D. F. Hamilton (eds) *The Meritocratic Intellect*, Aberdeen: Aberdeen University Press, 1980. D. Morrison and R. Henkel (eds) *The Significance Test Controversy*, London: Butterworths, 1970.

15. G. Glass *et al. School Class Size*, Beverley Hills; Sage, 1982. R. E. Young, 'Ideology critique: Necessary complement to empirical meta-analysis', *Discourse*, **4** (2), 1984: 52–8.

16. F. Kerlinger, *Foundations of Behavioural Research* (2nd edn) New York: Holt, Rhinehart and Winston, 1973.

17. D. Phillips, 'Toward an evaluation of the experiment in educational contexts', *Educational Researcher*, June/July, 1981: 13–20.

18. *Ibid.* and R. E. Young, 1984.

19. P. Duhem, in H. Feigl and M. Brodbeck (eds) *Readings in the Philosophy of Science*, New York: Scribner, 1953.

20. L. Cronbach *et al.* (eds) *Toward Reform of Program Evaluation*, San Francisco: Jossey-bass, 1980. N. Gage, *The Scientific Basis of the Art of Teaching*, New York: Teachers' College Press, 1978.

21. U. Bronfennbrenner, 'Towards an experimental ecology of human development', *American Psychologist*, **32**, 1977: 513–30.

22. A. Hargreaves, 'The significance of classroom coping strategies' in L. Barton and R. Meighan (eds) *Sociological Interpretations of Schooling and Classrooms: A reappraisal*, Driffield: Nafferton Books, 1978. G. Whitty, 'Sociology and the problem of radical educational change: Towards a reconceptualization of the "new" sociology of education', in M. Flude and J. Ahier (eds) *Educability, Schools and Ideology*, London: Croom Helm, 1974.

23. M. Hammersley, 'On interactionist empiricism', in P. Woods (ed) *Pupil Strategies: Explorations in the Sociology of the School*, London: Croom Helm, 1980.

24. J. Walker, 'The politics of control in educational research', *mimeo*, University of Sydney, Department of Education, 1984. J. Walker and C. Evers, 'Professionalisation and epistemic privilege in the politics of educational research', a paper delivered to the Annual Conference of the Australian Association for Research in Education, Canberra, 1983.

25. R. Craig and K. Tracy, *Conversational Coherence: Form, Structure and Strategy*, Beverley Hills: Sage, 1983.

26. S. Ragan, 'Alignment and conversational coherence', in R. Craig and K. Tracy, *op. cit.*

27. J. Heritage and D. Watson, 'Formulations as conversational objects', in G. Psathas (ed) Everyday Language: Studies in Ethnomethodology, New York: Irvington, 1979. G. Jefferson, 'Side sequences', in D. Sudnow (ed) *Studies in Social Interaction*, New York: Free Press, 1972. A. Pomerantz, 'Telling my side: Limited access as a fishing device', *Sociological Inquiry*, **50**, 1980: 186–98.
28. S. Ragan, *op. cit.*
29. B. Erickson *et al.*, 'Speech style and impression formation in a court setting: The effects of "powerful" and "powerless" speech', *Journal of Experimental Social Psychology*, **14**, 1978: 266–79.
30. J. Nias and S. Groundwater-Smith, *op. cit.*

CHAPTER 8

THE ORGANISATION OF EDUCATIONAL ENLIGHTENMENT

> Imperfect action is better for men and societies than perfection in waiting, for errors wrought by action are cured by new action. And when the people acted upon are made true partners in the actions, and co-discoverers of the corrections of error, then . . . in spite of blunders, or even because of them, the vital energies are increased, confidence increases, experience builds towards wisdom, and, most potent of all principles and ideals, deep democracy, slowly wins the field.
>
> (J. Collier)[1]

Schools have always involved individual learning and development, but only in conditions of rapid social change does the need for organisational learning become readily apparent, because it is only then that the pressure to adapt brings normally subterranean theories-in-use to the surface where they can be changed. Educational research can be seen as a necessary part of the reflection which should guide both individual and organisational change, at least, if we are to raise the level of rationality at which organisations and individuals learn. In the previous chapter it was argued that reflection on the politics and validity problems of research leads us to greater recognition of teachers' and pupils' possible roles in it. Critical 'action research' – one of the most promising recent developments in critical theory of education – has been guided by a similar recognition of the potentially valuable role of teachers and learners in the processes of organisational change.

However, the action research example must be approached with some caution. Habermas, quite rightly, was suspicious of early calls for action research to become a new paradigm for educational and social research, on the grounds that they came from behavioural scientists who failed to recognise that alternative modes of understanding, such as the hermeneutic, were better adapted to the interactive reality of social science research activity.[2] Calls for action research, within the positivist framework were self-contradictory, since action research requires an interactive and communicative understanding of the research process.

Moser's later call for a new educational research paradigm based on critical action research appears to escape this stricture, since it relies on research procedures influenced by symbolic interaction and ideology critique, rather than control-oriented ones.[3] However, Moser's model may still be inadequate in a topsy-turvy way. It is inadequate because it fails to give a place to control-oriented knowledge at all (i.e. behavioural science research in education). To demonstrate why this is so, it would be necessary to take up Habermas' argument in *Knowledge and Human Interests* at some length, but this would result in a book-length epistemological excursus. All that will be attempted here is a sketch of such an argument.

As pointed out earlier, two things might be said about Habermas' identification of the three knowledge-forming interests and their accompanying research traditions. First, there has been a great deal of misunderstanding of Habermas' argument, even by those who sought to take it up and apply it.[4] Many such people came from a position of anti-scientism and anti-behaviourism – from the humanities. They seized on Habermas' critique of positivism (in the *Positivismusstreit*) to reject all forms of control-oriented knowledge in human affairs. But this was not Habermas' position (nor that of Adorno and Horkheimer before him). His critique was more subtle – it was a critique of the over-extension of the (positivist) self-understanding of the physical sciences, which worked less badly there than elsewhere, to the social world in all its aspects. This critique did not assert that there were no aspects of the human sciences where human beings might be treated like things, i.e. causally controlled, but that the cultural dimension of human life went beyond this level of understanding.

Second, it is often asserted that Habermas failed to criticise the positivist self-image of the physical sciences.[5] This is simply not true. The central thrust of Habermas' argument against Popper is that Popper did not take his recognition of the role of the community of critical discourse far enough. Elsewhere, Habermas advocates the employment of hermeneutic and critical understanding in the physical and biological sciences.[6] Clearly, he does not accept that control-oriented knowledge provides an adequate account of the human activity of doing physical science, which is a different thing from accepting that control-oriented knowledge can give you an account of the world of things and their interactions. The latter view appears to be one that Habermas adopts, but is it a flaw in his theory? Is there no residue of validity in the method and approach of nomothetic empirical science, despite its deficient self-understanding? Habermas approaches this question from a Peircian pragmatism, with a historically aware, fallibilist view of scientific theory and he reflexively imposes a communicative model of scientific consensus formation on the activity of the community of control-oriented inquiry.[7] This view can scarcely be said to be one which involves acceptance of the positivist research community's own self-image, but it does permit the retention of a notion that one of the possible bases of scientific theorising is the identification of stable, determinate relationships between empirically defined variables. Surely the validity of such an approach, however human and fallible in the execution, must rest on the ontological characteristics of the objects of research themselves. To the degree that there are, in fact, stable, determinate processes at work in human affairs, such an approach may have something to offer. It is premature to dismiss all empirical research in education, since the process of discourse is open to all arguments and all evidentiary considerations. Moser, among others, failed to recognise this. Action research cannot be *the* paradigm for educational research, since it is only one possible procedural realisation of hermeneutic and critical insights into the research process.

Other critical action researchers, such as Carr and Kemmis have also appeared to reject all alternatives, failing to make it entirely clear that technical research forms can and should play a role within broader critical research strategies.[8] This rejection, which would simultaneously be a rejection of all generalising research, tends to result in a corresponding restriction of action research to the microscopic or face-to-face level. A tendency, noted earlier, to fail to come to grips with the limitations of the ideal speech situation (ISS) as a critical tool, and an accompanying self-limitation of critique has also contributed to the impression of an unnecessarily narrow model of method.

DECENTRALISED LEARNING PROCESSES

For better or worse, we live in large-scale social systems. But a great deal of critical theory of education has been written as if social life consisted of an Arcadian village fantasy. Critical theory does not leave us without criteria for analysis at the system level. Different system configurations may be subjected to evaluation on the basis of criteria other than those of efficiency. For instance, large scale structures of co-ordination and social will-formation, such as those exemplified by democratic electoral processes (secret ballot, one person, one vote) may be evaluated in terms of their universalism. Among the questions which arise at this stage is whether each vote is of equal value. Similarly, the administrative processes which manage the day-to-day realisation of the democratically influenced social will may be evaluated in terms of their efficiency, fairness and impartiality, and so on. But a crucial criterion for the evaluation of the administration of a democratically influenced social will is whether or not the manner of administration preserves and enhances the *general* democratic participation in social will-formation or threatens it. There is an internal pedagogical link between administrative style and the learning level of social evolution represented by democracy – the level of will-formation based on open, rational discussion. Authoritarian administrative styles within an organisation important to people's lives, such as their workplace, or school, can diminish people's capacity for participation in other, more public processes of social development.

As was suggested in the previous chapter, the idea of the ISS can contribute, indirectly, to the analysis of structures which go beyond the face-to-face level of organisation. Structures can be evaluated in the light of their capacity to enhance truth, justice and authenticity at the level of the situated communicative action they enable or hinder. But it must be remembered that, in a given historical context, the fact that a structure limits the face-to-face realisation of, say, justice, is not by itself a sufficient basis for critique; if it were, critique would be idealistic and utopian. What the ISS can do is make such a state of affairs *accountable*, that is, it becomes problematic for critical analysis and must be accounted for in terms of historical circumstances. Perhaps conditions exist which mean that the degree of justice obtaining is all that is structurally possible until such time as other changes ensue. The argument that the proletariat must first express itself through a dictatorship until such time as unregenerated capitalists have been regenerated is an argument of this kind. The problem of safeguards remains – guarantees of increasing the degree of justice at the appropriate time, i.e. the first possible time. But some problems of participation in will-formation and meaning-creation remain; these are problems of scale: you cannot co-ordinate an organisation of the historical scale of modern societies on the basis of face-to-face discussion alone. The problem of safeguards is a problem of the expression of interests. The dictatorship of the proletariat provides no mechanism for the continuous democratic expression of the will of the whole proletariat and the vanguard of the proletariat cannot be trusted to preserve the interests of the proletariat they lead, or, at least, not to develop new interests, specifically as a vanguard in remaining as a vanguard. The problem becomes one of solving the problem of the expression of interests by those whose interests they are, while at the same time permitting a structure of co-ordination, even leadership.

Walker's development of John Burnheim's notion of democratic decentralisation or 'demarchy', and his application of it to curriculum decision-making provides a useful model for the further development of critical theory which permits the problem of its application to large-scale processes to be addressed.[9] Walker's approach is characterised by a Quinean epistemological pragmatism and he has also repeated Quine's adoption of materialist-behaviourism, but it is possible to set aside

Walker's materialism for the purposes of the present discussion, as Walker agrees.

But Habermas' endorsement of democratic problem-solving processes is based on a slightly different set of considerations from Walker's. Although Habermas would no doubt agree with the general Deweyian insight that democratic modes of problem-solving are superior to others, he does so on the basis of an argument about the inherent character of communicative acts rather than on that of Dewey's more pragmatic analysis. Habermas' analysis, while concurring with the Deweyian one, and for generally similar reasons, rests, additionally, on a specific analysis of the way in which intersubjectively criticiseable validity claims in cognitive, interpersonal and expressive validity domains are resolved in communicative action.

Walker's analysis is a development of Quine's more psychologistic account in the direction of a Luhmannian systems-theory. However, unlike Luhmann's theory, it is based on a typically Anglo-Saxon 'analytical materialism' which employs sophisticated extensions of 'physicalist or other scientistic background convictions [to] underwrite the demand that everything intuitively known be alienated from the perspective of a natural-scientific observer' (*PDM*: 384). In contrast, Habermas' analysis proceeds from a phenomenological recognition of the world seen by participants in a 'performatory attitude'. The difference is profound but often confusing to the scientific mind. Reflexively, it is that mind, and its attitudes, which is at stake here. Is the self image of participants, in the flow of participation, to be one of self as machine, and indeed, is it possible to *participate* while in such a state of mind, or are we to recognise that the scientific attitude is itself a [non-participatory] state of mind?

Walker's analysis still suffers from the problems of the philosophy of consciousness and the commitment to democracy in it is a product of the same methodological prohibition as is found in Luhmann's theory, of any notion of a consciousness embracing the whole of society. Of course, earlier subjective holisms created a merely fictive total consciousness, and one can see in the nature of differentiated societies that 'the very demanding types of knowledge directed to the totality of society occur at most within specialised systems of knowledge, but not at the centre of society, as a self-knowledge on the part of the whole society' (*PDM*: 376).

It is for this reason, among others, that effective social problem-solving demands a participatory model. This is expressed by Habermas in the concept of a public sphere as a sphere of intersubjectively criticisable validity claims which includes claims arising from existential interests. This intersubjective domain is a cultural object, a 'common consciousness, however diffuse and controversial it may be, [in which] the society can gain normative distance from itself and can react to perceptions of crisis' (*PDM*: 377).

It is through the universalisation of uncoerced participation in this domain that the existential experience and interests of all individuals are involved. In this context, a problem is regarded as solved (tentatively) when the validity claims inherent in a proposed solution are accepted by all participants. Democratic will-formation through an open public sphere is not merely a more efficient way to achieve problem solutions, which could also, in principle, be achieved by an elite. Nor is is a convenient way of short circuiting the necessity of an elite 'marketing' such solutions to the masses. In Habermas' theory, democratic participation is a necessary part of maximising the likelihood of making valid judgements. Democracy is a necessary condition of the constitution of what will count as a solution, particularly in so far as the problems concerned reflect the need to reconcile existential interests.

However, Walker's analysis suggests ways in which we can move from the general level of Habermas' analysis, based as it is on a hypothetically socially undifferentiated domain, where the division of labour, etc., does not exist, to an analysis more appropriate for complex, socially-differentiated societies such as our own. Walker reminds us of the distinction between different kinds of interests in a public decision-making process:

> Not all matters of public interest are of legitimate interest to all members of the public; not all are matters of general interest. The general public comprises of more than one particular public, and the general interest consists only of those concerns of legitimate interest to all citizens, and therefore to all publics. It is a well-understood principle of democratic theory that all those members of a public sharing that public interest should have a say in decisions affecting it. As Burnheim has pointed out, however, there is much less appreciation of a correlative principle: that only those members of the public sharing that interest should have a say. (Walker, 1988: 7)

From this point he distinguishes between those issues which must be decided at the most general social level and those which can be functionally devolved onto sub-publics (only some of which are geographically localised publics). Walker further distinguishes between public and private interests and between matters where a decision 'directly causally affects someone's problem-solving capacity and cases where a decision affects someone's problem-solving capacity only by changing the problem-solving capacity of another' (Walker, 1988: 7).

In a somewhat ad hoc way from the standpoint of his meta-theory, Walker then accepts Kant's notion that we should 'act as to treat humanity, whether in your own person or that of another, always at the same time as an end, and never merely as a means' (Walker, 1988: 7). He goes on to give an example which makes this point clearer:

> an employer might have an interest in the production through education of a group of workers with certain narrowly specified skills and attitudes. This is an indirect interest, in contrast to the direct interest of the students in a broad, general education, which provides them with greater flexibility and satisfies, other, non-vocational needs. (Walker, 1988: 7)

To give priority to the employer's interest would be to treat the student as a 'means' to the employer's 'end' of solving his or her manpower problems. Thus, direct interests must take priority over indirect ones. But, Walker cautions,

> The moral priority of direct individual or sectional interests is only prima facie, however. Although it cannot be overridden by indirect private . . . interests, it can be overridden by a general interest, which is equally shared and equally direct for all, and which is identified with the area of shared, or overlapping private interests, and in particular, with the infrastructural conditions for the pursuit of private interests. Such infrastructural conditions are commonly believed to include peace, personal security and, in liberal democratic thought, an educated population. (Walker, 1988: 7–8)

Applied to curriculum decision-making, this model permits us to develop a justification for a functional differentiation of centralised and decentralised (including local) decision-making scopes. Of course, a model of this kind is quite different from those produced by more naive interpretations of critical theory, which rest upon an idealistic model of entirely open communication among all participants, regardless of social scale. However, in a culturally pluralist, economically differentiated, real world the impossibility of resolving all questions in a plenary rather than structured system of communication must be recognised, as must the existence of non-plenary yet public, e.g. regional or sectional, interests. A hierarchy of interests is unavoidable. Only democratic forms of organisation at each level could prevent this hierarchy of the generality of interests turning into a sedimented hierarchy of sectional interests, or bureaucratic power. Or, historically speaking, since hierarchies of sectional interest and bureaucratic power already exist, only developmental change can turn existing hierarchies of power into hierarchies of democratic co-ordination.

The developmental task before us must consist first of all in a critique of existing administrative structures and ideologies, involving, *inter alia*, the identification of interests and interest groups. This must be guided by the critical reconstruction of a justifiable democratic co-ordination process, and followed by political movements aimed at

1. separating out functionally decentralisable decision-making processes,
2. ensuring democratic participation in these new structures, e.g. school curriculum committees,
3. identifying those with legitimate direct and indirect interests in the problems solvable at a particular organisational level, and
4. gaining direct represention of interest groups in both centralised and decentralised decision-making functions.

(In this regard Burnheim's suggestion of statistical democracy through the random choice for fixed terms of office of representatives of particular interests provides an example of a possible mechanism.)

Before leaving Walker's analysis it might be useful to mention just one additional feature of it. He gives close attention to the kind of legitimate interests different categories of participants in education might be thought to have – parents, teachers, students, etc. When it comes to teachers' interests at the school level he makes a number of telling points:

> It seems clear that students have legitimate direct interests (perhaps to be represented by their parents) in their own education. What, though, of those who perform educational functions? Teachers . . . certainly have professional interests in educational decision-making. As professionals they are concerned with the quality and efficiency of the educational process. As workers, they have industrial interests in their own working conditions . . . the professional interest is an indirect interest in promoting the direct and indirect interests of others (students, employers, the general public); the industrial interest is a direct interest . . . in not allowing . . . educational practitioners [to be treated] merely as means to the end of others. . . . Do educational professionals, then, have a right to participation or represention in curriculum decision-making? On the present account, this can only be in so far as the decisions affect the [industrial] welfare of professionals. (Walker, 1988: 10)

Lacking a direct interest themselves, Walker is arguing, the participation of professionals in curriculum decision-making could only rest on the delegation to them of such powers from those who have them as a result of direct interest – students, parents and the general public. That is, they could participate only as selected representatives of that public, chosen perhaps, for their professional knowledge. But this does not mean that students and parents would have a much greater say. Where the general interest overlaps particular interests there must be either a consensus or a compromise. In practice, too, the emergence of schools with differing philosophies would be likely to be accompanied by opportunities for teachers to achieve a rough match between their own views and those of a particular community (and vice versa). From the standpoint of critical theory, there would also be an internal limitation on the influence of parents – if pedagogy is to be critically guided and truth-based, there must be room for the teacher's own, authentic participation in resolving validity questions. Still, the initial impact of parental participation is likely to be conservative. Only after parents have been educated by teachers to changes which have occurred in the decade or so since their own school experience will this conservatism be dissipated.

KLAFKI'S MODEL OF DECENTRALISED CURRICULUM DECISION-MAKING

Armed with the foregoing, it is possible to criticise Klafki's 1970s model of curriculum decision-making.[10] In many ways, Klafki's 'critical-constructive' model of education attempts to achieve just the sort of balance that the present author values. It also involves a model of action research which encompasses the macro-level as well as that of face-to-face groups. Any criticisms of Klafki's work should be tempered by a recognition that it is only from the perspective granted by the passage of time and political events that we are able to see the flaws in his earlier work so clearly.

In 'Decentralised curriculum development in the form of Action Research', Klafki describes a project (1969–71) which attempted to revise the curriculum for schools in the German state of Hessen. This project was politically cut short prior to the installation of a combination of supra-regional planning and local curriculum development, broadly similar to the kind of division of functions model outlined by Walker.

However, there were a number of features of the Hessen model which appear to clash with the Walker model. It was, at least in the initial phases, an educator dominated model:

> The term 'decentralised' implies that this kind of curriculum development takes place not only in cooperation with teachers but also in direct connection with their teaching practice, and, *if possible*, with the cooperation of pupils and parents (Klafki, 1975: 14; emphasis added)

and the participation in it of those with the most direct interests, pupils and parents, was regarded as presenting so many difficulties that it was structurally peripheral to the critical development processes. In addition, it was believed that few teachers were equipped to participate in the development of curriculum at school level:

> *Here* we are mainly interested in the situation of the teachers. Up to now, they have generally been able to acquire the qualifications for cooperation in curriculum development only to a very limited extent during their studies. (Klafki, 1975: 16)

These two factors left the initiative very much in the hands of the academic experts, a group with a narrow political base, and interests which were not only mostly indirect, but which might legitimately be regarded as constituting an obstacle to accurate perception of the direct interests of those whose interests they sought to advance. With the virtue of hindsight, we can see this to have been a recipe for political failure.

In the context of the politics of the state of Hessen, the Klafki model always went beyond the politics of the possible. Only the circumstances of the 1960s could have led educational experts to believe that such a system could work. It lacked extensive support from groups with potential or actual political power, including industrialists who have a strong, indirect interest in curriculum.

As a democratic, grass-roots approach it could be judged defective, since it was largely the construction of an intellectual vanguard, and did not grow out of a working through of the problem by participants at all levels. In many ways, despite idealism and the possession of democratic and participatory intentions, the manner in which the various projects proceeded was not unlike many policy implementation processes produced by the more humanistic sections of the technocracy. The more modest proposals for teacher in-service development which followed the collapse of the Hessen project have more long-term potential for a change of professional consciousness.[11] Since these later proposals are similar in outline to the work of Carr and Kemmis, which is more readily available in English, the discussion will now turn to the latter.

CRITICAL ACTION RESEARCH – THE CARR–KEMMIS MODEL

Action research is a self-conscious or reflective process of rationally guided experimentation. The fact that the act of research itself changes situations, and that the knowledge yielded by observation and reflection on the results of action permits the further change of situations through plans based on the understanding of participants, can be systematically incorporated in the process of change. What can make such research and reflection potentially critical is the participatory and communally discursive structure the cycle of action and reflection can take. It may well be the case that the observation and reflection stages of the action research cycle can yield only a situated form of knowledge rather than a generalisable one, but it may equally be the case that typical aptitude–treatment–interaction research models cannot yield information readily adaptable to particular situations. Perhaps one of the weaknesses of the Carr–Kemmis model is that it does not give us much of an idea of how such research might proceed at the large-scale level, although they take the view that it is applicable there. It seems better adapted to the situation where a small group is engaged in school improvement, and, indeed, its main use has been in small group work in in-service teacher education.

One of the longer-term benefits of the kind of teacher in-service programmes with which Kemmis and the Deakin University (Australia) group have been associated is the building up of an educated constituency for critical action research and critical theory generally. The participatory and discursive character of problem-solving in the Deakin model is laying the foundation for the development of the 'deep democracy' of which Collier spoke in 1945. Carr and Kemmis' ideology critique of traditional theory and practice in school development is also valuable, since it arms teachers with an understanding of the oppressive character of technicist and manipulative modes of administration. The Carr–Kemmis model, like Klafki's, systematically distinguishes critical research from positivist and interpretive modes of research and makes the point that only as participants can people be enlightened, because universal participation is the final guarantee of validity. However, they do tend to see action research and participation in a narrow way. There is not enough of the breadth that Habermas had in mind when he added the phrase 'in principle' to his discussion of participation in will-formation: 'Since action research is research into one's own practice, it follows that only practitioners and groups of practitioners can carry out action research.'[12]

There is a failure here to be quite clear that practice is interactional. The role of outside (i.e. academic) facilitators is recognised, while hedging this about with safeguards intended to permit the practitioner group to maintain control of the research process. One of the most important of these safeguards is the prohibition of 'externally formulated questions and issues which are not based in the practical concerns of practitioners'.[13] But the fact is that external agencies and authority structures *do* make claims on the practice of local groups of practitioners – at the very least, claims to play a necessary co-ordinating role among such groups. While external concerns should never displace the concerns which arise out of the direct interests of practitioners in solving the concrete problems of their practical situations, the absence from their discourse of the claims which arise from the general interest, or from the interests of others, such as those of administrators in co-ordinating activity, can only predispose their reflection to a one-sided and unrealistic set of outcomes. Such concerns and claims actually exist and impinge on practice, and in so far as the interests being expressed are either direct interests or are general interests, may have a legitimate role in teacher critique. While Carr and Kemmis recognise the existence of this level of analysis, they tend to see it as a set of constraints for the practitioner rather than a set of claims, some of which may be valid.[14]

Another limitation of the Carr–Kemmis analysis is the apparent identification of what happens in action research with 'strategic action' – risky, rationally-directed practical action.[15] But the process of action and inquiry need not be so relentlessly external and political. There is an inward dimension, the importance of which can easily be underestimated. Practitioners need to understand themselves and one another; they need to 'grow up' and develop greater ego strength. Carr and Kemmis' analysis is a little too 'cognitive', in the sense that the stumbling blocks to the development of practice in group settings, such as schools, are by no means only to be found in the misuse of authority by power figures or in resistance to change by traditionally-minded colleagues – some of the obstacles lie within those who desire emancipation. Max Miller's analysis of post-war antisemitism in Germany opens up a communicative and social-psychological understanding of this dimension of critical development, reminiscent of Adorno.[16]

CRITICAL ACTION FOR CURRICULUM DEVELOPMENT

The action research model has been applied to curriculum development by Shirley Grundy.[17] Using a typology and case studies of technicist, interpretive and critical approaches to curriculum decision-making, she shows, quite concretely, how each is constituted by a link between an epistemological approach and a corresponding form of action. In turn, each model of curriculum development supports or permits only certain kinds of structures of participation in curriculum formation. She shows that there is a broad correspondence between Habermas' discussion of the organisation of enlightenment and the principles of critical action research.

Grundy argues that critical action research provides a model of curriculum development consistent with what she regards as the principles of critical pedagogy and that practitioners are engaged in a process of self-education or mutual pedagogy, in which:

1. they confront the real problems of their existence,
2. they engage in a process of conscientisation,
3. they confront ideological distortions and
4. they incorporate actions as a part of knowing.[18]

From the standpoint of the account of critical pedagogy presented in Chapter 6 of the present work, however, Grundy's account of critical pedagogy is actually an account of the stages of ideology critique. It is not characterised by the universal or transcendental arguments of a critical reconstruction. This suggests a possible weakness in the account of critical curriculum praxis in Grundy's work – while Grundy envisages that teachers should engage with students' needs during the curriculum development process, they do so from their own perspective. Grundy would be among the first to object to teaching being considered solely from the administrators' perspective, no matter how much they tried to see things the teachers' way. The analysis needs a more explicit account of the communication structures appropriate to the parents' and pupils' participation in curriculum development – after all, they have a direct interest in it and this can only be overridden by a universal or general interest shared by the whole society. If we follow our rule of thumb on safeguarding the expression of interests, we cannot accept that teachers are appropriate representatives of pupils' interests. In the view advanced in Chapter 6, I envisaged a communicative process of progressively deeper involvement by pupils in curricular decisions. In the earlier part of the present chapter the possibility of a parental role at the school level was canvassed. This would lead to a critical partnership between parents, students, teachers and administrators, and a functional hierarchy of kinds of curriculum decisions, with, say, parental involvement varying from direct involvement at the school level to representative involvement at the system level. Parent involvement would diminish as students' capacities to participate developed.

Scrupulous attention to the need for participation of all types of participants (especially students) and for the democratic articulation of levels of organisation may be the slow way compared to the rapid reforms attempted in the 1960s, but it is perhaps a more certain and lasting way. There is no substitute for a discourse of all directly interested participants. Klafki's version of action research, like Carr and Kemmis', tends to recognise this in principle but not procedurally. Both the German and the Australian work focuses on the researcher–teacher relationship to the detriment of politically effective but difficult and slower models for change. Conservative critics in Germany, who charged that the parents had been left out of the process were right, but I doubt whether they would have also been worried by the fact that the pupils had been left out, too.

THE NEED FOR AN EMPIRICAL PRAGMATICS

It is clear from much of the foregoing discussion that actual, situated processes of enlightenment will involve finely-tuned communicative structures, appropriate organisational forms, and a politics which concerns itself with the establishment of rational structures of consultation and representation. The symbolic character of human organisation also calls for a communicative analysis. The critical principles produced by reconstruction of ideal discourses and developmental paths for individuals and societies must be supplemented by the identification of distorted structures of communication – by an ideology critique, directed, *inter alia*, at those distorted structures which nonetheless claim to be democratic or consultative. For this process of critique we need something more than the critical reconstruction of ideal possibilities – we need an empirical pragmatics to guide systematic observation and analysis. The use of such an empirical pragmatics is one of the major sources from which we can obtain feedback about our progress. Its exercise is one of our most important safeguards against manipulative uses of apparently critical processes.

EMPIRICAL PRAGMATICS AS REFLECTIVE METHOD

Critical empirical pragmatics provides a guide for the critique and progressive development of communication structures and practices. It can provide a reflective method for teachers and administrators, the rudiments of which can be taught to pre-service teacher educands. It can also provide a basis for in-service education. While it can provide a safeguard of sorts, what it cannot do is provide the courage to make specific critique in risky, real situations or the judgement to know at which point structures are most likely to yield.

In the case of the ISS there is no force but that of the better argument, but in institutionally-bound (real) speech, which is the concern of a critical empirical pragmatics, the speakers and hearers rely on the binding force of pre-existing norms and rules as a basis for action and interpretation. The presence of such norms usually fixes the interaction at the given learning level of the social group, but when the taken-for-granted world is disrupted, or perceived as problematic, the possibility of a discourse going behind the norms emerges. At any given level, the existing norms both enable the extant learning level and act as a barrier to higher learning levels.

Often the theory-in-use of interaction is present in the unmarked or un-objectified component of communication. As Habermas has pointed out, it 'is not possible to simultaneously perform and objectify an illocutionary act' (*C & ES*: 43). Normally, the surface form of the talk – often the discussable, statement-containing part of the talk – does not contain the expressive, imperative or regulative illocutions, except on those rare occasions when commands are being given, or people are giving direct expression to their emotions. This is particularly so in classrooms, which are characterised by a degree of emotional neutrality and a high level of constative (statement) talk. This pattern of explicitness/implicitness is one which conceals the power structure (regulative, imperative) beneath an apparently natural and objective level of talk.

In constative talk the possibility of a discussion of the grounds of propositional content is closer than that of a discussion of power structures. It is only when the regulative assumptions of the talk are violated, by someone talking 'out of turn', being 'rude', or the like, that the power structure of the communication becomes available for comment. Usually this comment goes only as far as an invocation of the norms governing relations in the situation – 'Don't speak to your father like that!' The successful communication of power is done through the assumptions of speech which objectifies something else. In turn, the power structure acts back on the exploration of factual validity questions, keeping the doors to questioning of 'the nature of things' firmly shut.

The process of the construction of power through speech is analogous to ritual. In a situation defined as ritual, action is based on a story (myth) of the natural and efficacious forms of action available to a group. A ceremony is gone though and actions performed which are believed to bring about, say, an improvement in the growth of crops. But if the reasoning behind the story is set aside, we can ask 'What effects does the ritual have if we discount the believed-in effects?' A common ethnological answer is that the emotionally charged event acts back on the participants to bring about some latent effect, such as a release of social tension, or an increase in group loyalty.[19] The propositional content of the myth is set aside and the ethnological meaning found in the latent, unobjectified, undiscussable meanings.

This acting back on participants is also a call for them to do symbolic 'work' on themselves. We can see this structure in school classrooms, where children co-operate in their own indoctrination, as discussed in Chapter 5, or in many school staff meetings, where the illusion of consultation is created in a communication structure dominated by the principal's agenda and chaired by him or her. Similar dialogic asymmetries have been located in organisational talk of many kinds, presenting the critical participant with an important obstacle in the conduct of effective critical dialogue.

The maintenance of power requires the engineering of acceptance. Reflexive communication about the status of texts must be prevented if what has been implicit is to remain so. This is the 'not-learning process' to which Habermas refers.[20] It would seem appropriate to extend our earlier discussion of ideology from a reference to symbolic systems which advantage one section of society at the expense of others, to a more specific reference to the practices whereby this is achieved – through a structure of blocked-off forms of validity exploration inherent in the personal and interpersonal aspect of speech roles. The opening up of such discourses is the business of critique, but it is better if such opening up is organised, since the individual who attempts to do it will at best be seen as an eccentric. As Habermas argued in *Legitimation Crisis*:

'The level of development of society is determined by the institutionally permitted learning capacity, in particular by whether theoretical–technical and practical questions are differentiated, and whether discursive learning processes take place' (*LC*: 8).

It is no accident that it is precisely the practical dimension of speech which is most often implicit in organisational talk. Undemocratic processes and processes which are contrary to the interests of categories of participants in them typically conceal the power relations that sustain them while, at the same time, restraining any deep exploration of the factual validity questions which arise from the explicit, constative level of the talk.

Critically informed communication analysis, working from classroom audio and video tapes, or transcripts, can provide an understanding of the talk practices that inhibit participation by students and others in the exploration of validity questions. I am presently developing and using critical communication analysis of this kind with my own students. As well as workshop experiences of communication study, the pre-service education of teachers should contain skills of organising self-directed, problem-solving learning, learning-promoting peer support structures, and, of course, more traditional study of the problems and processes involved in presenting new material in particular disciplines, diagnosing difficulties and assisting students with problems, etc. Teacher educators must also explore new ways of permitting student teachers to explore problematic aspects of their life-world without, at the same time, through utopian critique, heightening the already great anxieties many of them feel. The sensitive use of biographical methods of personal exploration is an appropriate means of fostering this kind of growth, as is the critical extension of clinical supervision of practice teaching being developed by Smyth and his students in Australia.[21]

Similar analyses of organisational communication, whether of meetings, or wider consultative processes, including analyses of the patterns of the flow of written information, can also permit the identification of constraints, the procedural censoring of input, and the limitation of speech. Such analyses, especially if made by relatively oppressed groups, can be quite powerful, since structures of domination everywhere depend not only on the exercise of legal authority but on communicative procedures of legitimation such as 'wide consultation' involving the 'opportunity to have your say' and the like. Let us look at an example.

As pointed out above, power in such organisations is largely ritual power. It is power over the communicative formation of sentiment and accompanying legitimacy. One of the commonest sources of legitimacy is an appeal, overt or covert, to ideals of democracy, and of 'belonging' or 'membership'. These appeals are often made through activities of pseudo-consultation and pseudo-participation.

Views on a question (often on an already formulated plan) are sought, and after a short period of time, with little possibility of lateral communication and sharing of views between affected groups, are collected by a small, elite group, which 'takes them into account' in redrafting the document. Since views are sought from individuals, there is no knowledge outside the executive group of the actual kind and number of views. This can be misrepresented or ignored, sometimes by unconscious selectivity. In any event, it is often the case that no mechanism exists for dealing with views in an open way even within the executive. There is no requirement for the executive to *engage* with views, even if they are those of a majority of those 'consulted'. In effect, the executive gets a free, private opinion poll, which it is at liberty to ignore if it wishes. Teachers might consider refusing to participate in such rituals, either individually or through an organised response. They should forgo the illusion of 'having a say' and thus prevent such processes having legitimacy. At the same time, they should make the nature of real consultation clear. For instance, they can call for systematic opinion polling, by independent or scrutinised agencies, with agreed questions and published results. They can also demand some engagement with the views presented; at the least a published response from executive groups, which can then be subjected to appraisal. Those who seek legitimacy through consultation and the calling up of the shade of democracy should be forced to pay the price – that the consultation be genuine. The same currency that legitimating rituals trade in can be cashed in to force the issue of differences between actual practices and the ideal. This becomes a vehicle for educational changes in the community being consulted as well as among those in power who are also persons of good will.

NOTES

1. J. Collier, 'United States Indian administration as a laboratory of ethnic relations', *Social Research*, **30**, 1945, 265–305, 298, quoted in S. Grundy, *Curriculum: Product or praxis?*, London: The Falmer Press, 1987, 143.
2. *T & P*: 11.
3. H. Moser, *Aktionforschung als kritische Theorie der Sozialwissenschaft*, München, 1975.
4. J. Van Maanen, 'Linking ways of knowing with ways of being practical', *Curriculum Enquiry*, **6** (3), 1977: 205–28.
5. *RTC*. See also D. La Capra, 'Habermas and the grounding of critical theory', *History and Theory*, **16**, 1977: 237–94.
6. See Note 49, Chapter 3; also *K & HI*: 69.
7. *K & HI*: Chapter 5, especially 97.
8. W. Carr and S. Kemmis, *Becoming Critical: Knowing Through Action Research*, Geelong: Deakin University Press, 1983. S. Kemmis and L. Fitzclarence, *Curriculum Theorising: Beyond Reproduction Theory*, Geelong: Deakin University Press, 1986.
9. J. Walker, 'Curriculum decision making at school level: Functional decentralisation

and democratic control', paper presented to the Conference on School-based Decision Making and Management, Melbourne, 1988, also as 'Functional autonomy and democratic control', in J. D. Chapman and C. W. Evers (eds) *School Based Decision Making and Management*, Sydney: Wiley, 1989.

10. W. Klafki, 'Decentralised curriculum development in the form of action research', *Information Bulletin*, Council of Europe, **1**, 1975: 13–22.

11. *Ibid.*: 16.

12. Carr and Kemmis, *op. cit.*, 1983: 173.

13. *Ibid.*: 174.

14. *Ibid.*: 185–6.

15. *Ibid.*: 160–1, 168.

16. M. Miller, 'Kollektive Erinnerungen und Gesellschaftliche Lernprozesse', Colloquium über Nachkreigsantisemetismus der Reimerstiftung, Bad Homburg, March 1988.

17. S. Grundy, *op. cit.*, also S. Kemmis and L. Fitzclarence, *op. cit.*

18. S. Grundy, *op. cit.*: 156–7.

19. See D. Hofffmann, *Kritische Erziehungswissenschaft*, Stuttgart: Kohlhammer, 1978: 90–4, and H. J. Heydorn, 'Zum Bildungsproblem in der Gegenwärtigen Situation', in H. J. Heydorn (ed.) *Zum Bildungsbegriff der Gegenwart*, Frankfurt, 1967.

20. *LC*: 14–17.

21. See L. Beyer, 'Field experience, ideology and the development of critical reflectivity', *Journal of Teacher Education*, **35** (3), 1984: 36–41, also W. J. Smyth *A Rationale for Teacher's Critical Pedagogy*, Geelong: Deakin University Press, 1987 for a different but valuable approach, and specifically on teacher education see *Leadership and Pedagogy*, Geelong: Deakin University Press, 1986. See also A. Berlak and H. Berlak, 'Toward a nonhierarchical approach to school inquiry and leadership', *Curriculum Inquiry*, **13** (3), 1983: 267–94, which represents an earlier attempt to come to grips with these issues.

CONCLUDING REMARKS

In certain traditions, above all in Jewish, . . . mysticism [such as the mysticism of Jakob Boehme] . . . the God of Origin, a quite candid and playful God, becomes external to himself, not by stepping outside . . . and becoming externalised, but rather by going into exile within himself . . . emigrating into the darkness of his own endlessly deep foundations, and . . . becoming His Other . . . man, left to himself must simultaneously carry out the redemption of nature with his own powers, and even the redemption of . . . God . . . it is only at this cost that God has initiated the world process as History.

(Habermas)[1]

The aim of this book was to construct a relatively complete and coherent account of a critical theory of education based on the work of Jürgen Habermas. To this point, criticisms of Habermas' work, or educational thinking based on it, have not occupied centre stage. This abstention was to allow the untrammelled development of the theory, but such a privilege can only be permitted for so long. The time has come to open up a wider discourse among all those who, considered broadly, could be said to be of a critical cast of mind. By this I mean those who have been attracted by Habermas' project of uniting moral and scientific thought in an understanding of an at least partially self-forming species, whether or not they have found his particular attempt to do this persuasive. I am sufficiently dogmatic about one thing: any lasting change for the better can only emerge from an open discourse among those interested in education. What has been written, then, is not merely accidentally programmatic and exploratory, it is necessarily so. To begin this process of dialogue I have chosen to turn to the views of Ian Lewis, who I take to be exemplary of critics of good will.[2]

In his review of Carr and Kemmis' *Becoming Critical: Knowing Through Action Research*, Ian Lewis identified what he saw to be the central contradictions of their work (99–102).[3] He might well see the same contradictions in the present book. The first of the perceived faults is that

> the authors take seriously their claim to be working toward the emancipation of teachers, and identify, as one of the criteria which their action research has to satisfy, acceptability of emerging theories to these same teachers. It seems odd, therefore, that only critical theory, derived externally to the study of education, can lead to this emancipation.[4]
> (Lewis, 1987: 100)

In this criticism Lewis makes a number of mistakes. He mistakes a mode of exposition for a recommended process, and in doing so confuses critical reconstructions with ideology critique and the organisation of enlightenment. The reconstruction of critique as immanent, from which the recommendation that the interested parties must validate a critique comes, is derived from a general consideration of the nature of critique. It offers little guidance for the substantive ideology critiques that may emerge from teachers' dialogues and which must be validated by them. Action research is simply a vehicle for this process of involvement of teacher interests. It is still the specific critique, derived not externally but from the teachers' concrete situations, which leads to their emancipation. Lewis' complaint boils down to the idea that critical theory is dogmatic because it imposes the necessity of avoiding dogma. In any case, as I argued earlier, Carr and Kemmis do get themselves in a trap when they emphasise the teachers' validation of critique as against that of other participants. The essence of discourse is that it occurs across the whole domain of intersecting interests, which in the field of education is, in part, a public domain.

Lewis also complains of the abstractness of the analysis. Perhaps he underestimates teachers. But is the mode of communication ill-matched to the intended audience? Carr and Kemmis, says Lewis,

> are very much at home in the confines of an academic library . . . [but] . . . we do not find much evidence of . . . the authors' familiarity with the practical world of teachers and the real problems which teachers face, and from which they are to be rescued.[5]

I could point out that I know something of the very practical success that the Carr–Kemmis programme has had, at least in Australia, and the fact that teachers there have found it far from abstract, but this would not serve to express how poor an argumentative move I believe Lewis has made. Practice is inevitably theorised, it is just a question of whether one theorises it in the taken-for-granted categories of the status quo, with their aura of naturalness and, indeed, of being uncontaminated by anything so unrelated to a peaceful life as 'theory' or whether one tries to distinguish between the inevitable and the constructed aspects of reality. This sort of criticism boils down to either the accusation that critical theorists write books, or that they write them badly. It is also worth nothing that almost all of Lewis' criticisms have been made *internally*, among German critical theorists of education, as long ago as 1969. Perhaps it is partly a problem of the economics of publishing that it is often necessary to combine two addressees for the one book – teacher educators and student teachers. This sometimes leads to communicative overstretch.

But Lewis does put his finger on what is, perhaps, the central, political problem for critical theory of education – the question of its intended audience.[6] In Marx's theory, the intended audience – the revolutionary subject or agent of change – was the proletariat. There was a point in addressing a message to them because they had not only a vested existential interest in changing the political–economic structure which oppressed them but also the numbers to bring this change about. However, anyone who has read *Das Kapital* might well have despaired of Marx's communication too. His analysis required restatement before it could reach the masses. Marx, with Engels, undertook this kind of writing himself in *The Communist Manifesto*. While the ultimate addressee of Marx's theory was the proletariat, it is clear historically that there was an intermediate addressee, the disaffected intelligentsia, to which Marx himself belonged. The intermediate addressee of critical theory of education has also been the intelligentsia, particularly academic educators; but Lewis is right to this extent, if this group remains the sole effective addressee, critical theory will fail. When conservative educators are finding the necessary metaphors to communicate with the general public, can critical educators be far behind?

Some of these points might be made about the addressee of critical theory, with two crucial differences. First, the addressee of critical theory is clearly universal; it is, in the Hegelian mode, all those oppressed by the master–slave relationship, including masters. This breadth of address is echoed in the methodology for change which critical theory favours, at least, where it is historically possible. Critical theory abhors the idea of a dictatorship, even one of the masses. The preferred mode of critical theory, in its theoretical and sometimes academic moment, is to recommend procedural changes which unmask and change oppressive communicative practices on a day-to-day basis. Its crucial point of practical attack, in societies which display the evolutionary level of the possibility of democratically open discourses, is the identification and removal of the distortions of speech. In a sense, critical theory is the level of critique appropriate for societies which have already institutionalised areas of open practical discourse – democracies. One might have to look elsewhere for models appropriate to the revolutionary situations of dictatorships, as Habermas, among others, acknowledged. For far too long revolutionary movements have held the attention of those who seek radical change in societies like our own, but critical theory seeks to adopt the values of democracy and individual rights, as both method and sign. As method, the democratic process will characterise the process of reform. As sign, the present level of imperfect realisation of the democratic ideal and human rights points to a better future.[7] It must never be forgotten by English speaking readers that the 'theory' in critical theory is more like 'method' – it is the method of critique. If this is forgotten, its critics will reproach it for not providing the substantive criticisms and practical reforms which only *situated practitioners* can provide, *after and through* critique.

That is why the central problem for critical theory remains that of the adequacy of Habermas' analysis of distorted communication. This has been subjected to a great deal of critique, sometimes by those who are unaware how much support linguistic pragmatics gives to the idea of a group of universally co-present functions of speech, along the lines that Habermas describes (e.g. Halliday's 'field, tenor and mode').[8] A strong case can also be made out for the notion that everyday communication normally assumes a consensual background of truth, appropriateness and sincerity so that their opposites become noticeable and accountable – truth, etc. is the 'ground' and departures from it the 'figure', as it were. Where many part company with Habermas is in the assertion that this fact can provide a universal quasi-normative basis for validity exploration:

> The human interest in autonomy and responsibility is not mere fancy, for it can be apprehended a priori. What raises us out of nature is the only thing whose nature we can know: language. Through its structure, autonomy and responsibility are posited for us. Our first sentence expresses unequivocally the intention of universal and unconstrained consensus. (*K & HI*: 314)

It may be that the idea of perfect *commune*-ication contains within it some notion of open, non-deceptive, reasonable speech, and so presents this possibility to us every time we speak, but surely the possibility of untruth, deception and abnormal speech also presents itself, with equal logical force. The everyday normality of an assumption of truth, etc. does not amount to a basis upon which we can overcome the need to decide for truth as against falsehood each time we speak. At the most it is a testimony to folk wisdom. A meta-decisionism is still necessary. We cannot avoid the need to choose the general course of our lives. This is clear enough from Habermas' acceptance that the ISS cannot provide a basis for judging whole ways of life or biographies. But once the meta-decision is made, and we turn to more limited spheres, Habermas' argument about how we may validly form our wills becomes more compelling – we do it together, sharing our experience and on the basis of treating others as ends not means, as interlocutors not objects.

If this modification is accepted, and the possibility of fallibility is maintained, there is room for aesthetic and moral vision – even for the mystical theodicy of Jakob Boehme – to take on something more than the aspect of a mere analogy for the history of emancipation. Some of its genuinely theological content might be reinstated. If so, the possibility of a Jewish, Christian or Muslim critical theory must be taken seriously.

Under these circumstances, the possibility of emancipation rests even more clearly on the courage and will of individuals; who knows, perhaps it rests even upon the grace of God, in the classical sense of the concept of grace – an ultimate, spiritual reality, which, as Rilke saw, is struggling to come into being in our lives and our history.

NOTES

1. *T & P*: 215.
2. I. Lewis, 'Encouraging reflexive teacher research', *British Journal of the Sociology of Education*, **8** (1), 1987: 95–105. See also R. Gibson, *Critical Theory and Education*, Sevenoaks: Hodder and Stoughton, 1986, which employ an eclectic definition of critical theory. Despite the different view of Habermas, Gibsons' chapters on aesthetic education and related topics, based largely on Adorno, are worth attention.
3. I. Lewis, *op. cit.*: 99–102.
4. *Ibid.* 198, 100.
5. *Ibid.* 100.
6. See Note 25, Chapter 2.
7. I. Lewis, *op. cit.*: 101. See also Habermas' remarks in P. Dews (ed.) *Habermas: Autonomy and Solidarity*, London: Verso, 1986: 68, on the appropriation of ideas of democracy and rights.
8. E.g. M. Halliday and R. Hasan, *Language, Context and Text*, Geelong: Deakin University Press, 1985.

INDEX

administrative context of schooling, 130–2
adolescence, motivational crisis of, 48–9
Adorno, T., 34, 150, 160
  critique, 58–61, 79
  on modern educational crisis, 16–18, 21
  on theories of knowledge, 72–4
alignment devices in job interviews,
  141–3
Arendt, H., 26, 29–30
Argyris, C., 132
Austin, 100–1, 107
autonomy
  and children, 110–12
  ego and rational, in communication,
  119–21

Bernstein, B., 95
Blankertz, H., 62, 81
Broyard, A., 14
Brumlik, 78

capitalism, 29–31
  critiques of, 34–6
  response to, 36–40
Carr, W., 151, 158–61, 167–8
Castles, S., 55
child, problem context of, 128–9
children and autonomy, 110–12
Chomsky, N., 39
coherence, concept of in interviews,
  140–1
Collier, J., 149, 159
colonisation of life-world frameworks, 95
communication
  bound and distorted, 112–14
  ego and rational autonomy in,
  119–21
systematically distorted, 106–9
traditional classroom, 90–1
communicative action, theory of, 99–104
communicative competence, 114–18

crisis
  educational, 1–25
  motivational, of adolescence, 48–9
tendencies in capitalism, 3–5
theories of and ungovernability, 53–4
critical development and teaching, 121–3
critique
  of capitalism, 34–6
  of Habermas, 37–40
  ideology, 34
  method of, 78–81
    of schooling, 81–2
  of Popper, 32
Cronbach, L., 138
curriculum
  context of, 133–4
  decision-making, model of, 157–8
  questions for, 118–19

Dearden, R., 111, 117
democratisation of universities, 63–4
Dewey, J., 68, 87
  on children's capacity, 111–12, 114, 122
  democracy and education, 46–8, 153
  problem-solving methods, 71
Dilthey, W., 42, 78
Duhem, P., 138
Dummett, 100

education
  democratisation of the university, 63–4
  development of critical theory, 56–61
    German critics of, 61–2
  and emancipation, 45–67
  and enlightenment, 41–3
  left authoritarianism, 55–6
  modernity, crisis of, 5–7
  motivational crisis of adolescence, 48–9
  research community, 135–7
  theory of, 82–4
  ungovernability and theory of crisis,
    50–5

educational enlightenment, organisation
    of, 149–66
  and critical action, 158–61
  decentralised curriculum decision-
      making, 157–8
  decentralised learning processes, 151–7
  empirical pragmatics, 161–5

Edwards, A., 93
emancipation, and education, 45–67
empirical pragmatics, 104–6
empirical–analytical sciences, 33
enlightenment and education, 41–3
  organisation of, 40–1, 149–66
Evers, C., 139

formulation in speech, 92–3, 94
Foucault, M., 8, 61, 75, 80
Frankfurt School, 14–21, 30–1, 34
Frege, 99, 100
Freire, P., 75, 96, 129
Furlong, V., 93

Gadamer, 36
Germany, critical theory of education in,
    56–61
  critics of, 61–2
Giroux, H., 21
Groothof, H.H., 68–9
Grundy, S., 160

Habermas, J.
  autonomy in communication, 120
  communication, systematically
      distorted, 106–9
  communicative action, theory of,
      99–104
  communicative competence, 114–15
  on crisis tendencies of capitalism, 3–4
  criticism of, 36–40, 87–8
  on critique of knowledge, 78–80
  curriculum context for research, 133
  democratic problem-solving, 153–4
  development of views of, 31–6
  developmental reconstruction, 111
  on discourse, 68–9
  on education, 45, 48–9
    development of theory, 56–61
    universities, 63–4
  on empirical pragmatics, 162–4
  and enlightenment, 40–3
  formative influences on, 26, 28–31
  Hegel, Marx and the Frankfurt School,
      15, 17, 19
  ideal speech situation, 75–8
  on the life–world, 69–70
  on modernity, 7–10
  on New Right and Old Left, 10–14
  theories of knowledge, 72–3

universal and empirical pragmatics,
    104–6
universal ideals and historical reality,
    127
Hegel, G. W. F., 2, 29, 78, 145
  growth of critical thought, 14–21
hermeneutic sciences, 33, 35–6
Hesse, M., 79
Heydorn, H. J., 62
historical reality, 126–8
Horkheimer, M., 34, 58, 59, 150
  methods of critique, 79
  modern educational crisis, 16–18, 21–3
  theories of knowledge, 72–4
human interests, and knowledge, 31–6
Husserl, E., 38

ideal pedagogical speech, 99–100
ideal speech situation, 75–8, 126–7
ideas, universal, 126–8
ideology, critique, 34
indoctrination, 89–90
interviews
  concept of coherence, 140–1
  job, and alignment devices, 141–3
  as social process, 140

job interviews *see* interviews

Kant, E., 17, 29, 78, 154
  on emancipation, 45, 46
  and knowledge, 37, 39, 42
Keckeisen, W., 56
Kellner, D., 36–8
Kemmis, S., 151, 158–61, 167–8
Klafki, W., 62, 157–9, 161
knowledge, 28–9
  and human interests, 31–6
  theories of, 72–5
Kohlberg, 39, 111, 115

Lakatos, I., 90
learning
  critical, and teaching, 99–125
  processes, decentralised, 151–7
  traditional, and teaching, 87–98
Lewis, I., 167, 168–9
life-world, 29
  colonisation of, 95
  and ideal speech situation, 75–6
  modern fate of, 69–72
Lukacs, G., 17

McCarthy, T., 32
Marx, K., 2, 58, 78, 169
  audience for, 40
  and capitalism, 3
  criticism of, 34–5, 37
  growth of critical thought, 14–21

Marx, K., *continued*
    on modernity, 8
methodology, reconstructing , 137–40
Mill, J. S., 7, 111, 117
Miller, M., 115–17, 120, 131–2, 160
Misgeld, D., 46
model(s)
    critical action research, 158–60
    curriculum decision-making, 157–8
    for research, 143–4
modern educational crisis, 1–25
    crisis tendencies of capitalism, 3–5
    critique, limitations of, 21–4
    educational crisis of modernity, 5–7
    Hegel, Marx and Frankfurt School,
        14–21
    New Right and Old Left, 10–14
modernity, 5–7, 7–10
Mollenhauer, K., 57–8, 62, 81
Moser, H., 58, 150–1

Nietzsche, F., 45, 61, 78
New Right and Old Left, 10–14

Oelkers, J., 87–8
Offe, C., 50–2, 54–5, 58

pedagogy
    contexts, 129–30
    traditional, 96–7
Peters, R., 88, 111, 117, 119–20
plurality in society, 26–7
Popper, K., 31–2, 73, 137, 150
pragmatics, empirical
    need for, 161–2
    as reflective method, 162–5
psychoanalysis, 36, 38

question/answer cycle, structure of, 91–4
Quine, 138, 153

Ragan, S., 141–2
recontextualisation and question/answer
        cycle, 94–5
reflection, 34, 37
research
    action and contexts, 126–48
    critical action, 158–60
    educational, community, 135–7
    interviews, 140
    model for, 143–4
    technical questions, 143–6

Rilke, R. M., 1, 24, 126, 171

Schleiermacher, F. D., 45
schooling, traditional, 68–86
    and critical theories of knowledge, 72–5
    critique, method of, 78–81
    and education, theories of, 82–4
    ideal speech situation, 75–8
    life-world, modern fate of, 69–72
    social development, rational, 82–4
Schutz, A., 29
Searle, 100–1
self and others, context of, 134–5
Sennett, R., 14
Shor, I., 71
social development, rational, 82–4
Spaemann, R., 62, 69, 133
Steinfels, P., 13
Streeck, J., 91, 93–4

teachers, thinking of, 95–6
teaching
    children and autonomy, 110–12
    classroom communications, 90–1
    colonisation, 94–5
    communication
        distorted, 106–9, 112–14
        ego and rational autonomy, 119–21
    communicative action, theory of,
        99–104
    communicative competence, 114–18
    critical, and learning, 99–125
    critical development, 121–3
    curriculum questions, 118–19
    developmental reconstruction, 110–23
    expressive functions, 109–10
    ideal pedagogical speech, 99–110
    and indoctrination, 89–90
    and pedagogy, 96–7
    question/answer cycle, structure, 91–4
    recontextualisation, 94–5
    and teachers' thinking, 95–6
    traditional, and learning, 87–98
    universal and empirical pragmatics,
        104–6

ungovernability, 53–5
universal pragmatics, theory of, 104–6
universities, democratisation of, 63–4

Walker, J., 139, 152–7
Wüstenberg, W., 55